ENGLISH LYRIC POETRY

(1500–1700)

FREDERIC IVES CARPENTER

ENGLISH
LYRIC POETRY

1500—1700

WITH AN
INTRODUCTION
BY
FREDERIC IVES CARPENTER

Granger Index Reprint Series

BOOKS FOR LIBRARIES PRESS
FREEPORT, NEW YORK

First published 1906 in
The Warwick Library of English Literature Series
Reprinted 1969

STANDARD BOOK NUMBER:
8369-6006-8

LIBRARY OF CONGRESS CATALOG CARD NUMBER:
77-76942

MANUFACTURED
BY
HALLMARK LITHOGRAPHERS, INC.
IN THE U.S.A.

TO MY FATHER

INTRODUCTORY NOTE

Dr. F. I. Carpenter, the Editor of the present
volume, is a distinguished Lecturer on English
literature at the University of Chicago. He is
known to American readers, and to students of
English literature in general, by a very subtle and
comprehensive investigation of the poetic speech
of the Elizabethans—*Metaphor and Simile in the
Minor Elizabethan Drama.* After all the labours
of Mr. Bullen and others, the rich lyric literature of
the Elizabethan age, and of the ages which went
before and after, still remains relatively little known.
It is hoped that the present survey of it, by a scholar
who has made it his special study, will help to make
its countless beauties more generally familiar, and
an appreciation of the " mind and art " of our elder
song-writers more readily attainable.

C. H. Herford
General Editor,
The Warwick Library

TABLE OF CONTENTS AND INDEX
OF AUTHORS

	Page
INTRODUCTION, - - - - - - - -	xix
ANONYMOUS LYRICS, 1588–1603—	
The Quiet Life, - - - - - -	69
Love's Perfections, - - - - - -	70
Sweet Lamenting, - - - - - -	70
The Test, - - - - - - -	70
The Shepherd's Praise of his Sacred Diana, - -	71
The Shepherd to the Flowers, - - - -	72
To Zepheria, - - - - - - -	73
Hence, Care! - - - - - -	73
The Month of Maying, - - - - -	74
Brown is my Love, - - - - -	75
Come Away! Come, Sweet Love! - - -	75
Madrigal: Lady, when I behold, - - -	76
I saw my Lady weep, - - - - -	76
Love and May, - - - - - -	77
Love's Realities, - - - - - -	77
Madrigal: My Love in her Attire, - - -	78
The Grace of Beauty, - - - - -	78
Lullaby, - - - - - - -	79
ANONYMOUS LYRICS, 1604–1675—	
Summer, - - - - - - -	163
In Laudem Amoris, - - - - -	163
Ye little Birds that sit and sing, - - -	164
There is a Lady, - - - - - -	165
Revels, - - - - - - -	165
Fain I would, - - - - - -	166
The Bellman's Song, - - - - -	166
Two in One, - - - - - -	166
A-Maying, - - - - - - -	167
The Hunt is Up, - - - - - -	168

	Page
The Urchins' Dance,	168
The Elves' Dance,	168
The Fairies' Dance,	169
The Satyrs' Dance,	169
Sweet Suffolk Owl,	169
The Merry Bells of Oxford,	170
Love in thy Youth,	170
Parting,	171
Hey Nonny No!	171
The Great Adventurer,	172
The King's Progress,	173
Waly, Waly,	174

FRANCIS BACON—
| The World, | 148 |

BARNABE BARNES—
| Ode: Behold, out walking in these valleys, | 105 |
| Sonnet: Ah, Sweet Content, | 106 |

FRANCIS BEAUMONT—
| On the Life of Man, | 152 |
| Lines on the Tombs in Westminster Abbey, | 153 |

NICHOLAS BRETON—
A Sweet Lullaby,	65
I would thou wert not fair,	66
Lovely kind and kindly loving,	67
What is Love?	68

EARL OF BRISTOL—
| Song: See, O see! | 231 |

RICHARD BROME—
| The Merry Beggars, | 227 |

WILLIAM BROWNE—
Carpe Diem,	135
The Song in the Wood,	135
The Siren's Song,	136
Love's Reasons,	137
Epitaph on the Countess of Pembroke,	137
Epitaph,	137
Welcome,	138
Vision of the Rose,	139

"J. C."—
| Beauty and Time, | 107 |

THOMAS CAMPION—   Page
    To Lesbia, - - - - - - - - 126
    Come Away ! - - - - - - - - 127
    The Measure of Beauty, - - - - - - 128
    The Shadow, - - - - - - - - 128
    When thou must home, - - - - - - 129
    Day and Night, - - - - - - - 130
    The Man of Life Upright, - - - - - 130
    A Hymn in Praise of Neptune, - - - - 131
    Winter Nights, - - - - - - - 132
    The Charm, - - - - - - - - 132
    There is none, O none but you, - - - - 133
    Follow your Saint ! - - - - - - 134
    Rose-cheeked Laura, - - - - - - 134

THOMAS CAREW—
    Song : Ask me no more where Jove bestows, - - 219
    Disdain Returned, - - - - - - 220
    The Primrose, - - - - - - - 220
    Epitaph on the Lady Mary Villers, - - - 221

GEORGE CHAPMAN—
    Her Coming, - - - - - - - 104
    Of Circumspection, - - - - - - 104

CHARLES COTTON—
    Ode : Laura Sleeping, - - - - - 228

ABRAHAM COWLEY—
    Ode : On Solitude, - - - - - - 234

RICHARD CRASHAW—
    Wishes : To his Supposed Mistress, - - - 245
    The Flaming Heart, - - - - - 247
    Two went up into the Temple to Pray, - - 248

SAMUEL DANIEL—
    Sonnet to Delia : Beauty, sweet Love, - - 94
    Sonnet : Care-charmer Sleep, - - - - 95
    Song : Are they shadows that we see? - - 95
    Love's Birth and Becoming, - - - - 96

ROBERT DAVENPORT—
    A Requiem, - - - - - - - 161

SIR JOHN DAVIES—
    To the Rose, - - - - - - - 104

Thomas Dekker— Page
Troll the Bowl! - - - - - - - 109
The Merry Month of May, - - - - 110
Content, - - - - - - - 111
Lullaby, - - - - - - - 111
The Gifts of Fortune and Cupid, - - - 112
Robert Devereux: see Essex, Earl of.
John Dickenson—
A Pastoral Catch, - - - - - - - 64
George Digby: see Bristol, Earl of.
John Donne—
A Valediction Forbidding Mourning, - - 113
The Funeral, - - - - - - - 114
Ode: Absence, hear thou my protestation, - - 115
Song: Sweetest Love, I do not go, - - - 116
The Undertaking, - - - - - - 117
The Blossom, - - - - - - - 118
Sonnet: Death, be not proud, - - - 119
Hymn to God the Father, - - - - 119
Michael Drayton—
Sonnet: To the Lady L. S., - - - - 97
Sonnet: To the River Ankor, - - - - 98
Sonnet: Since there's no help, come, - - 98
To the Cambro-Britons and their Harp: his Ballad
of Agincourt, - - - - - - 99
William Drummond of Hawthornden—
Sonnet: To the Nightingale, - - - - 139
Sonnet: Spring, - - - - - - 140
Sonnet: Posting Time, - - - - - 140
Sonnet: Sweet Bird, - - - - - 141
Sonnet: On Solitude, - - - - - 141
Sonnet: Repent, Repent! - - - - 142
Sonnet: To Sir W. Alexander, - - - 142
Madrigal: This Life, which seems so fair, - - 143
Song: Phœbus, arise! - - - - - 143
Madrigal: Sweet Rose, whence is this hue, - - 144
John Dryden—
Alexander's Feast, or the Power of Music, - - 256
A Song for St. Cecilia's Day, - - - - 262
Song: Ah, Fading Joy! - - - - - 264
Incantation from Œdipus, - - - - 264
Song from King Arthur, - - - - - 266

SIR EDWARD DYER—   Page
   My mind to me a Kingdom is,   -   -   -   -   48

EARL OF ESSEX—
   "A Passion of my Lord of Essex",   -   -   -   112

JOHN FLETCHER, or BEAUMONT AND FLETCHER—
   Sweetest Melancholy,   -   -   -   -   -   154
   Love's Emblems,   -   -   -   -   -   155
   Invocation to Sleep,   -   -   -   -   -   155
   Song to Bacchus,   -   -   -   -   -   156
   Drink To-Day,   -   -   -   -   -   156
   Beauty Clear and Fair,   -   -   -   -   157
   The Charm,   -   -   -   -   -   157
   To his Sleeping Mistress,   -   -   -   158
   Weep no More,   -   -   -   -   158
   Dirge,   -   -   -   -   -   -   158
   Marriage Hymn,   -   -   -   -   159

PHINEAS FLETCHER—
   Hymn: Drop, drop, slow tears,   -   -   -   160

JOHN FORD—
   Calantha's Dirge,   -   -   -   -   160
   Penthea's Dying Song,   -   -   -   161

GEORGE GASCOIGNE—
   The Lullaby of a Lover, -   -   -   -   8

JAMES GRAHAM: see Montrose, Marquis of.

ROBERT GREENE—
   Sephestia's Song to her Child,   -   -   53
   Fawnia, -   -   -   -   -   54
   Philomela's Ode, -   -   -   -   55

WILLIAM HABINGTON—
   To Castara: The Reward of Innocent Love, - -   200
   To the Moment Last Past,   -   -   -   201
   Nox Nocti Indicat Scientiam, -   -   -   202
   Cogitabo pro Peccato Meo,   -   -   -   203

LORD HERBERT OF CHERBURY—
   Love's Eternity,   -   -   -   -   -   238

GEORGE HERBERT—
   Virtue, -   -   -   -   -   -   239
   The Collar, -   -   -   -   -   239
   Love, -   -   -   -   -   -   241

ROBERT HERRICK—   Page

   The Argument of the Hesperides, -   -   -   - 205

   Upon the Loss of his Mistresses,   -   -   - 205

   To live Merrily, and to Trust to Good Verses,   - 206

   An Ode for Ben Jonson,   -   -   -   - 208

   His Prayer to Ben Jonson,   -   -   -   - 208

   To Anthea, -   -   -   -   -   -   - 209

   The Night Piece, -   -   -   -   -   - 210

   Cherry Ripe, -   -   -   -   -   -   - 210

   To Electra, -   -   -   -   -   -   - 211

   Delight in Disorder,   -   -   -   -   - 211

   Upon Julia's Clothes,   -   -   -   -   - 211

   To the Rose, -   -   -   -   -   -   - 212

   To Dianeme, -   -   -   -   -   -   - 212

   This Age Best,   -   -   -   -   -   -   - 212

   Divination by a Daffodil,   -   -   -   - 213

   To the Virgins, -   -   -   -   -   - 213

   To Blossoms, -   -   -   -   -   -   - 213

   To Daffodils, -   -   -   -   -   -   - 214

   To Violets, -   -   -   -   -   -   - 215

   To Meadows, -   -   -   -   -   -   - 215

   Anacreontic, -   -   -   -   -   -   - 216

   Upon a Child that Died,   -   -   -   - 216

   Upon a Child, -   -   -   -   -   - 216

   Grace for a Child, -   -   -   -   - 217

   The Litany, -   -   -   -   -   -   - 217

THOMAS HEYWOOD—

   Pack Clouds, Away,   -   -   -   -   - 108

   Song of the Bell, -   -   -   -   -   - 108

HENRY HOWARD: see Surrey, Earl of.

BEN JONSON—

   Echo's Lament of Narcissus, -   -   -   - 120

   Hymn to Diana, -   -   -   -   -   - 121

   Hymn to Pan, -   -   -   -   -   - 121

   Song: To Celia, -   -   -   -   -   - 122

   How near to what is good is what is fair,   - 123

   Buzz! quoth the Blue-fly,   -   -   -   - 123

   The fairy beam upon you,   -   -   -   - 123

   Charis' Triumph, -   -   -   -   -   - 124

   The Measure of the Perfect Life,   -   -   - 125

   Hymn: Hear me, O God!   -   -   -   - 125

THOMAS LODGE—   Page
    Rosader's Description of Rosalynd, -   -   -   -   61
    The Harmony of Love, -   -   -   -   -   63
    Whilst Youthful Sports are Lasting,   -   -   -   63

RICHARD LOVELACE—
    Going to the Wars,   -   -   -   -   -   223
    To Althea from Prison, -   -   -   -   -   223
    The Rose,   -   -   -   -   -   -   224

JOHN LYLY—
    Apelles' Song,   -   -   -   -   -   50
    Spring's Welcome, -   -   -   -   -   51
    Hymn to Apollo, -   -   -   -   -   51
    Fairy Revels, -   -   -   -   -   52

JOHN MILTON—
    Hymn on the Nativity, -   -   -   -   176
    L'Allegro, -   -   -   -   -   -   183
    Il Penseroso, -   -   -   -   -   187
    Song: O'er the smooth enamelled green, -   -   192
    Song: Nymphs and Shepherds, dance no more,   -   193
    Song: Sweet Echo, sweetest Nymph,   -   -   193
    Incantation: Sabrina fair,   -   -   -   194
    The Land of Eternal Summer,   -   -   195
    Song on May Morning, -   -   -   -   196
    Sonnet: To the Nightingale, -   -   -   196
    Sonnet: On his Blindness, -   -   -   197
    Sonnet: On the Late Massacre in Piedmont, -   -   197

MARQUIS OF MONTROSE—
    My dear and only Love, -   -   -   -   -   236

HENRY MORE—
    The Philosopher's Devotion, -   -   -   -   243

THOMAS NASH—
    Spring, the sweet Spring,   -   -   -   58
    Death's Summons, -   -   -   -   -   59
    Fading Summer, -   -   -   -   -   60

GEORGE PEELE—
    Song of Paris and Œnone,   -   -   -   56
    Harvestmen A-Singing, -   -   -   -   57
    Farewell to Arms, -   -   -   -   -   57

FRANCIS QUARLES—
    Phosphor, bring the Day,   -   -   -   -   241

Page

Sir Walter Raleigh—
    Pilgrim to Pilgrim, -   -   -   -   -   -   43
    Even such is Time, -   -   -   -   -   -   45

Earl of Rochester—
    Song: Dear, from thine Arms, -   -   -   -   253
    To his Mistress, -   -   -   -   -   -   254
    Love and Life, -   -   -   -   -   -   254

Sir Charles Sedley—
    To Celia, -   -   -   -   -   -   -   255

William Shakespeare—
    When icicles hang by the wall, -   -   -   80
    Over hill, over dale, -   -   -   -   80
    You spotted snakes, -   -   -   -   -   81
    Who is Silvia? -   -   -   -   -   81
    Tell me where is fancy bred, -   -   -   -   82
    Under the greenwood tree, -   -   -   -   82
    Blow, blow, thou winter wind, -   -   -   83
    Sigh no more, ladies, -   -   -   -   -   84
    O mistress mine, -   -   -   -   -   84
    Come away, come away, death, -   -   -   85
    How should I your true love know, -   -   85
    Take, O take those lips away, -   -   -   86
    Hark, hark! the lark, -   -   -   -   -   86
    Fear no more the heat o' the sun, -   -   86
    Full fathom five thy father lies, -   -   87
    Where the bee sucks, -   -   -   -   -   87
    Sonnets Nos. 29, 30, 33, 60, 66, 71, 73, 104, 106,
        107, 109, 116, 129, 146, -   -   -   -   88–94

Samuel Sheppard—
    Epithalamium, -   -   -   -   -   -   230

James Shirley—
    A Dirge, -   -   -   -   -   -   225
    Peace Restored, -   -   -   -   -   -   226

Sir Philip Sidney—
    Sonnet: Philomela, -   -   -   -   -   45
    Sonnet: Heart-Exchange, -   -   -   -   46
    Sonnet: To the Moon, -   -   -   -   46
    Sonnet: Love is Enough, -   -   -   -   47
    Sonnet: Inspiration, -   -   -   -   -   47
    Sonnet: Eternal Love, -   -   -   -   -   48

JOHN SKELTON—   Page
    To Mistress Margery Wentworth, - - - - I
    To Mistress Isabel Pennell, - - - - - 2

ROBERT SOUTHWELL—
    The Burning Babe, - - - - - - 103

EDMUND SPENSER—
    The Song of Enchantment, - - - - - 13
    From the Daphnaida, - - - - - - 14
    Sonnets (8, 34, 68, 79), - - - - - - 16
    Prothalamion, - - - - - - - 18
    Epithalamion, - - - - - - - 24
    From an Hymn in Honour of Beauty, - - - 37
    From an Hymn of Heavenly Beauty, - - - 42

WILLIAM STRODE—
    Song: In Commendation of Music, - - - 229

SIR JOHN SUCKLING—
    Orsames' Song, - - - - - - - 221
    Constancy, - - - - - - - 222

EARL OF SURREY—
    Sonnet: Description of Spring, - - - - 3
    Sonnet: Geraldine, - - - - - - 4
    Sonnet: Complaint of a Lover Rebuked, - - - 4
    The Means to Attain Happy Life, - - - - 5

GEORGE TURBERVILE—
    The Lover to his Lady, - - - - - - 9

NICHOLAS UDALL—
    Pipe, merry Annot, - - - - - - 12

HENRY VAUGHAN—
    The Retreat, - - - - - - - 249
    The World, - - - - - - - 250
    Peace, - - - - - - - 250
    Beyond the Veil, - - - - - - 251
    The Chosen Path, - - - - - - 252

"A. W."—
    A Dialogue between the Soul and the Body, - - 162

EDMUND WALLER—
    On a Girdle, - - - - - - - 232
    Song: Go, lovely Rose, - - - - - - 232
    To a Lady in Retirement, - - - - - 233
    The Last Prospect, - - - - - - 234

Simon Wastell—
 Of Man's Mortality,   -   -   -   -   -   Page 145

John Webster—
 Dirge: Call for the robin redbreast,   -   -   - 146
 Hark, now everything is still, -   -   -   - 146
 Vanitas Vanitatum,   -   -   -   -   - 147

James Wedderburn—
 Go, Heart,   -   -   -   -   -   - 10
 Leave me not,   -   -   -   -   - 11

John Wilmott: see Rochester, Earl of.

George Wither—
 The Author's Resolution in a Sonnet,   -   - 198
 The Flower of Virtue,   -   -   -   - 199

Sir Henry Wotton—
 The Character of a Happy Life,   -   -   - 149
 On his Mistress, the Queen of Bohemia, -   - 150

Sir John Wotton—
 Damætas' Jig in Praise of his Love,   -   - 151

Sir Thomas Wyatt—
 Forget not yet,   -   -   -   -   -   5
 An Earnest Suit to his Unkind Mistress, -   - 6
 The Lover sheweth how he is Forsaken, -   - 7

Index of First Lines,   -   -   -   -   -   - 268

INTRODUCTION

THE English Lyric has been late in coming into its own. For a full century the exquisite song of the lesser Elizabethan choir lay perdue History of the appreciation of the English Lyric. while the great critics of the classical period, following in the way of the later Aristotelian tradition, solemnly discussed theory and practice in epic and drama only. Dryden, ever a jealous defender of English literary performance, has next to nothing to say of the English Lyric. The eighteenth-century imitators of Milton and Spenser catch not so much at the lyric vein of these masters as at their tricks of diction and at their narrative or their idyllic manner. Percy's *Reliques*, in 1765, however, began to bring back into esteem the wilding flavour of sixteenth- and seventeenth-century verse, both art-lyric and popular song and ballad. And perhaps the obscurer collections of verse which earlier in the century preceded the *Reliques*, such as Allan Ramsay's *Evergreen*, also helped to insinuate something of the spirit of the older lyric, and something of its peculiar cadence and rhythm of song, into the minds of impressionable youths like Burns and Blake and Chatterton, and to prepare the taste of the new generation little by little for the new things which

were coming in poetry. The Romantic revolution
was certainly in part a literary revolution, involving
a return to higher sources of inspiration and to
older poetic ideals than had prevailed for so long.
Wordsworth, writing in 1815, testifies as to the
effect wrought by Percy's *Reliques,* that "For our
own country its poetry has been absolutely re-
deemed by it". The lyrical spirit of modern
English poetry is in considerable measure a develop-
ment from the lyrical spirit of the Elizabethan age;
and the appreciation of the Elizabethan lyric has
grown with the growth of the modern lyric.

The term 'Lyric' in modern times has always
been of uncertain usage. In the broadest sense it
What is Lyric? is often taken to cover all poetry which
does not fall under the species Epic or
Drama, or any of their allied forms. Vagueness of
connotation has attached to the term, also, from the
implicit acceptance by some modern writers of the
lyric form and mood as the poetic form and mood
par excellence. In this sense lyrical expression is
conceived as the very soul and essence of poetical
expression. Thus Gray in a letter to Mason,
December 19th, 1756, writes: " The true lyric style,
with all its flights of fancy, ornaments, and heighten-
ing of expression, and harmony of sound, is in its
nature superior to every other style; which is just
the cause why it could not be borne in a work of
great length, no more than the eye could bear to
see all this scene that we constantly gaze upon—
the verdure of the fields and woods, the azure of
the sea and skies—turned into one dazzling ex-
panse of gems". The same idea has been elaborated

by Poe in his essay on *The Poetic Principle*; and Coleridge, in his summary of the characteristics of Shakespeare's work, calls attention to the "interfusion of the lyrical—that which in its very essence is poetical".

In the stricter sense of the term, however, two essential ideas attach to the lyric: the idea of its musical character and associations, and The Lyric and the idea of the lyric as the peculiar poetic Music. instrument for the expression of personal mood and feeling. In its origins generally, no doubt, and in its highest development as an unmixed species in the lyrical poetry of the Greeks, the lyric is always closely associated with music. Wordsworth, indeed, asserts that in all lyric kinds, "for the production of their full effect, an accompaniment of music is indispensable": although he modifies this statement by adding that in most of his own verse, "as a substitute for the classic lyre or romantic harp, I require nothing more than an animated or impassioned recitation, adapted to the subject". In the modern lyric accordingly there are two classes: on the one hand such verse as in form and spirit is most nearly associated with the idea of musical delivery or accompaniment, like the Elizabethan song-lyric; and on the other hand such verse as most closely imitates the form and spirit of verse in other tongues, especially Greek or Italian, which originally was associated with that idea, like the modern ode or sonnet.[1] From the variety of its funda-

[1] See the discussion of the relations of music and poetry by Mr. Theodore Watts in the article on 'Poetry' in the *Encyclopædia Britannica*.

mental musical associations, direct or remote, flows
that variety of metrical form which is characteristic
of the lyric species. In the perfect or ideal lyric,
whether poem or song, the form must be the perfect
expression of the mood. " In the last resort," as M.
Brunetière writes,[1] "this conformity of the move-
ment with the emotion in a poem is all that is
needed to constitute it a true lyric." Similarly,
as music is perhaps the most delicate and wonder-
ful artistic instrument for the expression
of æsthetic mood, the lyric, which is
the poetic form most nearly allied to music, is that
in which æsthetic individualism and subjectivity
attain their fullest utterance.

Whence Lyric subjectivity.

In his famous preface of 1815, Wordsworth con-
fines the lyric to " the hymn, the ode, the elegy, the
song, and the ballad ", and postulates,
in addition to narrative poetry, to the
drama, and to the lyric, three other
main poetic divisions, viz., ' the idyllium ', didactic
poetry, and satiric poetry. The ballad in the
stricter sense—the communal or folk-epic, innocent
of the personal and subjective note—is obviously
allied rather with narrative than with lyrical poetry,
Wordsworth's *Lyrical Ballads* to the contrary not-
withstanding. On the other hand the sonnet, which
Wordsworth oddly enough ranks with the idyl,
should be classed with the modern lyric, where it
belongs by right both of its ultimate musical origin
and of the lyrical subjectivity of its inspiration.
The idyl, represented by such poems as *L'Allegro*
and *Il Penseroso*, is a class obviously allied to both

The several Lyric kinds: doubtful varieties.

---

[1] *L'Evolution de la Poésie Lyrique en France* (Paris, 1895), vol. i., 152.

narrative and lyric, and much of the composite poetry of the present century which is usually classed as lyrical is rather idyllic in form and spirit.[1] Didactic poetry and satiric poetry, finally, the two leading poetic types of the English 'classical' period, are also the two pre-eminently anti-lyrical forms, and consequently under no classification can they be properly ranked as any part of that literary residuum sometimes[2] called 'lyrical poetry'.

Conformance to the external marks of any recognized lyric kind constitutes perhaps 'a lyric', *pro forma*; but such is not the criterion of 'the lyrical'. Quality, on the contrary, quality and inspiration, are the subtle tests of all lyrical writing. Lyric poetry is pre-eminently the outcome of " the best and happiest moments of the happiest and best minds ". Apply this test never so strictly, and it is still amazing what extent and variety of product remains from the two great periods of English poetry. And outside of these periods also, there are important lyrical gleanings, especially in the poetry of the pre-Elizabethan period.

The Anglo-Saxon poetry, which, like all primitive poetry, is mostly of an indeterminate and undifferentiated species, is streaked here and there by lyricism. It presents perhaps no lyric in the

[1] The Idyl of course is of classical origin. The species in modern poetry is discussed in the interesting essay, entitled "A Comparison of Elizabethan with Victorian Poetry", by the late Mr. J. A. Symonds (in his *Essays Speculative and Suggestive*, 399 f.). See also his *Greek Poets*, ch. xx.

[2] As, for example, by Landor (*Works*, iv. 56):—"all that portion of our metre, which, wanting a definite term, is ranged under the capitulary of lyric ".

modern sense, but various short pieces, mostly
in the elegiac manner, approach the lyric in form,

Lyricism in
Anglo-Saxon
poetry. and are of interest for what they re-
veal of the fundamental subjective and
poetic temper of the Saxon mind.   In
the poem called *Deor's Lament*, the compelling
impulse of the lyric mood breaks through the re-
straint of the common alliterative measure in which
almost all Old English poetry is written and forces
the lines into a rude strophic movement:

> Ðas ofereode, Ðisses swa maeg—
>
> That was overpassed; and so this I may endure

the poet sings as the burden of his lament at the
conclusion of each irregular stanza, in a mood like
the mood of that man of many wiles, the much-
enduring Odysseus, when he cries out: "Endure,
my heart, for already a worse thing than this hast
thou endured!"   This fragment, however, as well
as a few others, may be relics of an earlier poetry
no longer extant, wherein greater variety of lyric
measure prevailed.   Other Anglo-Saxon poems,
*The Wanderer, The Ruin, The Seafarer, The Wife's
Complaint,* and *The Husband's Message,* in the
elegiac manner, are fundamentally lyrical, and fore-
shadow much that is permanent in the lyrical
moods of the English poetic genius.[1]   They may
be compared with some of the passages of an
elegiac or lyrical cast in the *Beowulf,* as, for ex-
ample, the valedictory lament of the last owner of
the hoard, over the hidden treasure of the departed

---

[1] Versions of considerable portions of these poems may be found in
Stopford Brooke's *History of Early English Literature.*

warriors (lines 2247–2266). *The Battle of Brunan-
burgh*[1] and the fragment entitled *The Fight at
Finnsburgh*,[2] may fairly be classed as lyrical ballads.
In *The Song of Azarias*[3] of the Exeter   The Anglo-Saxon
MS., we have a lyric in everything   Religious Lyric.
except metrical form.   It is a nature-song of praise
and thanksgiving addressed to the Creator of this
universe of wonders:

> Ðe gebletsige, bylywit Faeder,
> Woruldcraefta wlite, and weorca gehwilc—
>
> To Thee, O Father, blest and merciful,
> Face of wisdom and created things;
> To Thee the heavens and the seas beneath,
> And all the angels of the better world
> Among the stars, together render praise!

—so the hymn begins (in the longer version quoted
in the Caedmonic poem of *Daniel*), revolving in an
artless maze of fervent and earnest repetition around
this simple theme to the end.   Another poem shows
this tendency to the lyrical mood and manner in a
still more marked degree. This is the *Christ*, ascribed
to Cynewulf.[4] It is a typical early mediæval poem,
founded in parts on the model of the Christian Latin
poetry, and may be described as a sort of elaborate
hymn on a narrative and didactic groundwork.[5]

The eager aspiration for poetic and above all for

[1] Everyone is familiar with Tennyson's version of this poem.

[2] A version may be consulted in Garnett's *Translation of Beowulf*, p. 97.

[3] A paraphrase of the Apocryphal book of The Song of the Three Children.

[4] Accessible in an admirable edition with modern version by Mr. I. Gollancz (London, 1892).

[5] Recent authorities argue that the *Christ* is properly to be regarded as three separate poems, of which the last doubtless is not by Cynewulf. Cf. Profs. Trautmann and Blackburn in *Anglia*, vols. xviii. and xix., 1896.

lyric utterance is apparent throughout the Anglo-
Saxon period, without articulate and adequate
artistic form for such utterance.[1] Potentiality of
mood, however, and the ideality of temperament
requisite for a great national school of poetry are
plainly in the race, and it will require but the slight
alloy and fusion of foreign blood and culture to
bring them to utterance at a later day.

After the Norman conquest the influence of
mediæval asceticism and of the Latin poetry of the
church is still apparent in the Middle
English religious lyric. Under French
influence, however, a new lyric kind
gradually develops, and, under the poetic impulse
of Troubadour and Trouvère, a new range of feelings
and motives is introduced into English poetry.
The lyric production of this period in England was
undoubtedly very considerable, although the greater
part of it has disappeared. What is left falls into
three principal classes: the religious lyric, produced
under strict Latin and ecclesiastical influence; the
political songs, best exemplified in the poems of
Laurence Minot,[2] which are racy and original
enough in matter and manner, but which are rather
satirical than lyrical in spirit; and the secular and
amatory lyrics, produced under French and courtly

Middle English Lyrical Poetry: the chief kinds.

[1] In the Gnomic Verses occurs the following passage (Brooke,
History of Early English Literature, p. 10): "To all men wise words
are becoming; songs to the gleemen and wisdom to men. As many as
men are on the earth, so many are their thoughts; each to himself has
a separate soul. So then he who knows many songs and can greet the
harp with his hands, hath the less of vain longing, for he hath in himself
his gift of joy which God gave to him."

[2] Edited by Mr. Joseph Hall (Clarendon Press Series, 1887).

influence—often, however, composed by wandering students and minstrels,—among which are to be classed a considerable number of miscellaneous lyrics, mainly *adespota* of unnamed authors, as well as the more formal poetry in lyrical measures, but with meagre lyrical inspiration, of Chaucer and his English followers.[1]   All these kinds receive their chief development in the thirteenth and fourteenth centuries, when finally the new nation comes into a heritage of language and culture adequate to such uses.

The spirit of the Middle English religious lyrics is still that of Christian asceticism, inspired and solaced by a piety fervent and intense if also narrow and conventionalized.   The *The Middle English Religious Lyric.* greater number are hymns to Christ and to the Virgin.   Occasionally there is abundant lyric sweetness and a persuasive grace of movement, revealing the influence of Latin hymnody, as in the following stanza, slightly modernized, from *The Virgin's Complaint*, a poem of the fifteenth century:

> I abode and abide with great longing,
> I love and look when man will crave,
> I plain me for pity of pining;
> Would he ask mercy, he should it have;
> See to me, soul, I shall thee save;
> Bid me, child, and I will go;
> Prayedst me never, but I forgave,—
> *Quia amore langueo.*

[1] There is as yet no convenient anthology of Middle English Lyrics. Consequently they must be sought for generally in the volumes of the Early English Text Society and in similar publications.   Boeddeker's edition of MS. Harl. 2253 (Berlin, 1878), however, contains many of the best of the miscellaneous lyrics.   A few in modern versions may be found in Fitzgibbon's *Early English Poetry* (Canterbury Poets), and in Dr. MacDonald's *England's Antiphon*.

Significant of the mood of these religious lyrics is the fact that frequently an autumnal or winter background is chosen. The conventional background of the new love-poetry, on the other hand, is always spring or summer,

> Tasting of Flora and the country-green,
> Dance, and Provençal song, and sunburnt mirth!

for the new lyric had its birth in Provence, and still favours its southern ancestry. The union of incipient dramatic conception with affecting pathos and religious fervour is exemplified in the poem entitled, after its first line,

Stond wel, moder, under rode

—an English variation on the theme of the *Stabat Mater Dolorosa*:

> 'Stand well, mother, under the rood;
>   Behold thy son with gladë mood;
>   Blithë mother mayst thou be.'
> 'Son, how should I blithë stand?
>   I see thy feet, I see thy hand
>   Nailëd to the hard tree.'
>
>   .   .
>
>   When he rose then fell her sorrow;
>   Her bliss sprung the third morrow:
>   Blithë mother wert thou tho!   *then*
>   Lady, for that ilkë bliss,
>   Beseech thy son of sunnës liss   *for sin's release*
>   Be thou our shield against our foe![1]

The English mystery plays perhaps should be classed as crude dramatic lyrics. The form of them throughout is generally stanzaic, and they often

---

[1] The version in its entirety, in Dr. Mac Donald's *England's Antiphon*, together with the accompanying comments, may be profitably consulted by the reader.

aim at poetical and lyric effects. Occasionally a
passage is distinctly lyrical, as, for example, the
Hymn of Adoration by the Magi in the York plays.[1]
In the *Pearl*, however, that most poetical of all
Middle English poems outside of Chaucer, we have
the most perfect specimen of the religious poetry of
the age.[2] It is a lyrical allegory, elegiac in strain,
and full of religious symbolism—a sort of primitive
In Memoriam and *Paradiso* in one. Under the
form of the conventional mediæval vision, it gives
expression to the tender grief of a father for the
loss of his child (the Pearl), with the final consola-
tion accorded to his faith and love through a vision
of her bliss in Paradise. The intensity and the
elegiac subjectivity of the feeling of the poem,
accentuated by its new sense of poetic form and the
recurrent stanzaic effects, as of a sonnet-sequence,
raise it in many parts to a high lyric pitch.

> Pearl! pleasant to princes' pay   *for princes' pleasure*
> Too cleanly closed in gold so clear,
> Out of the Orient I boldly say,
> Ne provëd I never her precious peer.
>
> .   .   .   .   .
>
> Alas! I lost her in an erbere;   *arbour*
> Through grass to ground it from me yot;   *went*

[1] The York Plays, ed. Lucy Toulmin Smith (Oxford, 1885), pp. 135–6.
See also the chorus of eight burgesses who worship Jesus, pp. 216–18,
and the Prayer of the Priest and Anna's Welcome, p. 443:

> "Welcome! blessed Mary and maiden aye,
> Welcome! most meek in thine array,
> Welcome! bright star that shineth bright as day,
> All for our bliss!"

[2] Mr Gollancz has given us a very attractive edition of the *Pearl* with
a modern rendering (London, 1891). A synopsis of the poem may be
found in Dr. Mac Donald's *England's Antiphon*, pp. 34 f.

I dwindle, fordokked of love-dangere, *{ despoiled of love's-control*
Of that privy pearl withouten spot.

. . . .

'O Pearl', quoth I, 'of rich renown,
So was it me dear that thou con deem, *{ what thou didst judge*
In this very avisiön;
If it be a very and sooth sermoun *{ if the relation be verily true*
That thou so goest in garlands gay,
Then well is it me in this doel-dungeon, *dungeon of woe*
That thou art to that Prince's pay!'

Chaucer's few poems in lyrical measures are exotic trifles, lacking seriousness; but outside of Chaucer there is a secular lyric of considerable extent, and presenting much variety and freshness of feeling. Spring songs like "Sumer is icumen in", songs of politics and of patriotism, love-songs, snatches of refrain like the following:

The Middle English Secular Lyric.

Blow, northern wind;
Send thou me my sweeting!
Blow, northern wind
Blow! blow! blow!

and short pieces in many other sorts can be found among the scanty remains of this poetry. The greater number, perhaps, are love-lyrics, songs of a somewhat conventional cast, after the Norman model, but still with an old-world sweetness and charm.

A sweetly suyre she hath to holde, *neck*
With armës, shouldre, as man wolde,
And fingers fair to folde;
God woldë she were mine!

She is crystal of clannesse,
And banner of beautë;

> She is lily of largesse,
> She is paruenke of prouesse,   { *periwinkle of courage*
> She is selsecle of sweetnesse,   *heliotrope*
> And lady of lealtë.

The Normans are teaching the Englishmen the
arts of gallantry and the graces of the lyric turn,
and are visibly subduing the serious northern mind
to the spirit of romantic love! The lyric manner,
however, is not yet free. A narrow conventionalism
lies behind it all—behind the religious lyric the
cloistered pessimism and Manicheeism of mediæval
Christianity; and the artless artificiality and form-
alism of mediæval court-life and chivalry behind
the secular lyric. Thus in these love-songs there
are scarcely more than two normal motives: the
praise of the beloved set forth in a fixed poetry-
stuff of conventional similes for her beauty:

> She is crystal of clannesse,
> And banner of beautë;
> She is lily of largesse;

and love-plaints, turning on the hopeless aspiration
of the lover for a lady whose qualities set her far
above possibility of attainment, presented usually
in a spring-tide setting, and full of conventional
lover's hyperbole. Through all this, indeed, the
poetic emotion may still be felt, but it is not strictly
original. Mediæval poetry, except in the hands of
great masters, like Dante and Chaucer, is highly
impersonal. Lyric subjectivity is the gift of the
Renaissance. The emotion of the mediæval poet
takes the form of a set theme, whether of praise
or plaint, as in the love-lyric, or of ascetic renuncia-

tion, as in the religious lyric, or of evanescence, of
mutability, the melancholy reflection of the passing
of things—theme beloved alike by the poets of the
Greek Anthology, by the minstrels of the Middle
Ages, and by the poets of the Renaissance—which
Spenser, as last of the mediævals, has sung so
eloquently.   Nowhere in the mediæval lyric do we
find the note of personal revelation and confession,
the subjective and individualistic note of the son-
nets of Sidney and Drummond and Shakespeare,
or of the lyrics of Donne; nowhere anything like
the purely personal accent of Shelley's lyric cry,
that concentrated utterance of the soul's despair
of the modern idealist, sounding like the wail of a
lost spirit:

> O world, O life, O time,
> On whose last steps I climb,
> Trembling at that where I had stood before;
> When will return the glory of your prime?
> No more; ah! nevermore!

The Middle English period was, doubtless, a
period of artistic and poetic education for the race,
and the gains are not a few, but most of them
seem to be lost before the sixteenth century—lost
from disuse, and fading into insignificance before
the new and brilliant gains of the poetry founded
on Italian art, that more fortunate offspring and
development on a foreign soil of the happy first
influence of the Troubadour song.   The Middle
English lyric is but the twittering of birds before
the dawn.   The full lyric chorus is not yet heard.

From the death of Chaucer to the advent of
Wyatt and Surrey there is practically an inter-

regnum in the history of the English lyric as in
that of most other literary forms, marked only by
a few belated specimens of the earlier
religious and secular lyrical style, by the   Scotch Lyrists
                                                  of the Fifteenth
ballads and other verses in imitation of   Century.
exotic French forms written by Gower, Lydgate,
Occleve, and similar contemporaries or disciples of
Chaucer, by the rare and remarkable phenomenon
of laureate Skelton's few lyrics of occasion, and,
most noteworthy of all, by the lyrical attempts of
the Scotch imitators of Chaucer—James I. of Scot-
land, Henryson, and Dunbar.   In the allegories
and visions of these Scotch poets the influence of
French mediæval culture is still predominant; but
here first, nevertheless, we begin to feel that a new
light is already dawning. We feel this, for example,
in Dunbar's *Lament for the Makers*, in some of his
shorter lyrics, nay, even in his grotesque and terribly
mediæval *Dance of the Seven Deadly Sins*; we feel
it also in many passages of the *King's Quair*:

> Worshipë, ye that lovers been, this May,
> For of your bliss the kalends are begun;
> And sing with us, 'Away, Winter, away!
> Come, Summer, come, the sweet season and sun!'
> Awake, for shame! that have your heavens won,
> And amorously lift up your headës all;
> Thank Love, that list you to his mercy call.

But in relation to the main growth of the English
lyric, the poetry of this group of singers seems to
have been an isolated phenomenon.[1]

---

[1] The poetry of this Scotch School may be conveniently read in the
volume of *Mediæval Scottish Poetry* in the Abbotsford Series of the
Scottish Poets, edited by Mr. George Eyre Todd (Glasgow, 1892).

Many strands, new and old—strands of Middle English song, and strands of ballad music and The Elizabethan folk-song, as well as the innumerable Lyric. iridescent threads of Italian and Renaissance poetry—go to the weaving of the great Elizabethan lyric. This lyric, indeed, in its perfected form, is an art-lyric, a cultivated lyric, and not an autochthonous popular lyric or *volkslied*. A national lyric it is at its best, but its appeal is always really to artistic and sophisticated sensibilities, and not to the rustic, nor even to *l'homme sensuel moyen*, inhabitant in court or in town. As Italian Sources a poetic art-form the Elizabethan lyric of Elizabethan owes its first inspiration almost ex-Lyric Forms. clusively to the influence of Italian poetry. Until the full Elizabethan chorus is heard, until Spenser and Sidney have begun their song, it is mainly an imitative lyric, a lyric in its formative stage. Matter and manner are largely paraphrased from the Italian throughout Surrey, Wyatt, and Watson, and in much of Gascoigne and Turbervile, and the writers in the early miscellanies. The predominant influence in England, as it had been throughout Europe for so long before, is that of Petrarch and his Italian followers. Petrarch's treatment of romantic love, his use of Nature, his management of the sonnet-sequence, and his chief poetic forms—the sonnet, the canzone or ode, the sestina, and the madrigal—are all adopted, with only slight modifications at first, in this early Renaissance poetry of England. This influence of the earlier Italian lyric is received and assimilated by a vigorous poetic brood. If the note of direct

imitation prevails in the earliest Elizabethans, in
Spenser and in the best lyrists contemporary with
Spenser it is already subdued to the colour of the
genius of the individual poet.   Indeed from the
beginning the voices we hear are the voices of
Englishmen, and the native accent breaks through
the foreign idiom.   Skelton, your uni-
versity laureate and the first of the   Manner of the
moderns, is English and idiosyncratic   Early Eliza-
bethan Lyrists.
with a vengeance! The mood of English reflection
marks much of the poetry of Wyatt, of Gascoigne,
and of the anonymous contributors to the mis-
cellanies; while many of the old conventions and
many of the old poetic forms, such as the couplet,
rime royal, Poulter's measure, ballad measure, and
the fourteeners are retained, and appear sporadically
throughout the period.   Before Spenser and Sid-
ney, however, everything is tentative and experi-
mental.   The lyric has not attained to freedom of
feeling and of expression.   The heavy atmosphere
of the fifteenth century is not yet dissipated.   The
early lyrists write in an idiom neither mediæval
nor yet quite modern.   The manner of continental
culture is with difficulty caught.   But the change
when it does come is very rapid.   Gaiety, expan-
siveness, fanciful ease, richness, and music, all at
once startle the timid ear of the early twilight,
when, about 1580, the level sun begins to shine
across the skies.   The imaginary courts of love,
the allegoric visions, the cavalcades, and the
didactic commonplaces of the mediæval age dis-
appear in an instant, or shine in a tender afterglow
in the pages of Spenser's romance.   Poetry all of

a sudden becomes subjective, personal, reflective, alive, intense. The individual is liberated from the blighting anonymity of mediævalism. He seeks the free expression of himself in art. The arts accessible to him in England are music, the drama, and lyric poetry, and these accordingly are the chief arts developed during the succeeding period.

In the broadest sense lyricism, the salient, personal, and rhythmical expression of the individual passion and sense of things, is the pervading note of the Elizabethan times. English history at all times has been largely the struggle of the individual for emancipation and self-manifestation. Hence lyric art in all its composite forms is peculiarly an English art, and the lyricism of English poetry is its most constant and permanent element. So we find that the very drama of the Elizabethans is pervaded by this prevailing lyric mood.[1]

Lyricism the Note of Elizabethan Literature.

The Elizabethan lyrical impulse seeks expression in a great variety of poetical forms.[2] The lyric proper appears, now under the pastoral convention, now as sonnet and sonnet-sequence, now in various composite

Leading forms of the Elizabethan Lyric.

---

[1] See the ingenious essay by the late Mr. J. A. Symonds on 'The Lyrism of the English Romantic Drama' (in *The Key of Blue and other Prose Essays*, London and New York, 1893).

[2] The extensive lyrical production of the Elizabethan period is to be found scattered through innumerable publications, such as the works of individual poets, the various miscellanies and anthologies of the day, occasional songs in prose romances, in the drama, in the masques (in itself a quasi-lyrical species), and in the song-books which supplied and delighted the musical tastes of our forefathers. In addition to all this many pieces in manuscript yet remain unpublished. More specific bibliographical indications are to be found in the body of the present volume in the brief introductory notes accompanying the text.

literary forms, such as formal ode and epithalamium, and again as the pure song-lyric of the Elizabethan song-books, in madrigal, canzon, 'ode', roundelay, and catch, that altogether delightful and exquisite outburst of bird-like music, exotic and Italianate, and yet, to modern ears, at the same time so freshly English and native.[1] Further than this, many elegiac and idyllic variations, prolonged to more than lyric length, are frequently heard.

The variety and scope of Elizabethan lyrical production as a whole are as remarkable as its distinction and perfection of style in many parts. The more purely literary lyric in almost every kind of form known at the present day is produced in abundance, in addition to the lyric in which the pastoral manner, or the note of song, or the sonnet convention predominates. Lyrics in these forms reach their chief perfection, perhaps, in the more literary poets, such as Spenser, Daniel, Drayton, Browne, Drummond, and Milton. In Spenser's *Epithalamion* and the *Four Hymns*, especially, is exemplified what has been called the Greater Lyric,[2] the long-breathed lyric of elaborate involutions in subject-matter and in metrical form, which in the seventeenth and eighteenth centuries is represented principally by the formal ode, Pindaric and otherwise. No one in English has managed this difficult form of art with such constancy of

[1] On the various forms of the Elizabethan lyric Professor Schelling's Introduction, pp. xiv f., to his charming anthology of Elizabethan lyrics (Boston, 1895), may be consulted with advantage by the reader interested in the further study of the subject.

[2] See Mr. Ernest Rhys's Introduction to his volume of selections from the lyric poems of Spenser.

poetic inspiration, and such unfailing harmony of
the parts and of the whole, as has Spenser.

The Elizabethan period, in the whole history of
the English lyric, is the great period of the shaping
and development of lyrical forms and rhythms.
With the wandering minstrels and university wits
like Peele and Greene, and with the song-writers,
the lyric becomes popular and racy of English life
and sentiment. They attain, as by instinct, to the
perfect touch and phrase of the artist in words.
The language is still something plastic, and can be
mastered and made ductile to song and to measure.
Euphuism and word-play of every sort are practised
and parodied and then practised again. But it is
a Euphuism not yet intellectualized nor crystallized
into a rigid mannerism. And so artful phrasing
becomes a gift and a passion with writers, and the
taste for it spreads to all classes, until the lyric
perfection of diction of even the minor Elizabethan
song is made possible. In Spenser the musical
development of English speech is at its highest,
until Milton comes and adds a harmony unknown
even to Spenser. The refinement of form, it is
true, continues through the next two reigns, and
many new effects are caught, as in Herrick and in
Milton, but the lyrical form and spirit of the first
period is *sui generis* and distinctive.

The essential artistic impulse and the accepted
conventions of any literary form are
always more or less at variance. In the
Elizabethan lyric this discrepancy of
form and inspiration is less marked than
in many other literary kinds, for the reason that

Pastoral and
Sonnet Forms:
Conventional
Aims and Real
Aims.

the lively sense of beauty and delight which marked
the lyric mood of the time more easily accom-
modated itself to and revitalized fixed and exotic
literary modes than would have been possible with
a colder and more literal generation. Conventional
meaning and real meaning, however, we find rapidly
shifting and changing from decade to decade
throughout this age of rapid change and swift
development, whether in the vein of pastoral, of
sonnet, or of song. The earlier romantic idealism
rests chiefly in the pastoral convention, which,
indeed, tinges the Elizabethan lyric throughout.
In the best of the pastoral lyrics pastoralism is
but a setting or background, subtly suggesting the
tone of romantic idealism and of golden-age other-
worldliness, which is the fundamental mood of the
piece. Likewise, also, amid all the amatory con-
ventionality of the sonnet-sequences, we feel that
the recurrent formulæ of love, of lover's despair and
lady's praise, are but the obbligato accompaniment
of the real, the underlying theme, which, through
all the artifices of art, is purposing the lyric re-
velation and self-expression of the poet's inner
mood and nature. It is so in the sonnets of Shake-
speare, and in the best of those of Sidney, Spenser,
and Drayton. And for the reason, doubtless, that
love is the great awakener of the soul—

Beauty breeds love, love consummates a man,

as Chapman sings—we find in these sonnets more
of the modern note, more of the introspective
and analytical spirit, than had yet appeared in
the lyric. They are the first full expression in

English poetry of the subjective spirit of modern
lyricism.

In the song-lyric of the Elizabethan age con-
ventionality is melted into pure lyric mood, or only
The Elizabethan adds a further ornament and grace to
Song-Lyric. a musical utterance without it some-
what formless and unstayed. The exquisite accord
of music and words in this lyric has been noted by
all competent judges. Elizabethan music was a
music perfectly fitted to song, slight and melodic,
full of local colour and suggestiveness, and admir-
ably adapted to commend and ensure and fortify
lyric poetry of as perfect a quality in its particular
kind as probably has been or ever will be written
to the accompaniment of musical notes in so in-
tractable a language as English. The Elizabethan
song-lyric is a form of pure art—poetic emotion
stirred by the sense of beauty and of musical
delight, with the slightest possible admixture of
the temporal and the adventitious. These haunting
measures of song, the secret of which seems to be
now lost from our speech, are never overweighted
with meaning, nor at their best are they over-
charged with convention or with ornament. The
Elizabethan song-writer understands instinctively
the laws of the kind in which he works. How free
are the lyrics in Shakespeare's plays, for example,
from the subtleties and the compressions of the
dramatic style of that master. Meaning here is
masked in pure mood, is suggested and potential,
not hardened into thought. "The apothecaries",
writes Thomas Campion in the preface to his *Fourth
Book of Airs*, "have Books of Gold, whose leaves,

being opened, are so light as that they are subject
to be shaken with the least breath; yet, rightly
handled, they serve both for ornament and use.
Such are light Airs." And yet, in all this lyric-song
there is almost never the suggestion of the mere
exercise in versification. It has everywhere the
note of spontaneity. A flying mood is caught in
its passage, is slightly idealized, and then is fitted
to diction and verse which by association and by
cadence exactly render it to the hearer or reader.
If the mood be inconsequential and fleeting, it is so
much the more the proper material for musical and
lyric expression. The mere music of words, allied
to the exact quantum and substance of feeling and
idea, has never elsewhere been equalled in English
for lightness and grace, and an indescribable charm
and singularity of verbal expressiveness. In Shake-
speare, Campion, Heywood, Dekker, and Breton,
and in the single masterpieces of a host of minor
or unnamed singers, is found in unapproachable
perfection that peculiar artless art, that first fine
careless rapture, that exquisite harmony and union
of form and substance, which in the last resort, as
M. Brunetière rightly says, is all that is needed in
poetic form to constitute the true lyric, and which
in any form seems to be the crowning attainment
of art. In its day the Elizabethan song-lyric is a
holiday lyric, the sweetener and solace of life in
hall and bower, in court and city. It responds to
the superabundant play-instinct of the age—the
instinct of men seeking free expression after the
long ascetic repression of the Middle Ages. The
Elizabethan period is partly, and for a few brief

years, what Taine calls it, the period of a Pagan
Renaissance. Life all at once has come to have a
new joy and interest for men, here, now, and of
itself. The senses reassert their rights. And it is
still a half-century before the relapse into the black
remorse of Puritanism. And so, meanwhile, the
romantic comedy of life is played out to the sound
of the lyre and of song.

This sense of joyous elation, this spontaneity and
careless ease of the early Elizabethan song, is that
which gives it high permanent worth to us; and no
one can appreciate its richness and inspiration who
does not drink somewhat deeply of it—who cannot
for the moment give himself up to the mood of it,
rejoice in its joy, and admire its seeming-careless
art and its happy music. It supplies something
not elsewhere found in English poetry. Afterwards,
and all too soon, the eternal note of sadness is
brought in.

The chief lyric writers typical of the first great
poetic period extending to the death of Elizabeth
Chief Elizabethan are Spenser, Sidney, Raleigh, Lyly,
Lyrists. Greene, Peele, Nash, Lodge, Breton,
Shakespeare, Daniel, Drayton, Southwell, Barnes,
Heywood, and Dekker. Others—Donne, Jonson,
Campion, and Sir John Davies, for example—fall
partly within the same period, but their lyric
manner, as well as in a less degree also the lyric
manner of Shakespeare, Chapman, and Daniel,
points rather to the special style of the lyric of
the Jacobean period, and is rather transitional than
typically Elizabethan. Spenser and Sidney fitly
usher in the great period of the lyric. In the

Shepherd's Calendar the lyric and the pastoral notes are blended. Fresh and elate, if also slightly conscious and naïve, like the voice of youth, it struck out a new music in English verse. The Lyrics of Spenser's characteristic lyric, however, Spenser. is the Greater Lyric, the prolonged lyric. His art requires ample room for its evolutions. Accordingly his lyric utterance, as in the *Epithalamion*, is large, harmonious, and splendidly impassive. The sharper lyrical cry, the strenuous utterance of brief but deep emotion, first comes from Of Sidney. Sidney, as in the sonnet beginning:

Leave me, O Love, which reachest but to dust.

After this the way is open to all comers, and the full choir of song is heard in the land. In this choir are many notes and many voices: Of Minor the delicate melody of Lyly, perfect in Lyrists. diction, light and refined; the richer note of Greene, full of English feeling, strangely heightened with pastoral and Renaissance fancies, varied in rhythm, but somewhat languorous and overwrought; Peele's few lyrics, golden in cadence, that go on murmuring in the memory; the fresh voice of Nash, now rollicking and open, and again musically melancholic; Lodge, more inclined to pastoralism, trying experiments in motives and rhythms that evade failure by a hand's-breadth, and too copious in his vein of song to be uniformly felicitous; Breton, as fresh as Nash, as copious as Lodge, but endowed with a finer artistic feeling, and altogether captivating in his ready grace and buoyancy; Dekker and Heywood, lyrical and Elizabethan in spirit, humane,

lovers of sunshine and song, and carrying down
into the midst of the perplexities of the Jacobean
age the simpler lyrical snatches that had pleased
their youth; Drayton, grave-minded, with the
ethical poet's fuller ambition, and touched with the
new and deeper lyric feeling that utters itself most
perfectly in Shakespeare's sonnets; Daniel, pure in
utterance, refined and meditative, and typical minor
master of the closet lyric; and, lastly, the sum of
all these parts and master of the poetic schools of
both periods, the lyric Shakespeare, most poignant
and intense of sonnetteers, through all whose
moods runs a hidden noble harmony, bitter-sweet,
ever broken and ever synthesized anew, the fire of
desire and the calm of æsthetic contemplation
alternately active and quiescent, large, self-sacrific-
ing, and Promethean,—and on the other hand, and
in the same breath, subtlest and aptest singer of a
lyric song, tuned to the whole gamut of singable
emotions, from the woodnotes wild of the lyrics in
As You Like It to the last solemn perfect simplicity
of the Dirge in *Cymbeline*.

The history of its lyrical poetry exhibits a
strenuous and fervent idealism as one of the con-
stant traits of the English mind. We
feel the first breath of this spirit in
the heroic resignation and loyalty of
Beowulf; it reappears in the eager hymns
of Cynewulf's *Christ*; we may find it in a score of
Hail Marys in the period before Chaucer; it shines
like a cathedral lamp through the tender symbolism
of the *Pearl*; it is loftiest in Spenser's *Hymns of
Heavenly Love and Beauty*; it is felt in the lyrics of

*Leading Moods
and Motives of
the Elizabethan
Lyric: Moral
Idealism.*

Milton and in the verse of Herbert and Vaughan; until, with the decline of the lyrical spirit in the poetry of the English classical period, it disappears for a time, only to come to a new birth in the lyrical revival of the modern romantic period. This peculiarly English note of idealism, ethical and earnest, and yet ardent and enthusiastic—this serious and moral acceptance and interpretation of things, underlies even the lightness and insouciance of the Elizabethan song-lyric. We find it even in Campion; we find it, for all his Paganism, in Herrick. From *Beowulf* to *Hamlet*, from *Hamlet* to the *Ode to Duty* and *The Two Voices*, this is the dominant mood of English poetry. It underlies even Chaucer's playfulness and breezy delight in the panorama of external existence. In the midst of discordant conditions, it impels the essentially English nature of Dryden to dissatisfied satire and self-reproaches; Pope is driven by it to write didactic *Essays on Man*; and it is the very breath of nineteenth-century lyricism. When this temperamental mood of the race attains to adequate objective expression, as in the great poetry of the Elizabethan age, when it projects itself into concrete forms of the imagination, as in Shakespeare and Spenser, in Keats and Tennyson, the result is an art at once English and universal. Something of this universality of æsthetic validity, combined with the native flavour of a national art, attaches even to the minor lyrical production of the Elizabethan period.

The England of the Renaissance is a new-old world; every element is mixed in it; and its poetry reflects this mixture. In its greater writers, in

Spenser, Sidney, and Shakespeare, in its lyrical drama and its Greater Lyric, we study its weightier poetic interpretation of life. But when we wish merely to catch the freshness and lighter music of its native mood, we go to its minor lyrists, to Greene, Peele, Breton, and Lodge, and the other contributors to *England's Helicon* and *Davison's Poetical Rhapsody*.

Mixture of Moods.

The themes of this song are the eternal themes of lyric poetry. Praise of the gods—whatever gods may be,—patriotism, war, revelry, and rejoicing, and above all, love: these are the set descants of the lyric poet in every age. The subject in a lyric poem, of course, is of less account than in any other kind of poetry. The feeling, the music, the mood, is everything. Simple and perpetually recurrent is the range of themes in any collection of Elizabethan lyrics: pastorals and pastoral piping, presenting spring, May-time and maying, shepherds' feasts, shepherds' loves, and the joys of country-life; ditties of careless delight, and blithe praises of contentment and ease; flowers and birds, fairy life, songs of pagan gods and myths,

Lyric Themes.

> Where flowers and founts, and nymphs and demi-gods,
> And all the Graces find their old abodes,

siren-songs and kisses, and the easy admonition to seize the passing hour; until lastly all these themes in their turn give place to others of deeper and more sombre meaning. But in the earlier Elizabethan poetry at least we discover proof that the English sense of pure beauty has found expression in lyric poetry more perfectly than in any other art.

Love is the first subject of the Elizabethan lyrics. In the sonnets it is refined and elaborate and romantic, as with Spenser and Sidney, or deep and passionate and perplexed as with Shakespeare. The song-lyric, as developed in accord with the musical art of the time, is too light an instrument to utter the deeper notes of passion, and its theme is fanciful love, love that laughs and entreats and sings from very blitheness of soul. It is pagan love and Renaissance love, and the love of English man and maiden, that sounds through these lyrics; nothing deeply sentimental or mediæval. After love there are many themes, treated in many moods; but in the Elizabethan period, with a few significant exceptions, love is the expected theme, the *point de repère* of all lyrical verse. Its apotheosis is reached in Spenser's *Hymn in Honour of Love*.

Lyric Love.

The chief lyric writers who mark the transition to the new poetic period, the period of James and Charles I., as we have already noticed, are Donne, Jonson, Campion, Sir John Davies, and in less measure, Shakespeare, Daniel, Chapman, and perhaps also Drummond, Browne, and Drayton. Those who are typical of the period are the younger Fletchers, the Beaumonts, Ford, Shirley, Randolph, Suckling, Lovelace, Herrick, Habington, Carew, Crashaw, Quarles, Vaughan, the two Herberts, and Wither. Pointing to the impending classical manner in poetry, and generally non-lyrical in genius, are Waller, Denham, Davenant, and Cowley.

The Jacobean and Carolan Lyric.

The change from the earlier to the later period

is rapid and unmistakable, but is partly hidden by
The Change in
Poetic Mood. the divergent and sometimes slightly
anachronic aims and tendencies of
different writers and schools. It is, indeed, as
much a change in national temper and mood as it
is in poetic form. The characteristic spirit of the
early times is one of freshness, elation, and the
great joy of curiosity and of satisfied discovery. A
new view of the world always promises so much at
first! And as the eagerness and facility of youth
mark the opening of this poetic period, so some-
thing of the soberness and deepening cast of thought
of maturity are characteristic of the last years of
Elizabeth and of the times of James and Charles.
Life becomes no longer an Arcadian pastoral or
a fairy pageant. It grows many-sided, vast and
weighty. It has problems after all which mere
audacity and elateness are incapable of solving.
Experience brings thought, and thought, reflective
thought, too often brings sorrow. The carnival of
the Renaissance, the joyous bravado of the new
awakening in England was soon over. The Puritan
undercurrent in the national character begins again
to make itself felt. Life drunk to the lees casts us
back into remorse and revulsion of feeling. The
lyric poetry of the new period reflects the entire
process, just as the drama does,—just as the drama
of Shakespeare alone does when studied in its
chronological development.[1] The several copies of
verses ascribed to Bacon, to Essex, and to Raleigh,
express the new *Weltschmerz*, just as *Hamlet*

---

[1] As in Prof. Dowden's *Shakspere's Mind and Art*; or in Prof. Barrett
Wendell's *William Shakspere* (New York, 1894).

expresses it.   The generation yearns for rest.   The time-spirit speaks, for example, through Donne. After a hot and extravagant youth, he turns ardent devotee and sings a palinode to poetry and the other kickshaws of youth in a *Farewell to the World*,[1] in which he voices the growing discontent of the times with the overstrained hurly-burly of life, and its yearning for rest in some idyllic retreat. It is the inevitable reaction of mood which always attends Romanticism. The same yearning reappears two centuries later in Rousseau and Byron, in Shelley and Wordsworth.   Milton, from the calm perspective of his retired youth, voices the eternal antithesis of the two ideals of life in *L'Allegro* and *Il Penseroso*.

Expressive of this change in life, the lyrical poetry of the seventeenth century from the very beginning rapidly becomes more subjec- The Change in tive, more reflective, and more weighted Art. with conscious meaning. The old manner of lyrical writing is still attempted; there is still pastoral and song; but even pastoral and song are affected by the new something in the moral atmosphere; they become more literary and less spontaneous, less amateurish and more deliberate; there is a growth of manner and of self-consciousness, until in the end art begins to supersede nature and native inspiration, and by the time of Charles the golden cadence of Breton and Lyly and Peele is heard no more. Pastoral and song expand with the expanding content of life and thought less than other

---

[1] Claimed by Dr. Grosart for Donne; but variously ascribed also to Wotton, to Raleigh, and to others.

literary kinds, in proportion to their less immediate attachment to the actual forms of life; so that inevitably they give place more and more to the weightier lyric forms, to ode and elegy, and reflective monody, which become characteristic poetic types of the new age, just as pastoral and song are the representative forms of the earlier period; while the sonnet is the connecting link of the two, and in its fuller development in Shakespeare perhaps antedates the spirit of the later changes by several years.[1] The lyric throughout exhibits a deeper moral substance. It is becoming modernized.

The influence of Petrarch and the early Italian lyric, so prominent in all Elizabethan poets of the first period, and the influence of Italian Platonism, so marked in the cases of Sidney and Spenser, make way first for the influence of the later Petrarchists of Italy, France, and Spain, such as Chiabrera, Marino, and Gongora, which is felt in the poets of the so-called Fantastic School in England, in Crashaw, Cowley, Quarles, and all the followers of Donne, and even, in a less degree, in poets like Drummond; later, or even beginning with Jonson, the normalizing and literate influence of Latin poetry grows stronger and stronger with poets who smack of the new classicism, until it allies itself in the end with the various French influences which are so noticeable in much of the literature of the last half of the seventeenth century.

New Foreign Influences.

The themes of lyric poetry do not greatly change.

---

[1] The date of Shakespeare's sonnets is uncertain; and may be anywhere from 1592 to 1608.

What does change in it is its spirit, its form, and
its mood. Just as we see Pindar's pomp
and artistic exaltation pass into the
choral elaboration and the measured
nobility of the Sophoclean ode, and just as Sappho's
passion gives way to the delicate lassitude and
melancholy of the poets of the Greek Anthology,
so we see the swift simplicity and the contented
grace of the poets of the reign of Elizabeth yielding
to the inimitable and indescribable 'seventeenth-
century touch' of Jonson, Donne, and Herrick,
uniting the common and the remote, the simple
and the 'metaphysical' in the nearest and most
uncommon conjunctions of lyrical verse that English
poetry has ever seen. The older and simpler themes
are still repeated, but a new range is added. Even
lyric love grows less lyrical and more intense. A
more masculine beauty and a new mood of reflec-
tion set in with Shakespeare's sonnets. Love is
no longer idyllic or even sentimental. It becomes
something fatal for good or ill. With Donne,
especially, it becomes subtleized; the thought of
it is a reverie; the lover dwells on the themes of
absence and inconstancy; it leads to all the passions,
and to the final consciousness of all the good and
ill of life. Other subjects enter the lyric: there are
tears and dirges; Shakespeare and Fletcher sing
the pleasures of melancholy; Sleep and Death are
compared and moralized; Jonson, Fletcher, Campion,
and Herrick sing of triumphs and bridals—for
ceremonies and masques, the pomp and pageantry
of external existence, still fill the public eye; so,
too, verse in elegy, ode, and epithalamium more

and more becomes occasional and ceremonial; the poet begins to address himself rather to the single patron or to the court than to the national public of Elizabeth's day.[1] Anacreontics, reflections on the pettiness of life, the theme of *vanitas vanitatum*, a lambent sentiment and a reversion to a gentle mood of ascetic submission in the new religious lyric of Herbert, Crashaw, and Vaughan, autumn and old age, winter and retirement, and death: such are the characteristic topics of this lyric.

Each lyrist of this period has his style and way of thinking to himself; there is little of the set manner of a school among any party of them; and yet certain tendencies in common naturally mark out two or three fairly well-defined groups for separate treatment. Thus Campion, Drummond, and Browne, nay even Herrick and Milton, although modifying and modified each by the influences of the time, continue and develop certain tendencies of the lyric school of Spenser and the early Elizabethans. Campion, whose song begins during the last decade of Elizabeth's reign, but continues down nearly to the end of that of James, is in one sense the representative song-writer of the age; although the quality of his imagination—shown, for example, in such a piece as that of his beginning,

Three Tendencies in Seventeenth-century Lyric Art: I. The Followers of Spenser and the Romantic Lyric.

Campion.

When thou must home to shades of underground—

---

[1] This tendency is especially marked in the Jacobean drama, as Mr. Fleay has pointed out. Royal patronage dominates all other, and the dramatist writes far more for the mere court and town party, and less to the greatly united nation, than in Elizabeth's day.

is touched not so much with the manner of the school contemporary with Spenser as with the new manner which comes with the turning of the century. Campion is a lyric poet of a rare sort. There is a sweet perfection in his phrase and feeling at his best, which reminds us of the best of his Scotch contemporary Drummond. His unambitious lyric is simple with the simplicity of true art. At his best, and within a narrow field, he is worthy to rank where Mr. Bullen places him—after Burns and Shelley,—or where Professor Schelling places him— with Herrick and Ben Jonson. The imagination of Drummond aspires to Spenser's rich standard of association and contrast; *Drummond.* he has a refined poetic sensuousness and delight in objective imagery; his sentiment is romantic, melancholy, and musical; but the new subjective and meditative emotion which pervades his verse, and a slight involuntary tendency to the new conceits and metaphysical quiddities mark him also as one of the new age. The idyllic and objective spirit of the early period is better reproduced in Browne, who is often admirably suave and melodious, but whose manner tends to a *Browne.* more than lyrical profusion and length; while the same spirit with the same attendant defect appears now and then also in the easy verse of Wither. The early paganism and delight in external beauty are continued likewise in Herrick and in the Cavalier poetry, transformed *Herrick.* however by a certain sophistication of style and feeling. Herrick is indeed the last expression of the pagan Renaissance, prolonged into the quiddities of the metaphysics, the self-reproaches of the mystics and the devotees, and the darkness of Puritanism. Herrick rises to no spiritual heights nor does he sink into spiritual glooms. He is frankly for this world while it lasts, piously content with its good gifts. His naïveté is partly art, partly nature, or rather it is nature refined by art; for he is out and out an artist—the most perfect specimen of the minor poet that England has ever known. He is purely a lyrist, and in his own vein he is really unsurpassed, whether in the English lyric or any other. Milton's lyric style is not so purely lyrical and personal; it is rather idyllic and objective. In this he is in a measure the poetic son of Spenser; and he, too, last of the Elizabethans, has a certain turn of lyric rhythm and phrase never afterwards recaptured. *L'Allegro* and *Il Penseroso* are the objective and idyllic presentations of the two fundamental sub-jective states of the human soul. In these poems all the rhythmical witchery and the subtle beauty of symbolism developed or suggested in the lyrics of Spenser, Shakespeare, Campion, Fletcher, Drum-mond, and Browne, is taken up and carried into the last perfection of English idyllic metre and fancy. And the *Lycidas* carries on the vein of earlier Ode and Elegy to a like perfection. Through all the concrete symbolism of these poems, however, we read the suggestion of the new ethical and subjec-tive mood of the time, saturated with and subdued to the genius of the man Milton.

Against the Renaissance ornamentation, the idyl-licism, and the exotic conventionality characteristic

Milton as a Lyrist.

of so much of the poetry of the first Elizabethan
period, two poets especially, Donne and   II. The influ-
Jonson, early set themselves in more or   ence of Jonson.
less conscious reaction, and by their strong personal
influence do much to change the character of the
poetry of the succeeding age.   Jonson's lyrical
outbursts are of a rare quality, and are informed
with a true poetic rhetoric and a sonorous fancy
that captivates the ear and the memory.   But even
at his best there is something elaborate and care-
fully prepared in his finest imaginings—something
of the pomp of deliberate art aiming at explicit
results and fired to a measured enthusiasm, as, for
example, in his *Triumph of Charis.*   His genius
does not readily flow; it has too many inhibitions
and lacks geniality.   So that his purely lyrical pro-
duction is scanty, in spite of a voluminous mass of
poetry to his credit neither dramatic nor narrative,
but couched in varied metrical forms, epitaphs, epi-
grams, epistles, epithalamia, odes, panegyrics, and
the like; even the purely lyrical element in his
masques is not persistent but sporadic.   His rare
singing lyrics thus are in the style of the period,
with a bias toward regularity and conscious art, but
the influence of his other verse is all for classicism
and restraint.   The truth is that neither Jonson nor
Donne was by temperament fundamentally lyrical,
and this fact was of unhappy augury for the lyrical
spirit of the succeeding age.   Jonson's immediate
followers are chiefly the minor dramatists, Brome,
Cartwright, and Randolph, although many others,
like Herrick and Suckling, are sealed of the tribe
of Ben, and show the impress of his strong person-

ality. In most cases, however, the influence of Jonson, strangely enough, is conjoined with that of Donne.

The lyric manner of Donne[1] certainly is in marked contrast with that of all preceding poets III. Donne and and of most of his early contemporaries, after. and the note of reaction in it is unmistakable. It was immediately recognized as a novelty, and, in that age of catholic tastes, it was very generally admired.[2] Protests, however, were not wanting. Drummond, in a passage in a letter which seems to be directed against the new movement which starts from Donne, writes: "[Poesy] subsisteth by herself, and after one demeanour and continuance her beauty appeareth to all ages. In vain have some men of late, transformers of everything, consulted upon her reformation, and endeavoured to abstract her to metaphysical ideas and scholastical quiddities, denuding her of her "The Metaphysi- own habits and those ornaments with cal School." which she hath amused the world some thousand years."[3] Donne's poetry, it cannot be denied, is denuded of most of the habits and ornaments which up till then had been considered *de rigueur* for polite verse. Whether the occasional ingenuity and remoteness of his imaginative turns deserve the appellation of "metaphysical ideas and

[1] Most of his poetry, in all probability, was written circa 1590–1600.

[2] See, as a very interesting example of contemporary verse-criticism, Thomas Carew's *Elegy upon the Death of Dr. Donne.* What Donne's reform was, in the eyes of his contemporaries, is fully explained in this piece.

[3] In Masson's *Life of Drummond*, p. 257 ; date of letter unknown, but before 1641.

scholastical quiddities" might to-day be made a
matter of question. Dr. Johnson, indeed, using what
appears to have been the traditional epithet—it is
used also by Dryden in the same connection,—calls
the manner 'metaphysical'; and, by a heroical
exercise of the time-fallacy (for the lyrical work of
Donne and of Cowley was separated by a full
quarter-century), ranks the poetry of Cowley under
the same head. As a matter of fact Cowley's verse
is, loosely speaking, 'metaphysical'; that is to say,
it is far-fetched, abstract, and intellectualized.
Cowley represents both the culmination and the
incipient degeneracy of the school of wit and
ingenuity in poetry. He is the reputed father of
the bastard Pindarique ode,[1] a species which repre-
sents the galvanic extravagance of individualism,
already potential in Donne, and also the dissolution
of organic poetic form, just as the conceits and the
abstract manner of his thought represent a similar
extravagance and decay in poetic substance.
Donne's quality, however, is quite different from
that of Cowley. His thought and his fancies
indeed are often strange and fantastic; but his
imagery is only too concrete and intense. It is
primarily in this respect that his conceits represent
an advance over the purely conventional and
Italianate conceits of the early lyric school, or over
the more elaborate and conscious prettinesses of
Marinists like Drummond. What marks the new
poetic style is an intensification of conceit, weight-
ing it with symbolism. Applied to more serious
conceptions the tendency results in the religious

[1] Jonson, however, wrote Pindariques before Cowley.

symbolism of Crashaw and Herbert. Donne is a
thoroughly original spirit and a great innovator; he
is thoughtful, indirect, and strange; he nurses his
fancies, lives with them, and broods over them so
much that they are still modern in all their distinc-
tion and ardour, in spite of the strangeness of their
apparel—a strangeness no greater perhaps than
that of some modern poets, like Browning, as the
apparel of their verse will appear two hundred
years hence. Ingenuity, allusiveness, the evocation
of remote images and of analogies that startle the
mind into a more than half acquiescence, phantoms
of deep thoughts, and emotions half-sophisticated
and wholly intense: these things mark the poetry
of Donne. His lyric is original and taking, but it
lacks simple thoughts; it does not sing. It is
ascetic and sometimes austere; the sense of sin, the
staple of contemporary tragedy, enters the lyric
with Donne. He is all for terseness and meaning;
and his versification accords with his thought and
is equally elliptical.

But as Donne's spirit is all for individualization,
so his influence is rather masculine and genetic
The influence of than formal. His influence is widely
Donne.   diffused, but he does not form a school.
Indeed, some of those who show the attraction of
his genius most are themselves in partial reaction
against what is bizarre and extravagant in the
rhythms and in the art of Donne. It is thus, for
example, with Waller and Carew, who derive from
Jonson in part and in part from Donne, and with
the growing band of those who practised the heroic
couplet and the formal graces of the new classical

manner, which was destined so soon to supersede
Elizabethan lyricism. With the cavalier The Cavalier
and courtier lyrists of the Carolan age, Lyrists.
however, the new lyric treatment of love and of the
lighter concerns of life which was begun by Donne
is carried to its inevitable if not its natural develop-
ment. The note of serious artistic effort is lost;
the man of the world supplants the poet. Cynicism,
persiflage, badinage, gallantry, and rococo conceits
mark the verses of Carew, Suckling, Lovelace, and
Randolph; when they succeed it is by a happy
lyric accident, but the result then is seen in little
masterpieces of inimitable charm.

Donne's poetic style, as well as the spirit of
symbolism and asceticism of his religious lyrics,
influences strongly all the seventeenth-
century religious poetry. George Herbert The Seventeenth-
is Donne's first disciple, and Herbert's century Religious Lyric.
poetry in turn exercises a strong influence on Cra-
shaw and Vaughan. There is, however, much more
poetic individualism in the religious lyrists than in
the cavalier lyrists, inasmuch as their lyrics are
more the expression of the inner life of the religious
thought of the times, and less the copies of polite
verse and the careless exercises of fancy of mere
men of the world. Herbert's sweet submissiveness
of mood, his spirituality, even his mannered quaint-
ness, have charmed generations of readers. Crashaw
is in poetry as in religion an emotional ritualist; a
rich and sensuous pathos characterizes his diction
and his rhythms, and redeems from tastelessness
conceits over-subtle and symbolical, and marked by
all the extravagance of the rococo vein. Vaughan's

verse is highly remarkable and original—that of a
genius *manqué*, but rising to gleams of inspiration.
In form he is careless and unequal, but his lyric is
meditative, fresh, and highly subjective, the deep
and pregnant reflection of a life and experience of
much sorrow. In feeling and in phrase he is often
strangely modern.

The poetry of Donne and the sonnets of Shake-
speare introduce an intense and self-consuming
Characteristics of subjectivity into English lyric poetry.
the Seventeenth- With others, such as Drummond and
century Lyrical
Style. Vaughan, there is something of the same
spirit, but not until the modern period is lyric sub-
jectivity ever again so deep and pregnant as with
these two masters of passionate introspection. It
is doubtless the union of this note of subjectivity,
subtlety, and sophistication with the idyllic and
objective manner of the early Elizabethans which
produces the potency and charm of the character-
istic seventeenth-century lyric—a lyric which is
the result of a fusion of styles; objective imagery
made strange and significant by remoteness and
unexpectedness on the one hand, on the other sub-
jective significance and depth touched by objective
grace and beauty. For the lyric is always char-
acteristic of the times; and the age, not yet freed
from all the influences of Mediævalism, was still
engaged in an attempt to penetrate into nature by
way of subtlety and indirection. The forcing pro-
cess which the cumulative Renaissance influences
had carried on, aided by the counter-irritant of the
Reformation movement, had sharpened and exas-
perated men's wits to an incredible degree. The

curiosity of the Elizabethans was on the *qui vive* at all points and continually. To meet and satisfy this avidity of intellectual and emotional appetite, literature was forced more and more to subtlety and to the purveyance of significant novelty. We see this process in the very substance and manner both of contemporary prose literature and of the drama. Thus Bacon's metaphors are analogically subtle and penetrating to a very high degree; Burton is strange and curious and abounds in odd juxtapositions of thought; Sir Thomas Browne ransacks the universe *The natural genesis of conceits in poetic style.* for surprising conceptions, and wings his way through remote spheres to an *O altitudo!* And so often of the dramatic style of Shakespeare and Webster. All this reacts upon both style and subject in the lyric. Conceits, as Professor Saintsbury remarks, are more in place in the lyric than in any other literary form; it is only when they are pursued for their own sake and become conventional and intellectualized that they lose their grace and cease to act as the saving salt of lyric style. There is a certain moment in seventeenth-century lyric literature when the fusion of two opposite styles is just at its perfection, and conceit and conception hang in happy equipoise. Before stand the simpler pastoral and Italian conceits of the early lyrists; immediately after follow the 'metaphysical' conceits and the decline of lyric style; between the two hovers the delicate style of seventeenth-century lyricism in its brief perfection.

Long before the new lyric style has reached its height, the elements which were to mark its decline have begun to appear. With Daniel and with

Jonson something of a classical and normalizing
tendency had already manifested itself.

More and more, too, the lyric begins
to stagger under an increasing weight of thought.
The vein of philosophical poetry opened in Spen-
ser's Platonic hymns is developed with Sir John
Davies, Chapman, Lord Brooke, Lord Herbert of
Cherbury, and Henry More. Didactic and gnomic
verse after Latin models grows in favour. The
very subjectivity of the lyric spirit, pushed to self-
consciousness, becomes a fatal gift for the final
destruction of the lyric. The fierce tension of life
begins to obliterate art. The singing mood recedes
before the new influences. Now and then, at the
end of the period, a poetic recluse, like Herrick or
like Milton, endeavours to resist the stress of life
and the forces making for prose, but with only
partial success. Both Herrick and Milton show
traces of the time-spirit, and are not lyrical with
the full-throated ease of earlier singers; in Herrick
especially there is a self-conscious artlessness which
is quite foreign to the best Elizabethan spirit.

Another influence which militates against the
lyric spirit in the Jacobean and Carolan age is
the spread of satire. Donne and Jonson are both
satirists. At first, perhaps, the self-consciousness
of the satiric spirit, while chilling slightly the naïve
ingenuousness of the early lyric enthusiasm, leads
to a new mastery over expression and a firmer tone
of real feeling; so that the modern reader feels
more at home with the seventeenth-century lyrists
than with the Elizabethan. The deeper satire and
cynicism of the Restoration period, however, seems

thoroughly to precipitate the lyric mood. The process of the change can be characteristically traced in the new lyric treatment of love. The dark pessimism of the Shakespeare of the *Sonnets* and the Donne of the *Elegies* passes into the persiflage and levity of the Cavalier lyrists, wherein conventional reminiscences of the old idyllicism and Petrarchan romanticism are strangely mingled with new and conflicting elements of satire, raillery, frank paganism, and a subtleized pseudo-Platonism. In the later Restoration times the Cavalier spirit is carried to the last point of cynicism, and lyric love becomes an idle convention for mere poetasters.

Changes in form resulting from changes in spirit affect the lyric later than other literary kinds, for the reason that Form in the lyric is more important than in other kinds and consequently more tenacious and persistent. The formal reversion to classicism, accordingly, affects the external appearance of narrative and dramatic poetry profoundly, but leaves the metres and conventions of the lyric substantially untouched; it has the more fatal effect, however, of restraining and finally of superseding that impulse to free, inspired, and personal poetic utterance which is the essential spirit of lyricism itself. With this spirit the spirit of modern classicism was fundamentally at variance. The change in poetic inspiration and tone, accordingly, is marked in the lyric as soon as in other literary forms. This change meant at first a deepening and complexity of thought and feeling. A finished and subtle art takes the place of the earlier free and fluent inspiration. The lyric

By way of Summary.

turn flows more and more from the remote and
the unexpected; the spontaneity and artlessness of
the simple emotions disappear; feeling becomes
sophisticated; men come to think in two ways: the
cavalier and courtier poets affect a light and cynical
gaiety and stake their all on the prizes of this
world; while to Donne and to the writers of the
religious lyric, Puritan, Anglican, and Catholic, the
natural and the mere external things of this world
grow less and less. Finally, the influence of the
classical reaction begins to make itself felt; the
conventional and the artificial in form and feeling
become of greater weight, and the normalizing
spirit of the reformers subdues the note of indi-
vidualism apparent in Donne and the poets of the
Fantastic School.   Then the Puritan reaction
follows and the Englishman sings no longer. He
has become prudential and he is in trouble about
his soul.

The lyrical product of the Restoration period is
of no great importance and offers few, if any,
The Restoration Lyric. original features. The poets who repre-
sent the transition from the preceding
age are Waller, Cowley, Denham, and Davenant.
The chief lyrical writers typical of the period are
Dryden, Dorset, Sedley, and Rochester. Dryden's
great odes are a marked advance in respect of
rhetoric, of harmonious versification, and of native
power, over the Pindariques of Cowley and of
Cowley's imitators. But otherwise the Restoration
lyric seems essentially to represent the mere sur-
vival and decadence of the Cavalier and Courtier

lyric of the age of Charles I. With the transfor-
mation of general poetic style and the predomi-
nance of the couplet, we observe the pinching-out
of the lyric vein and the disappearance of lyrical
inspiration. The sonnet is no longer written, and
the range of lyric form is greatly narrowed. Did-
actic, descriptive, and satiric verse take the place of
the varied lyrical kinds of the Elizabethan period.
There is no longer food for the lyrical spirit. The
nation is exhausted with its long civil discord.
Life is no longer new and fresh, nor is it intensely
earnest. Literature no longer voices any deep
national moods or aspirations. It appeals to 'the
town', and not to the nation, and 'wit', regulated
by judgment, rather than by imagination and fancy,
becomes the measure of literary performance. With
the new classicism the lyrical spirit has little in
common, and the true English lyric must wait for
its revival until the next romantic period.

ENGLISH LYRIC POETRY.

(1500–1700.)

JOHN SKELTON.

(1460?–1529.)

TO MISTRESS MARGERY WENTWORTH.

Skelton's slender but genuine lyric vein seems to have been obscured by the satirical tendency of most of his verse-writing. He is a genius *manqué*, but a genius, and may fitly be put first in point of time among modern representatives of English lyric poetry. His works are accessible in the second volume of Chalmers' edition of Johnson's *English Poets* (1810), and in a separate edition by Dyce (1843).

WITH marjoram gentle,
  The flower of goodlyhede[1],
Embroidered the mantle
Is of your maidenhede.
  Plainly I can not glose[2];
Ye be, as I divine,
The pretty primrose,
The goodly columbine.
  With marjoram gentle,
The flower of goodlyhede,
Embroidered the mantle
Is of your maidenhede.
  Benign, courteise, and meke,
With wordes well devised,
In you who list to seke,
Be virtues well comprised.

[1] goodlihead, goodness.   [2] flatter.

With marjoram gentle,
The flower of goodlyhede,
Embroidered the mantle
Is of your maidenhede.

TO MISTRESS ISABEL PENNELL.

MY maiden Isabel,
   Reflaring[1] rosabel,
The flagrant[2] cammamel,
  The ruddy rosary,
The sovereign rosemary,
The pretty strawberry,
  The columbine, the nept[3],
The jeloffer[4] well set,
The proper violet.
  Ennewed[5] your colouer
Is like the daisy flower,
After the April shower.
  Star of the morrow gray,
The blossom on the spray,
The freshest flower of May.
  Maidenly demure,
Of womanhede the lure,
Wherfore I make you sure,
  It were an heauenly health,
It were an endless wealth,
A life for God himself,
  To hear this nightingale
Among the birdes smale,
Warbeling in the vale,
Dug, dug, jug, jug,
Good year and good luck,
With chuck, chuck, chuck, chuck!

[1] perfumed.   [2] *i.e.* fragrant.   [3] catmint.   [4] gilliflower.   [5] Renewed

HENRY HOWARD, EARL OF SURREY.

(1517?–1547.)

DESCRIPTION OF SPRING.

(WHEREIN EACH THING RENEWS, SAVE ONLY THE LOVER.)

The selections from Surrey and Wyatt, with two exceptions, appeared first in the volume usually known as *Tottel's Miscellany* (1557). This was the first of the Elizabethan miscellanies, and a great landmark in the new poetry. Selections from most of the others, such as *England's Helicon* and *Davison's Poetical Rhapsody*, will be found on subsequent pages of the present volume. Both of the latter works may be read in the modern editions of Mr. Bullen. *Tottel's Miscellany* is included in Professor Arber's series of "English Reprints". The contributors include most of the poets of the time. The sonnet and the song are represented in these collections, but the pastoral note, at least in the later ones, seems to predominate. The poems in *Tottel's Miscellany*, written mostly 1527–1557, are partly in the amatory vein, imitative of Italian models, and partly in the native manner, didactic, reflective, and elegiac. There are separate modern editions of Surrey and Wyatt, and both are included in Chalmers' *English Poets*.

THE sootë[1] season, that bud and bloom forth brings,
  With green hath clad the hill, and eke the vale:
The nightingale with feathers new she sings;
The turtle to her mate hath told her tale;
Summer is come, for every spray now springs,
The hart hath hung his old head on the pale;
The buck in brake his winter coat he flings;
The fishes float with new repaired scale;
The adder all her slough away she slings;
The swift swallow pursueth the flies smale[2];
The busy bee her honey now she mings[3];
Winter is worn that was the flowers' bale.
  And thus I see among these pleasant things
  Each care decays, and yet my sorrow springs.

[1] sweet.   [2] small.   [3] mingles.

DESCRIPTION AND PRAISE OF HIS LOVE GERALDINE.

FROM Tuscane came my lady's worthy race;
　　Fair Florence was sometime her ancient seate;
The western isle, whose pleasant shore doth face
Wild Camber's cliffs, did give her lively heat[1]:
Foster'd she was with milk of Irish breast;
Her sire, an Earl; her dame of princes' blood:
From tender years, in Britain she doth rest
With kinges childe, where she tasteth costly food.
Hunsdon did first present her to mine eyen;
Bright is her hue, and Geraldine she hight:
Hampton me taught to wish her first for mine;
And Windsor, alas, doth chase me from her sight.
　　Her beauty of kind[2], her virtues from above;
　　Happy is he that can obtain her love!

COMPLAINT OF A LOVER REBUKED.

LOVE that liveth and reigneth in my thought,
　　That built his seat within my captive breast,
Clad in the arms, wherein with me he fought,
Oft in my face he doth his banner rest.
She, that me taught to love, and suffer pain,
My doubtfull hope, and eke my hot desire
With shamefast cloak to shadow and refrain,
Her smiling grace converteth straight to ire.
And coward Love then to the heart apace
Taketh his flight, whereas[3] he lurks, and plains
His purpose lost, and dare not shew his face.
For my lordes gilt thus faultless bide I pains,
Yet from my lord shall not my foot remove:
Sweet is his death, that takes his end by love.

[1] the warmth of life.　　　[2] nature.　　　[3] where.

THE MEANS TO ATTAIN HAPPY LIFE.

MARTIAL, the things that do attain
    The happy life be these, I find:
The riches left, not got with pain,
    The fruitful ground, the quiet mind,

The equal friend, no grudge, no strife,
    No charge of rule nor governance;
Without disease, the healthful life;
    The household of continuance;

The mean diet, no delicate fare;
    True wisdom joined with simpleness;
The night dischargèd of all care,
    Where wine the wit may not oppress.

The faithful wife, without debate[1];
    Such sleeps as may beguile the night;
Contented with thine own estate,
    Ne wish for death, ne fear his might.

SIR THOMAS WYATT.
(1503-1542.)

FORGET NOT YET.

FORGET not yet the tried intent
    Of such a truth as I have meant[2];
My great travail so gladly spent,
    Forget not yet!

Forget not yet when first began
The weary life ye know, since whan
The suit, the service none tell can;
    Forget not yet!

---

[1] quarrelling.   [2] fidelity as I have shown.

Forget not yet the great assays[1],
The cruel wrong, the scornful ways,
The painful patience in delays
    Forget not yet!

Forget not! oh! forget not this,
How long ago hath been, and is
The mind that never meant amiss,
    Forget not yet!

Forget not then thine own approved,
The which so long hath thee so loved,
Whose steadfast faith yet never moved:
    Forget not yet!

AN EARNEST SUIT TO HIS UNKIND MISTRESS NOT TO FORSAKE HIM.

AND wilt thou leave me thus?
    Say nay! say nay! for shame!
To save thee from the blame
Of all my grief and grame[2].
And wilt thou leave me thus?
Say nay! say nay!
    And wilt thou leave me thus?
That hath lov'd thee so long?
In wealth and woe among·
And is thy heart so strong
As for to leave me thus?
Say nay! say nay!
    And wilt thou leave me thus?
That hath given thee my heart
Never for to depart;
Neither for pain nor smart:

[1] trials.   [2] vexation.

And wilt thou leave me thus?
Say nay! say nay!
    And wilt thou leave me thus,
And have no more pity,
Of him that loveth thee?
Alas! thy cruelty!
And wilt thou leave me thus?
    Say nay! say nay!

"THE LOVER SHEWETH HOW HE IS FORSAKEN OF SUCH AS HE SOMETIME ENJOYED."

THEY flee from me, that sometime did me seek,
    With naked foote stalking within my chamber:
Once have I seen them gentle, tame, and meek,
That now are wild, and do not once remember
That sometime they have put themselves in danger[1],
To take bread at my hand; and now they range,
Busily seeking in continual change.

Thanked be fortune, it hath been otherwise,
Twenty times better; but once especial,
In thin array, after a pleasant guise,
When her loose gown did from her shoulders fall
And she me caught in her armes long and small[2],
And therewithal, so sweetly did me kiss,
And softly said, 'Dear heart, how like you this?'

It was no dream; for I lay broad awaking:
But all is turned now through my gentlenesse,
Into a bitter fashion of forsaking;
And I have leave to go of her goodnesse;
And she also to use newfanglenesse.
But, since that I unkindly so am served,
How like you this; what hath she now deserved?

[1] in my power.   [2] slender.

GEORGE GASCOIGNE.
(1530?–1577.)

THE LULLABY OF A LOVER.

Gascoigne wrote much in lyrical measures in the period immediately
preceding the advent of Spenser and Sidney.   His poems are contained
in volume ii. of Chalmers' collection, and there is a modern edition of
his works by W. C. Hazlitt (Roxburghe Library, 1869, 2 vols.).   The
selection is from Gascoigne's *Hundred Sundry Flowers*, 1572.

SING Lullaby, as women do,
   Wherewith they bring their babes to rest,
And Lullaby can I sing too,
As womanly as can the best.
With Lullaby they still the child,
And if I be not much beguiled,
Full many wanton babes have I,
Which must be stilled with Lullaby.

First Lullaby my youthful years,
It is now time to go to bed,
For crooked age and hoary heares[1],
Have won the haven within my head:
With Lullaby then youth be still,
With Lullaby content thy will,
Since courage quails, and comes behind,
Go sleep, and so beguile thy mind.

Next Lullaby my gazing eyes,
Which wonted were to glance apace;
For every glass may now suffice,
To shew the furrows in my face:
With Lullaby then wink[2] awhile,
With Lullaby your looks beguile:
Let no fair face, nor beauty bright,
Entice you eft with vain delight.

     [1] hairs.   [2] close the eyes.

And Lullaby my wanton will;
Let reason's rule now reign thy thought,
Since all too late I find by skill,
How dear I have thy fancies bought;
With Lullaby now take thine ease,
With Lullaby thy doubts appease;
For trust to this, if thou be still,
My body shall obey thy will.

.   .   .   .   .

Thus Lullaby my youth, mine eyes,
My will, my ware, and all that was,
I can no mo delays devise,
But welcome pain, let pleasure pass:
With Lullaby now take your leave,
With Lullaby your dreams deceive,
And when you rise with waking eye,
Remember then this Lullaby.

GEORGE TURBERVILE.

(1530?-1595?)

THE LOVER TO HIS LADY THAT GAZED MUCH UP TO THE SKIES.

These four lines are a translation of the well-known epigram ascribed to Plato. Turbervile's lyrical verse appeared in 1570 as *Epitaphs, Epigrams, Songes and Sonets*. Reprinted in volume ii. of Chalmers' *Poets*.

MY Girl, thou gazest much
Upon the golden skies:
Would I were Heaven, I would behold
Thee then with all mine eyes.

JAMES WEDDERBURN.

(1500?–1565?)

GO, HEART.

A Scots lyrist, author of *Ane Compendious Buike of Godly and Spiritual Songs*, 1597 (edition of circa 1549 no longer extant). In Dalyell's *Scottish Poems of the Sixteenth Century*, Edinburgh, 1801. The extracts may be found in Fitzgibbon's *Early English Poetry* (Canterbury Poets).

GO, heart, unto the lamp of light:
    Go, heart, do service and honour;
Go, heart, and serve him day and night;
    Go, heart, unto thy Saviour.

Go, heart, to thy only remede,
Descending from the heavenly tour,
Thee to deliver from pain and deid[1]:
    Go, heart, unto thy Saviour.

Go, heart, right humble and full meek,
Go, heart, as leal and true servitour,
To him that health is for all flesh,
    Go, heart, unto thy Saviour.

Go, heart, with true and whole intent,
To Christ, thy help and whole succour;
Thee to redeem He was all rent;
    Go, heart, unto thy Saviour.

To Christ, that rose from death to life,
Go, heart, unto my latter hour,
Whose great mercy can none descrive,
    Go, heart, unto thy Saviour.

[1] death.

LEAVE ME NOT.

Psalm xxvii. 9.

AH! my Lord, leave me not,
   Leave me not, leave me not,
Ah! my Lord, leave me not,
   Thus mine alone:
With ane burden on my back
I may not bear, I am so weak,
Lord, this burden from me take,
   Or else I am gone.

.   .   .   .   .   .

With Thy hands Thou hast me wrought,
Leave me not, leave me not,
With Thy hands Thou hast me wrought,
   Leave me not alone;
I was sold and Thou me bought,
With Thy blood Thou hast me coft[1]·
Now am I hither sought
   To Thee, Lord, alone.

I cry and I call to Thee,
To leave me not, to leave me not,
I cry and I call to Thee,
   To leave me not alone:
All they that laden be,
Thou bidst them come to Thee,
Then shall they saved be,
   Through Thy mercy alone.

[1] bought.

NICHOLAS UDALL (?).

(1504?–1556.)

PIPE, MERRY ANNOT.

This is a song from the early comedy of *Ralph Roister Doister* (printed 1566), of which Udall is thought to have been the author. The song seems to be of earlier date, and may not have been of Udall's composition. The play may be found in Hazlitt's Dodsley, vol. iii.

PIPE, merry Annot,
    Trilla, Trilla, Trillary.
Work, Tibet; work, Annot; work, Margery;
Sew, Tibet; knit, Annot; spin, Margery.
Let us see who will win the victory.

    Pipe, merry Annot,
    Trilla, Trilla, Trillary.
What, Tibet! what, Annot! what, Margery!
Ye sleep, but we do not, that shall we try;
Your fingers be numbed, our work will not lie.

    Pipe, merry Annot,
    Trilla, Trilla, Trillary.
Now, Tibet; now, Annot; now, Margery;
Now whippet apace for the maistry:
But it will not be, our mouth is so dry.

    Pipe, merry Annot,
    Trilla, Trilla, Trillary.
When, Tibet? when, Annot? when, Margery?
I will not,—I can not,—no more can I.
Then give we all over, and there let it lie!

EDMUND SPENSER.
(1552?–1599.)

THE SONG OF ENCHANTMENT.

Spenser's *Lyrical Poems* (the *Shepherd's Calendar, Astrophel*, the *Amoretti, Epithalamion, Four Hymns*, and *Prothalamion*) have appeared in a separate volume in Mr. Ernest Rhys' series of "The Lyric Poets" (London and New York, 1895). Extracts of a lyrical cast from the *Shepherd's Calendar*, 1579, appear in the volume of *English Pastorals* in the present series. The *Daphnaida*, "an elegy upon the death of the noble and virtuous Douglas Howard", appeared in 1591; the *Amoretti* or Sonnets in 1595 (written 1592–3); the *Epithalamion*, a song in celebration of the poet's own marriage, in 1595 (written 1594–5); the *Prothalamion*, or a "Spousal Verse, in honour of the double marriage of two honourable and virtuous ladies, the Lady Elizabeth and the Lady Katherine Somerset", in 1596; and the *Four Hymns* in the same year. The following is the famous Song of Despair from the *Fairy Queen*, book I., canto ix.

WHO travels by the weary wandering way,
    To come unto his wishèd home in haste,
And meets a flood that doth his passage stay,
Is not great grace to help him over past,
Or free his feet that in the mire stick fast?
Most envious man, that grieves at neighbour's good,
And fond, that joyest in the woe thou hast!
Why wilt not let him pass, that long hath stood
Upon the bank, yet wilt thyself not pass the flood?

He there does now enjoy eternal rest
And happy ease, which thou dost want and crave,
And further from it daily wanderest:
What if some little pain the passage have,
That makes frail flesh to fear the bitter wave?
Is not short pain well borne, that brings long ease,
And lays the soul to sleep in quiet grave?
Sleep after toil, port after stormy seas,
Ease after war, death after life does greatly please!

The lenger life, I wot, the greater sin;
The greater sin, the greater punishment:
All those great battles, which thou boasts to win
Through strife, and bloodshed, and avengement,
Now praised, hereafter dear thou shalt repent;
For life must life, and blood must blood repay.
Is not enough thy evil life forespent?
For he that once hath missèd the right way,
The further he doth go, the further he doth stray.

Then do no further go, no further stray,
But here lie down, and to thy rest betake,
Th' ill to prevent, that life ensewen may;
For what hath life that may it lovèd make,
And gives not rather cause it to forsake?
Fear, sickness, age, loss, labour, sorrow, strife,
Pain, hunger, cold that makes the heart to quake;
And ever fickle fortune rageth rife;
All which, and thousands mo, do make a loathsome life.

FROM THE DAPHNAIDA.

HOW happy was I when I saw her lead
      The shepherds' daughters dancing in a round!
How trimly would she trace and softly tread
The tender grass, with rosy garland crowned!
And when she list advance her heavenly voice,
Both Nymphs and Muses nigh she made astownd,
And flocks and shepherds causèd to rejoice.

But now, ye shepherd lasses! who shall lead
Your wandering troups, or sing your virelayes[1]?
Or who shall dight your bowers, sith she is dead
That was the Lady of your holy-days?
Let now your bliss be turnèd into bale,

---

[1] light songs.

And into plaints convert your joyous plays,
And with the same fill every hill and dale.

   .   .   .   .

Henceforth I hate what ever Nature made,
And in her workmanship no pleasure find;
For they be all but vain, and quickly fade,
So soon as on them blows the Northern wind;
They tarry not, but flit and fall away,
Leaving behind them nought but grief of mind,
And mocking such as think they long will stay.

I hate the heaven, because it doth withhold
Me from my love, and eke my love from me;
I hate the earth, because it is the mould
Of fleshly slime and frail mortality;
I hate the fire, because to nought it flies;
I hate the air, because sighs of it be;
I hate the sea, because it tears supplies.

   .   .   .   .

I hate to speak, my voice is spent with crying;
I hate to hear, loud plaints have dulled mine ears;
I hate to taste, for food withholds my dying;
I hate to see, mine eyes are dimmed with tears;
I hate to smell, no sweet on earth is left;
I hate to feel, my flesh is numbed with fears:
So all my senses from me are bereft.

I hate all men, and shun all womankind;
The one, because as I they wretched are;
The other, for because I do not find
My love with them, that wont to be their star:
And life I hate, because it will not last;
And death I hate, because it life doth mar;
And all I hate that is to come or past.

   .   .   .   .

To live I find it deadly dolorous,
For life draws care, and care continual woe;

Therefore to die must needs be joyeous,
And wishful thing this sad life to forgo:
But I must stay; I may it not amend;
My Daphne hence departing bade me so;
She bade me stay, till she for me did send.

Yet, whilst I in this wretched vale do stay
My weary feet shall ever wandering be,
That still I may be ready on my way
When as her messenger doth come for me;
Ne will I rest my feet for feebleness,
Ne will I rest my limbs for frailty,
Ne will I rest mine eyes for heaviness.

SONNETS.

MORE than most fair, full of the living fire,
   Kindled above unto the Maker near;
No eyes but joys, in which all powers conspire,
That to the world naught else be counted dear;
Through your bright beams doth not the blinded guest
Shoot out his darts to base affections wound;
But Angels come to lead frail minds to rest
In chaste desires, on heavenly beauty bound.
You frame my thoughts, and fashion me within;
You stop my tongue, and teach my heart to speak;
You calm the storm that passion did begin,
Strong through your cause, but by your virtue weak.
    Dark is the world, where your light shined never;
    Well is he born that may behold you ever.

———

LIKE as a ship, that through the Ocean wide,
   By conduct of some star doth make her way;
Whenas a storm hath dimmed her trusty guide,
Out of her course doth wander far astray!

So I, whose star, that wont with her bright ray
Me to direct, with clouds is overcast,
Do wander now, in darkness and dismay,
Through hidden perils round about me plast;
Yet hope I well that, when this storm is past,
My Helicë, the lodestar of my life,
Will shine again, and look on me at last,
With lovely light to clear my cloudy grief:
    Till then I wander careful[1], comfortless,
    In secret sorrow, and sad pensiveness.

MOST glorious Lord of life! that, on this day,
    Didst make thy triumph over death and sin;
And, having harrowed hell, didst bring away
Captivity thence captive, us to win:
This joyous day, dear Lord, with joy begin,
And grant that we, for whom thou diddest die,
Being with thy dear blood clean washed from sin,
May live for ever in felicity!
And that thy love we weighing worthily,
May likewise love thee for the same again;
And for thy sake, that all like dear didst buy,
With love may one another entertain!
    So let us love, dear love, like as we ought:
    Love is the lesson which the Lord us taught

FRESH Spring, the herald of love's mighty king,
    In whose coat-armour richly are displayed
All sorts of flowers, the which on earth do spring
In goodly colours gloriously arrayed;
Go to my love, where she is careless laid,
Yet in her winter's bower not well awake;
Tell her the joyous time will not be stayed,

[1] full of care.

Unless she do him by the forelock take;
Bid her therefore herself soon ready make,
To wait on Love amongst his lovely crew;
Where everyone, that misseth then her make[1],
Shall be by him amerced with penance due.
　　Make haste, therefore, sweet love, whilst it is prime;
　　For none can call again the passed time.

MEN call you fair, and you do credit it,
　　For that yourself ye daily such do see:
But the true fair, that is the gentle wit,
And virtuous mind, is much more praised of me:
For all the rest, however fair it be,
Shall turn to nought and lose that glorious hue;
But only that is permanent and free
From frail corruption, that doth flesh ensue.
That is true beauty: that doth argue you
To be divine, and born of heavenly seed;
Derived from that fair Spirit, from whom all true
And perfect beauty did at first proceed:
　　He only fair, and what he fair hath made;
　　All other fair, like flowers, untimely fade.

PROTHALAMION.

CALM was the day, and through the trembling air
　　Sweet-breathing Zephyrus did softly play
A gentle spirit, that lightly did delay
Hot Titan's beams, which then did glister fair;
When I (whom sullen care,
Through discontent of my long fruitless stay
In princes' court, and expectation vain
Of idle hopes, which still do fly away,
Like empty shadows, did afflict my brain)
Walked forth to ease my pain

[1] mate.

Along the shore of silver streaming Thames;
Whose rutty[1] bank, the which his river hems,
Was painted all with variable flowers,
And all the meads adorned with dainty gems
Fit to deck maidens' bowers,
And crown their paramours
Against the bridal day, which is not long:
  Sweet Thames! run softly, till I end my song.

There, in a meadow, by the river's side,
A flock of Nymphs I chanced to espy,
All lovely daughters of the flood thereby,
With goodly greenish locks, all loose untied,
As each had been a bride;
And each one had a little wicker basket,
Made of fine twigs, entrailed curiously,
In which they gathered flowers to fill their flasket,
And with fine fingers cropt full feateously
The tender stalks on hie.
Of every sort, which in that meadow grew,
They gathered some; the violet, pallid blue,
The little daisy, that at evening closes,
The virgin lily, and the primrose true,
With store of vermeil roses,
To deck their bridegroom's posies
Against the bridal day, which was not long:
  Sweet Thames! run softly, till I end my song.

With that I saw two swans of goodly hue
Come softly swimming down along the Lee;
Two fairer birds I yet did never see;
The snow, which doth the top of Pindus strew,
Did never whiter shew,
Nor Jove himself, when he a swan would be
For love of Leda, whiter did appear;

<hr>

[1] rooty.

Yet Leda was (they say) as white as he,
Yet not so white as these, nor nothing near;
So purely white they were,
That even the gentle stream, the which them bare,
Seemed foul to them, and bade his billows spare
To wet their silken feathers, lest they might
Soil their fair plumes with water not so fair,
And mar their beauties bright,
That shone as heaven's light,
Against their bridal day, which was not long:
    Sweet Thames! run softly, till I end my song.

Eftsoons the Nymphs, which now had flowers their fill,
Ran all in haste to see that silver brood,
As they came floating on the crystal flood;
Whom when they saw, they stood amazed still,
Their wondering eyes to fill;
Them seemed they never saw a sight so fair,
Of fowls so lovely, that they sure did deem
Them heavenly born, or to be that same pair
Which through the sky draw Venus' silver team;
For sure they did not seem
To be begot of any earthly seed,
But rather Angels, or of Angels' breed;
Yet were they bred of summer's heat, they say,
In sweetest season, when each flower and weed
The earth did fresh array;
So fresh they seemed as day,
Even as their bridal day, which was not long:
    Sweet Thames! run softly, till I end my song.

Then forth they all out of their baskets drew
Great store of flowers, the honour of the field,
That to the sense did fragrant odours yield,
All which upon those goodly birds they threw
And all the waves did strew,

That like old Peneus' waters they did seem,
When down along by pleasant Tempe's shore,
Scattered with flowers, through Thessaly they stream,
That they appear, through lilies' plenteous store,
Like a bride's chamber floor.
Two of those Nymphs, meanwhile, two garlands bound
Of freshest flowers which in that mead they found,
The which presenting all in trim array,
Their snowy foreheads therewithal they crowned,
Whilst one did sing this lay,
Prepared against that day,
Against their bridal day, which was not long:
    Sweet Thames! run softly, till I end my song.

'Ye gentle birds! the world's fair ornament,
And heaven's glory, whom this happy hour
Doth lead unto your lovers' blissful bower,
Joy may you have, and gentle hearts' content
Of your love's couplement;
And let fair Venus, that is queen of love,
With her heart-quelling son upon you smile,
Whose smile, they say, hath virtue to remove
All love's dislike, and friendship's faulty guile
For ever to assoil.
Let endless peace your steadfast hearts accord,
And blessed plenty wait upon your board;
And let your bed with pleasures chaste abound,
That fruitful issue may to you afford,
Which may your foes confound,
And make your joys redound
Upon your bridal day, which is not long:
    Sweet Thames! run softly, till I end my song.

So ended she; and all the rest around
To her redoubled that her undersong,
Which said their bridal day should not be long:

And gentle Echo from the neighbour ground
Their accents did resound.
So forth those joyous birds did pass along,
Adown the Lee, that to them murmured low,
As he would speak, but that he lacked a tongue,
Yet did by signs his glad affection show,
Making his stream run slow.
And all the fowl which in his flood did dwell
Gan flock about these twain, that did excel
The rest, so far as Cynthia doth shend[1]
The lesser stars.   So they, enranged well,
Did on those two attend,
And their best service lend
Against their wedding day, which was not long:
   Sweet Thames! run softly, till I end my song.

At length they all to merry London came,
To merry London, my most kindly nurse,
That to me gave this life's first native source;
Though from another place I take my name,
An house of ancient fame:
There when they came, whereas those bricky towers
The which on Thames' broad aged back do ride,
Where now the studious lawyers have their bowers,
There whilom wont the Templar Knights to bide,
Till they decayed through pride:
Next whereunto there stands a stately place,
Where oft I gained gifts and goodly grace
Of that great lord, which therein wont to dwell,
Whose want too well now feels my friendless case;
But ah! here fits not well
Old woes, but joys, to tell
Against the bridal day, which is not long:
   Sweet Thames! run softly, till I end my song.

[1] shame, confound.

Yet therein now doth lodge a noble peer,
Great England's glory, and the world's wide wonder,
Whose dreadful name late through all Spain did thunder,
And Hercules' two pillars standing near
Did make to quake and fear:
Fair branch of honour, flower of chivalry!
That fillest England with thy triumph's fame,
Joy have thou of thy noble victory,
And endless happiness of thine own name
That promiseth the same;
That through thy prowess, and victorious arms,
Thy country may be freed from foreign harms;
And great Elisa's glorious name may ring
Through all the world, filled with thy wide alarms,
Which some brave muse may sing
To ages following,
Upon the bridal day, which is not long:
   Sweet Thames! run softly, till I end my song.

From those high towers this noble lord issuing,
Like radiant Hesper, when his golden hair
In th' ocean billows he hath bathed fair,
Descended to the river's open viewing,
With a great train ensuing.
Above the rest were goodly to be seen
Two gentle knights of lovely face and feature,
Beseeming well the bower of any queen,
With gifts of wit, and ornaments of nature,
Fit for so goodly stature,
That like the twins of Jove they seemed in sight,
Which deck the baldrick of the heavens bright;
They two, forth pacing to the river's side,
Received those two fair brides, their love's delight;
Which, at th' appointed tide,
Each one did make his bride

Against their bridal day, which is not long:
  Sweet Thames! run softly, till I end my song.

EPITHALAMION.

YE learned sisters, which have oftentimes
  Been to me aiding, others to adorn,
Whom ye thought worthy of your graceful rimes,
That ever the greatest did not greatly scorn
To hear their names sung in your simple lays,
But joyed in their praise;
And when ye list your own mishaps to mourn,
Which death, or love, or fortune's wreck did raise,
Your string could soon to sadder tenor turn,
And teach the woods and waters to lament
Your doleful dreariment:
Now lay those sorrowful complaints aside;
And, having all your heads with garlands crowned,
Help me mine own love's praises to resound;
Ne let the same of any be envied:
So Orpheus did for his own bride!
So I unto myself alone will sing;
The woods shall to me answer, and my echo ring.

Early, before the world's light-giving lamp
His golden beam upon the hills doth spread,
Having dispersed the night's uncheerful damp,
Do ye awake, and, with fresh lusty-hed,
Go to the bower of my beloved love,
My truest turtle dove;
Bid her awake; for Hymen is awake,
And long since ready forth his mask to move,
With his bright tead[1] that flames with many a flake,
And many a bachelor to wait on him,
In their fresh garments trim,

[1] torch.

Bid her awake therefore, and soon her dight,
For lo! the wished day is come at last,
That shall, for all the pains and sorrows past,
Pay to her usury of long delight:
And, whilst she doth her dight,
Do ye to her of joy and solace sing,
That all the woods may answer, and your echo ring.

Bring with you all the Nymphs that you can hear,
Both of the rivers and the forests green,
And of the sea that neighbours to her near,
All with gay garlands goodly well beseen.
And let them also with them bring in hand
Another gay garland,
For my fair love, of lilies and of roses,
Bound truelove wise with a blue silk riband;
And let them make great store of bridal posies,
And let them eke bring store of other flowers,
To deck the bridal bowers.
And let the ground whereas her foot shall tread,
For fear the stones her tender foot should wrong,
Be strewed with fragrant flowers all along,
And diapered like the discoloured[1] mead;
Which done, do at her chamber door await,
For she will waken straight;
The whiles do ye this song unto her sing,
The woods shall to you answer, and your echo ring.

Ye Nymphs of Mulla, which with careful heed
The silver scaly trouts do tend full well,
And greedy pikes which use therein to feed;
(Those trouts and pikes all others do excel);
And ye likewise, which keep the rushy lake,
Where none do fishes take;

---

[1] variegated.

Bind up the locks the which hang scattered light,
And in his waters, which your mirror make,
Behold your faces as the crystal bright,
That when you come whereas my love doth lie,
No blemish she may spy.
And eke, ye lightfoot maids, which keep the door,
That on the hoary mountain used to tower;
And the wild wolves, which seek them to devour,
With your steel darts do chase from coming near;
Be also present here,
To help to deck her, and to help to sing,
That all the woods may answer, and your echo ring.

Wake now, my love, awake! for it is time;
The rosy morn long since left Tithone's bed,
All ready to her silver coach to climb;
And Phœbus gins to show his glorious head.
Hark, how the cheerful birds do chant their lays
And carol of love's praise.
The merry lark her matins sings aloft;
The thrush replies; the mavis descant plays;
The ouzel shrills; the ruddock warbles soft;
So goodly all agree, with sweet concent,
To this day's merriment.
Ah! my dear love, why do ye sleep thus long,
When meeter were that ye should now awake,
T' await the coming of your joyous make,
And hearken to the birds' love-learned song,
The dewy leaves among!
For they of joy and pleasance to you sing,
That all the woods them answer, and their echo ring.

My love is now awake out of her dreams,
And her fair eyes, like stars that dimmed were
With darksome cloud, now show their goodly beams
More bright than Hesperus his head doth rear.

Come now, ye damsels, daughters of delight,
Help quickly her to dight:
But first come ye fair hours, which were begot,
In Jove's sweet paradise of Day and Night;
Which do the seasons of the year allot,
And all that ever in this world is fair,
Do make and still repair:
And ye three handmaids of the Cyprian queen,
The which do still adorn her beauty's pride,
Help to adorn my beautifulest bride;
And as ye her array, still throw between
Some graces to be seen,
And, as ye use to Venus, to her sing,
The whiles the woods shall answer, and your echo ring.

Now is my love all ready forth to come:
Let all the virgins therefore well await;
And ye fresh boys that tend upon her groom
Prepare yourselves; for he is coming straight.
Set all your things in seemly good array,
Fit for so joyful day,
The joyful'st day that ever sun did see.
Fair Sun! show forth thy favourable ray,
And let thy life-full heat not fervent be.
For fear of burning her sunshiny face,
Her beauty to disgrace.
O fairest Phœbus! father of the Muse.
If ever I did honour thee aright,
Or sing the thing that mote thy mind delight,
Do not thy servant's simple boon refuse;
But let this day, let this one day be mine;
Let all the rest be thine;
Then I thy sovereign praises loud will sing,
That all the woods shall answer, and their echo ring.

Hark! how the minstrels gin to shrill aloud

Their merry music that resounds from far,
The pipe, the tabor, and the trembling crowd[1],
That well agree withouten breach or jar.
But, most of all, the Damsels do delight
When they their timbrels smite,
And thereunto do dance and carol sweet,
That all the senses they do ravish quite;
The whiles the boys run up and down the street,
Crying aloud with strong confused noise,
As if it were one voice,
Hymen, iö Hymen, Hymen, they do shout;
That even to the heavens their shouting shrill
Doth reach, and all the firmament doth fill;
To which the people standing all about,
As in approvance do thereto applaud,
And loud advance her laud;
And evermore they Hymen, Hymen sing,
That all the woods them answer, and their echo ring.

Lo! where she comes along with portly pace,
Like Phœbe, from her chamber of the East,
Arising forth to run her mighty race,
Clad all in white, that seems a virgin best.
So well it her beseems, that ye would ween
Some angel she had been.
Her long loose yellow locks like golden wire,
Sprinkled with pearl, and pearling flowers atween,
Do like a golden mantle her attire;
And, being crowned with a garland green,
Seem like some maiden queen.
Her modest eyes, abashed to behold
So many gazers as on her do stare,
Upon the lowly ground affixed are;
Ne dare lift up her countenance too bold,

[1] a kind of violin.

But blush to hear her praises sung so loud,
So far from being proud.
Nathless do ye still loud her praises sing,
That all the woods may answer, and your echo ring.

Tell me, ye merchants' daughters, did ye see
So fair a creature in your town before;
So sweet, so lovely, and so mild as she,
Adorned with beauty's grace and virtue's store?
Her goodly eyes like sapphires shining bright,
Her forehead ivory white,
Her cheeks like apples which the sun hath rudded,
Her lips like cherries charming men to bite,
Her breast like to a bowl of cream uncrudded,
Her paps like lilies budded,
Her snowy neck like to a marble tower;
And all her body like a palace fair,
Ascending up, with many a stately stair,
To honour's seat and chastity's sweet bower.
Why stand ye still, ye virgins, in amaze,
Upon her so to gaze,
Whiles ye forget your former lay to sing,
To which the woods did answer, and your echo ring?

But if ye saw that which no eyes can see,
The inward beauty of her lively spright,
Garnished with heavenly gifts of high degree,
Much more then would ye wonder at that sight,
And stand astonished like to those which read
Medusa's mazeful head.
There dwells sweet love, and constant chastity,
Unspotted faith, and comely womanhood,
Regard of honour, and mild modesty;
There virtue reigns as queen in royal throne,
And giveth laws alone,
The which the base affections do obey,

And yield their services unto her will;
Ne thought of thing uncomely ever may
Thereto approach to tempt her mind to ill.
Had ye once seen these her celestial treasures,
And unrevealed pleasures,
Then would ye wonder, and her praises sing,
That all the woods should answer, and your echo ring.

Open the temple gates unto my love,
Open them wide that she may enter in,
And all the posts adorn as doth behove,
And all the pillars deck with garlands trim,
For to receive this Saint with honour due,
That cometh in to you.
With trembling steps, and humble reverence
She cometh in, before th' Almighty's view;
Of her ye virgins learn obedience,
When so ye come into those holy places,
To humble your proud faces:
Bring her up to th' high altar, that she may
The sacred ceremonies there partake,
The which do endless matrimony make;
And let the roaring organs loudly play
The praises of the Lord in lively notes;
The whiles, with hollow throats,
The choristers the joyous anthem sing,
That all the woods may answer, and their echo ring.

Behold, whiles she before the altar stands,
Hearing the holy priest that to her speaks,
And blesseth her with his two happy hands,
How the red roses flush up in her cheeks,
And the pure snow, with goodly vermill stain,
Like crimson dyed in grain:
That even th' Angels, which continually
About the sacred altar do remain,

Forget their service and about her fly,
Oft peeping in her face, that seems more fair,
The more they on it stare.
But her sad eyes, still fastened on the ground,
Are governed with goodly modesty,
That suffers not one look to glance awry,
Which may let in a little thought unsound.
Why blush ye, love, to give to me your hand,
The pledge of all our band?
Sing, ye sweet Angels, Alleluia sing,
That all the woods may answer, and your echo ring.

Now all is done: bring home the bride again;
Bring home the triumph of our victory:
Bring home with you the glory of her gain
With joyance bring her and with jollity.
Never had man more joyful day than this
Whom heaven would heap with bliss,
Make feast therefore now all this live-long day;
This day for ever to me holy is.
Pour out the wine without restraint or stay,
Pour not by cups, but by the bellyful,
Pour out to all that will,
And sprinkle all the posts and walls with wine,
That they may sweat, and drunken be withal.
Crown ye god Bacchus with a coronal,
And Hymen also crown with wreaths of vine;
And let the Graces dance unto the rest,
For they can do it best:
The whiles the maidens do their carol sing,
To which the woods shall answer, and their echo ring.

Ring ye the bells, ye young men of the town,
And leave your wonted labours for this day:
This day is holy; do ye write it down,
That ye for ever it remember may.

This day the sun is in his chiefest height,
With Barnaby the bright,
From whence declining daily by degrees,
He somewhat loseth of his heat and light,
When once the Crab behind his back he sees.
But for this time it ill ordained was,
To choose the longest day in all the year,
And shortest night, when longest fitter were:
Yet never day so long, but late would pass.
Ring ye the bells, to make it wear away,
And bonfires make all day;
And dance about them, and about them sing,
That all the woods may answer, and your echo ring.

Ah! when will this long weary day have end,
And lend me leave to come unto my love?
How slowly do the hours their numbers spend!
How slowly does sad Time his feathers move!
Haste thee, O fairest planet, to thy home,
Within the western foam:
Thy tired steeds long since have need of rest.
Long though it be, at last I see it gloom,
And the bright evening-star with golden crest
Appear out of the East.
Fair child of beauty! glorious lamp of love!
That all the host of heaven in ranks dost lead,
And guidest lovers through the night's sad dread,
How cheerfully thou lookest from above,
And seem'st to laugh atween thy twinkling light,
As joying in the sight
Of these glad many, which for joy do sing,
That all the woods them answer, and their echo ring!

Now cease, ye damsels, your delights forepast;
Enough it is that all the day was yours:
Now day is done, and night is nighing fast,

Now bring the bride into the bridal bowers.
The night is come, now soon her disarray,
And in her bed her lay;
Lay her in lilies and in violets,
And silken curtains over her display,
And odoured sheets, and Arras coverlets.
Behold how goodly my fair love does lie,
In proud humility!
Like unto Maia, whenas Jove her took
In Tempe, lying on the flowery grass,
Twixt sleep and wake, after she weary was
With bathing in the Acidalian brook.
Now it is night, ye damsels may be gone,
And leave my love alone,
And leave likewise your former lay to sing:
The woods no more shall answer, nor your echo ring.

Now welcome, Night! thou night so long expected,
That long day's labour dost at last defray,
And all my cares, which cruel love collected,
Hast summed in one, and cancelled for aye:
Spread thy broad wing over my love and me,
That no man may us see;
And in thy sable mantle us enwrap,
From fear of peril and foul horror free.
Let no false treason seek us to entrap,
Nor any dread disquiet once annoy
The safety of our joy;
But let the night be calm and quietsome,
Without tempestuous storms or sad affray:
Like as when Jove with fair Alcmena lay,
When he begot the great Tirynthian groom:
Or like as when he with thyself did lie
And begot Majesty.
And let the maids and young men cease to sing;
Ne let the woods them answer, nor their echo ring.

Let no lamenting cries, nor doleful tears
Be heard all night within, nor yet without:
Ne let false whispers, breeding hidden fears,
Break gentle sleep with misconceived doubt
Let no deluding dreams, nor dreadful sights,
Make sudden sad affrights;
Ne let house-fires, nor lightning's helpless harms,
Ne let the Pouke[1], nor other evil sprights,
Ne let mischievous witches with their charms
Ne let hob goblins, names whose sense we see not,
Fray us with things that be not:
Let not the screechowl nor the stork be heard,
Nor the night raven, that still deadly yells;
Nor damned ghosts, called up with mighty spells,
Nor griesly vultures, make us once affeared:
Ne let th' unpleasant choir of frogs still croaking
Make us to wish their choking.
Let none of these their dreary accents sing;
Ne let the woods them answer, nor their echo ring.

But let still Silence true night-watches keep,
That sacred Peace may in assurance reign,
And timely Sleep, when it is time to sleep,
May pour his limbs forth on your pleasant plain;
The whiles an hundred little winged loves,
Like diverse-feathered doves,
Shall fly and flutter round about your bed,
And in the secret dark, that none reproves,
Their pretty stealths shall work, and snares shall spread,
To filch away sweet snatches of delight,
Concealed through covert night.
Ye sons of Venus, play your sports at will!
For greedy Pleasure, careless of your toys,
Thinks more upon her paradise of joys,

[1] Puck.

Than what ye do, albeit good or ill.
All night therefore attend your merry play,
For it will soon be day:
Now none doth hinder you, that say or sing;
Ne will the woods now answer, nor your echo ring.

Who is the same, which at my window peeps?
Or whose is that fair face that shines so bright?
Is it not Cynthia, she that never sleeps,
But walks about high heaven all the night?
O! fairest goddess, do thou not envy
My love with me to spy:
For thou likewise didst love, though now unthought,
And for a fleece of wool, which privily
The Latmian shepherd once unto thee brought
His pleasures with thee wrought.
Therefore to us be favourable now;
And sith of women's labours thou hast charge,
And generation goodly dost enlarge,
Incline thy will t' effect our wishful vow,
And the chaste womb inform with timely seed,
That may our comfort breed:
Till which we cease our hopeful hap to sing;
Ne let the woods us answer, nor our echo ring.

And thou, great Juno! which with awful might
The laws of wedlock still doth patronize
And the religion of the faith first plight
With sacred rites hast taught to solemnize;
And eke for comfort often called art
Of women in their smart;
Eternally bind thou this lovely band,
And all thy blessings unto us impart.
And thou, glad Genius! in whose gentle hand
The bridal bower and genial bed remain,
Without blemish or stain;

And the sweet pleasures of their love's delight
With secret aid dost succour and supply,
Till they bring forth the fruitful progeny;
Send us the timely fruit of this same night.
And thou, fair Hebe! and thou, Hymen free!
Grant that it may so be.
Till which we cease your further praise to sing;
Ne any woods shall answer, nor your echo ring.

And ye high heavens, the temple of the gods,
In which a thousand torches flaming bright
Do burn, that to us wretched earthly clods
In dreadful darkness lend desired light:
And all ye powers which in the same remain,
More than we men can feign!
Pour out your blessing on us plenteously,
And happy influence upon us rain,
That we may raise a large posterity,
Which from the earth, which they may long possess
With lasting happiness,
Up to your haughty palaces may mount;
And, for the guerdon of their glorious merit,
May heavenly tabernacles there inherit,
Of blessed saints for to increase the count.
So let us rest, sweet love, in hope of this,
And cease till then our timely joys to sing:
The woods no more us answer, nor our echo ring!

Song! made in lieu of many ornaments,
With which my love should duly have been decked,
Which cutting off through hasty accidents,
Ye would not stay our due time to expect,
But promised both to recompense;
Be unto her a goodly ornament,
And for short time an endless monument.

FROM AN HYMN IN HONOUR OF BEAUTY.

WHAT time this world's great Workmaster did cast
    To make all things such as we now behold,
It seems that he before his eyes had plast
A goodly pattern, to whose perfect mould
He fashioned them as comely as he could,
That now so fair and seemly they appear,
As nought may be amended anywhere.

That wondrous pattern, wheresoe'er it be,
Whether in earth laid up in secret store,
Or else in heaven, that no man may it see
With sinful eyes, for fear it to deflore,
Is perfect Beauty, which all men adore;
Whose face and feature doth so much excel
All mortal sense, that none the same may tell.

Thereof as every earthly thing partakes
Or more or less, by influence divine,
So it more fair accordingly it makes,
And the gross matter of this earthly mine
Which clotheth it, thereafter doth refine,
Doing away the dross which dims the light
Of that fair beam which therein is empight[1].

For, through infusion of celestial power,
The duller earth it quickeneth with delight,
And life-full spirits privily doth pour
Through all the parts, that to the looker's sight
They seem to please: That is thy sovereign might,
O Cyprian queen! which flowing from the beam
Of thy bright star, thou into them dost stream.

That is the thing which giveth pleasant grace
To all things fair, that kindleth lively fire,

[1] confined.

Light of thy lamp; which, shining in the face,
Thence to the soul darts amorous desire,
And robs the hearts of those which it admire;
Therewith thou pointest thy son's poisoned arrow,
That wounds the life, and wastes the inmost marrow.

How vainly then do idle wits invent,
That beauty is nought else but mixture made
Of colours fair, and goodly temp'rament
Of pure complexions, that shall quickly fade
And pass away, like to a summer's shade;
Or that it is but comely composition
Of parts well measured, with meet disposition!

Hath white and red in it such wondrous power,
That it can pierce through th' eyes unto the heart,
And therein stir such rage and restless stour[1],
As nought but death can stint his dolour's smart?
Or can proportion of the outward part
Move such affection in the inward mind,
That it can rob both sense, and reason blind?

Why do not then the blossoms of the field,
Which are arrayed with much more orient hue,
And to the sense most dainty odours yield,
Work like impression in the looker's view?
Or why do not fair pictures like power shew,
In which ofttimes we nature see of art
Excelled, in perfect limning every part?

But ah! believe me there is more than so,
That works such wonders in the minds of men;
I, that have often prov'd, too well it know,
And whoso list the like assays to ken,
Shall find by trial, and confess it then,
That Beauty is not, as fond men misdeem,
An outward show of things that only seem

[1] tumult.

For that same goodly hue of white and red,
For which the cheeks are sprinkled, shall decay,
And those sweet rosy leaves, so fairly spread
Upon the lips, shall fade and fall away
To that they were, even to corrupted clay:
That golden wire, those sparkling stars so bright,
Shall turn to dust, and lose their goodly light.

But that fair lamp, from whose celestial ray
That light proceeds, which kindleth lovers' fire,
Shall never be extinguished nor decay;
But, when the vital spirits do expire,
Unto her native planet shall retire;
For it is heavenly born and cannot die,
Being a parcel of the purest sky.

For when the soul, the which derived was,
At first, out of that great immortal Spright,
By whom all live to love, whilom did pass
Down from the top of purest heaven's height
To be embodied here, it then took light
And lively spirits from that fairest star
Which lights the world forth from his fiery car.

Which power retaining still or more or less,
When she in fleshly seed is eft[1] enraced[2],
Through every part she doth the same impress,
According as the heavens have her graced,
And frames her house, in which she will be placed,
Fit for herself, adorning it with spoil
Of th' heavenly riches which she robbed erewhile.

Thereof it comes that these fair souls, which have
The most resemblance of that heavenly light,
Frame to themselves most beautiful and brave
Their fleshly bower, most fit for their delight,
And the gross matter by a sovereign might

[1] afterwards.   [2] implanted.

Tempers so trim, that it may well be seen
A palace fit for such a virgin queen.

So every spirit, as it is most pure,
And hath in it the more of heavenly light,
So it the fairer body doth procure
To habit in, and it more fairly dight
With cheerful grace and amiable sight;
For of the soul the body form doth take;
For soul is form, and doth the body make.

Therefore wherever that thou dost behold
A comely corpse[1], with beauty fair endued,
Know this for certain, that the same doth hold
A beauteous soul, with fair conditions thewed[2],
Fit to receive the seed of virtue strewed;
For all that fair is, is by nature good;
That is a sign to know the gentle blood.

Yet oft it falls that many a gentle mind
Dwells in deformed tabernacle drowned,
Either by chance, against the course of kind[3],
Or through unaptness in the substance found,
Which it assumed of some stubborn ground,
That will not yield unto her form's direction,
But is deformed with some foul imperfection.

And oft it falls, (ay me, the more to rue!)
That goodly beauty, albe heavenly born,
Is foul abused, and that celestial hue,
Which doth the world with her delight adorn,
Made but the bait of sin, and sinners' scorn,
Whilst every one doth seek and sue to have it,
But every one doth seek but to deprave it.

Yet nathemore is that fair beauty's blame,
But theirs that do abuse it unto ill:

[1] frame.   [2] endowed with fair qualities.   [3] nature.

Nothing so good, but that through guilty shame
May be corrupt, and wrested unto will:
Natheless the soul is fair and beauteous still,
However flesh's fault it filthy make;
For things immortal no corruption take.

But ye, fair Dames! the world's dear ornaments
And lively images of heaven's light,
Let not your beams with such disparagements
Be dimmed, and your bright glory darkened quite;
But, mindful still of your first country's sight,
Do still preserve your first informed grace,
Whose shadow yet shines in your beauteous face.

.   .   .   .

For Love is a celestial harmony
Of likely hearts composed of stars' consent,
Which join together in sweet sympathy,
To work each other's joy and true content,
Which they have harboured since their first descent
Out of their heavenly bowers, where they did see
And know each other here beloved to be.

Then wrong it were that any other twain
Should in Love's gentle band combined be
But those whom heaven did at first ordain,
And made out of one mould the more t' agree;
For all that like the beauty which they see,
Straight do not love; for Love is not so light
As straight to burn at first beholder's sight.

But they, which love indeed, look otherwise,
With pure regard and spotless true intent,
Drawing out of the object of their eyes
A more refined form, which they present
Unto their mind, void of all blemishment;
Which it reducing to her first perfection,
Beholdeth free from flesh's frail infection.

FROM AN HYMN OF HEAVENLY BEAUTY.

THE means, therefore, which unto us is lent
    Him to behold, is on his works to look,
Which he hath made in beauty excellent,
And in the same, as in a brazen book,
To read enregistered in every nook
His goodness which his beauty doth declare;
For all that's good is beautiful and fair.

Thence gathering plumes of perfect speculation,
To imp[1] the wings of thy high-flying mind,
Mount up aloft through heavenly contemplation,
From this dark world, whose damps the soul do blind,
And, like the native brood of eagle's kind,
On that bright Sun of Glory fix thine eyes,
Cleared from gross mists of frail infirmities.

Humbled with fear and awful reverence,
Before the footstool of his Majesty
Throw thyself down, with trembling innocence,
Ne dare look up with corruptible eye
On the dread face of that great Deity,
For fear, lest if he chance to look on thee,
Thou turn to nought, and quite confounded be.

But lowly fall before his mercy-seat,
Close covered with the Lamb's integrity
From the just wrath of his avengeful threat
That sits upon the righteous throne on high;
His throne is built upon Eternity,
More firm and durable than steel or brass,
Or the hard diamond, which them both doth pass.

His sceptre is the rod of Righteousness,
With which he bruiseth all his foes to dust
And the great Dragon strongly doth repress,

---

[1] To enlarge by engrafting.

Under the rigour of his judgment just;
His seat is Truth, to which the faithful trust,
From whence proceed her beams so pure and bright
That all about him sheddeth glorious light.

.   .   .   .

Ah, then, my hungry soul! which long hast fed
On idle fancies of thy foolish thought,
And, with false beauty's flattering bait misled,
Hast after vain deceitful shadows sought,
Which all are fled, and now have left thee nought
But late repentance through thy follies' prief [1];
Ah! cease to gaze on matter of thy grief:

And look at last up to that Sovereign Light,
From whose pure beams all perfect beauty springs,
That kindleth love in every godly spright
Even the love of God; which loathing brings
Of this vile world and these gay-seeming things;
With whose sweet pleasures being so possessed,
Thy straying thoughts henceforth forever rest.

SIR WALTER RALEIGH (?).

(1552–1618.)

Most of the poems which pass under the name of Raleigh, like *Pilgrim to Pilgrim*, are of quite uncertain ascription. His career as author began about 1576. *Even Such is Time* is said by Oldys to have been written by Raleigh on the eve of his execution. His poems are included in the volume of *Courtly Poets*, edited by Rev. J. Hannah (Aldine Poets, 1870).

PILGRIM TO PILGRIM.

AS you came from the holy land
    Of Walsinghame,
Met you not with my true love
    By the way as you came?

[1] proof trial.

How should I know your true love,
  That have met many one,
As I came from the holy land,
  That have come, that have gone?

She is neither white nor brown,
  But as the heavens fair;
There is none hath a form so divine
  On the earth or the air.

Such a one did I meet, good sir,
  Such an angelic face,
Who like a queen, like a nymph, did appear,
  By her gait, by her grace.

She hath left me here all alone,
  All alone, as unknown,
Who sometimes did me lead with herself,
  And me loved as her own.

What's the cause that she leaves you alone,
  And a new way doth take,
Who loved you once as her own,
  And her joy did you make?

I have loved her all my youth,
  But now old, as you see:
Love likes not the falling fruit
  From the withered tree.

Know that Love is a careless child,
  And forgets promise past;
He is blind, he is deaf when he list,
  And in faith never fast.

His desire is a dureless content,
  And a trustless joy;
He is won with a world of despair,
  And is lost with a toy.

Of womenkind such indeed is the love,
  Or the word love abused,
Under which many childish desires
  And conceits are excused.

But true love is a durable fire,
  In the mind ever burning,
Never sick, never old, never dead,
  From itself never turning.

EVEN SUCH IS TIME.

EVEN such is time, that takes in trust
    Our youth, our joys, our all we have,
And pays us but with earth and dust;
Who, in the dark and silent grave,
When we have wandered all our ways,
Shuts up the story of our days;
But from this earth, this grave, this dust,
My God shall raise me up, I trust!

SIR PHILIP SIDNEY.

(1554–1586.)

Sidney's Lyrics are gathered into a volume in the series of Rhys'
Lyric Poets. The first selection below is found in the early editions of
the *Arcadia* among other poems of Sidney's not germane to that work.
Dr. Grosart ascribes it positively to the "Astrophel and Stella" series.
The second occurs in the *Arcadia*, 1590, written 1580, although it first
appears in slightly different form as quoted in Puttenham's *Arte of
English Poesie*, 1589. The sonnets of the "Astrophel and Stella" series
were written probably before 1582, and appeared in 1591. Dr. Grosart's
editions of Sidney's *Complete Poems* are the standard modern editions.

PHILOMELA.

THE nightingale, as soon as April bringeth
    Unto her rested sense a perfect waking,
While late bare earth, proud of new clothing, springeth,

Sings out her woes, a thorn her song-book making,
  And mournfully bewailing,
Her throat in tunes expresseth
What grief her breast oppresseth,
  For Tereus' force on her chaste will prevailing.
O Philomela fair, O take some gladness,
That here is juster cause of plaintful sadness:
Thine earth now springs, mine fadeth;
Thy thorn without, my thorn my heart invadeth.

HEART-EXCHANGE.

MY true-love hath my heart, and I have his,
  By just exchange one for the other given:
I hold his dear, and mine he cannot miss;
There never was a bargain better driven.
His heart in me keeps me and him in one,
My heart in him his thoughts and senses guides;
He loves my heart for once it was his own;
I cherish his because in me it bides.
His heart his wound receivèd from my sight;
My heart was wounded with his wounded heart;
For as from me on him his hurt did light,
So still methought in me his hurt did smart:
Both equal hurt, in this change sought our bliss,
My true love hath my heart, and I have his.

TO THE MOON.

WITH how sad steps, O Moon, thou climb'st the skies!
  How silently, and with how wan a face!
What, may it be that even in heavenly place
That busy archer his sharp arrows tries!
Sure, if that long-with-love-acquainted eyes
Can judge of love, thou feel'st a lover's case,
I read it in thy looks; thy languisht grace,

To me, that feel the like, thy state descries.
That, even of fellowship, O Moon, tell me,
Is constant love deem'd there but want of wit?
Are beauties there as proud as here they be?
Do they above love to be loved, and yet
Those lovers scorn whom that love doth possess?
Do they call virtue there ungratefulness?

LOVE IS ENOUGH.

NO more, my dear, no more these counsels try;
  O give my passions leave to run their race;
Let Fortune lay on me her worst disgrace;
Let folk o'ercharged with brain against me cry;
Let clouds bedim my face, break in mine eye;
Let me no steps but of lost labour trace;
Let all the earth with scorn recount my case —
But do not will me from my love to fly.
I do not envy Aristotle's wit,
Nor do aspire to Cæsar's bleeding fame,
Nor aught do care though some above me sit;
Nor hope nor wish another course to frame,
But that which once may win thy cruel heart:
Thou art my wit, and thou my virtue art.

INSPIRATION.

I NEVER drank of Aganippe well,
  Nor ever did in shade of Tempe sit,
And Muses scorn with vulgar brains to dwell
Poor layman I, for sacred rites unfit.
Some do I hear of poets' fury tell,
But, God wot, wot not what they mean by it;
And this I swear by blackest brook of hell,
I am no pick-purse of another's wit.
How falls it then, that with so smooth an ease

My thoughts I speak; and what I speak doth flow
In verse, and that my verse best wits doth please?
Guess we the cause! What, is it this? Fie, no.
Or so? Much less. How then? Sure thus it is,
My lips are sweet, inspired with Stella's kiss.

ETERNAL LOVE.

LEAVE me, O Love, which reachest but to dust;
    And thou, my mind, aspire to higher things;
Grow rich in that which never taketh rust;
Whatever fades, but fading pleasure brings.
Draw in thy beams, and humble all thy might
To that sweet yoke where lasting freedoms be;
Which breaks the clouds, and opens forth the light,
That doth both shine, and give us sight to see.

O take fast hold; let that light be thy guide
In this small course which birth draws out to death,
And think how ill becometh him to slide,
Who seeketh heaven, and comes of heavenly breath.
Then farewell, world; thy uttermost I see:
Eternal Love, maintain thy life in me!

SIR EDWARD DYER.
(1550?–1607.)

MY MIND TO ME A KINGDOM IS

This poem is found in *MS. Rawl.* 85 (date uncertain). Dyer's scanty
poetic remains are included in vol. iv. of Dr. Grosart's edition of the
Miscellanies of the Fuller Worthies Library.

MY mind to me a kingdom is,
    Such present joys therein I find,
That it excels all other bliss
    That earth affords or grows by kind:

Though much I want which most would have,
Yet still my mind forbids to crave.

No princely pomp, no wealthy store,
   No force to win the victory,
No wily wit to salve a sore,
   No shape to feed a loving eye;
To none of these I yield as thrall:
For why?   My mind doth serve for all.

I see how plenty surfeits oft,
   And hasty climbers soon do fall;
I see that those which are aloft
   Mishap doth threaten most of all;
They get with toil, they keep with fear;
Such cares my mind could never bear.

Content to live, this is my stay;
   I seek no more than may suffice;
I press to bear no haughty sway;
   Look, what I lack my mind supplies:
Lo, thus I triumph like a king,
Content with that my mind doth bring.

Some have too much, yet still do crave;
   I little have, and seek no more.
They are but poor, though much they have,
   And I am rich with little store;
They poor, I rich; they beg, I give;
They lack, I leave; they pine, I live.

I laugh not at another's loss;
   I grudge not at another's pain;
No worldly waves my mind can toss;
   My state at one doth still remain:
I fear no foe, I fawn no friend;
I loathe not life, nor dread my end.

Some weigh their pleasure by their lust,
    Their wisdom by their rage of will;
Their treasure is their only trust;
    A cloaked craft their store of skill:
But all the pleasure that I find
Is to maintain a quiet mind.

My wealth is health and perfect ease:
    My conscience clear my chief defence;
I neither seek by bribes to please,
    Nor by deceit to breed offence:
Thus do I live; thus will I die;
Would all did so as well as I!

JOHN LYLY.

(1554?–1606.)

These are the first of the numerous songs from the Elizabethan
Dramatists included in this volume. Mr. Bullen has edited a volume of
such *Lyrics from the Dramatists* (London, 1889). The first and second
occur in *Alexander and Campaspe*, 1584 (acted 1581). The *Hymn to
Apollo* is in *Midas*, 1592 (acted 1590): Mr. Symonds compares this
Hymn to the Processional Hymns of the Greek Parthenia, and says that
it "might well have been used at such a festival". The *Fairy Song* is
from *Endymion*, 1591 (acted circa 1580). The songs, however, were not
included with the plays until the collective edition of 1632. There is a
modern edition of Lyly's *Dramatic Works* edited by F. W. Fairholt
(London, 1858, 2 vols.).

APELLES' SONG.

CUPID and my Campaspe played
    At cards for kisses—Cupid paid.
He stakes his quiver, bow, and arrows,
His mother's doves and team of sparrows:
Loses them too; then down he throws
The coral of his lip, the rose

Growing on 's cheek (but none knows how);
With these the crystal of his brow,
And then the dimple of his chin—
All these did my Campaspe win.
At last he set her both his eyes.
She won, and Cupid blind did rise.
O Love, has she done this to thee?
What shall, alas! become of me?

SPRING'S WELCOME.

WHAT bird so sings, yet so does wail?
    O 't is the ravished nightingale.
"Jug, jug, jug, jug, tereu," she cries,
And still her woes at midnight rise.
Brave prick-song! who is 't now we hear?
None but the lark so shrill and clear;
Now at heaven's gates she claps her wings,
The morn not waking till she sings.
Hark, hark, with what a pretty throat,
Poor robin redbreast tunes his note;
Hark how the jolly cuckoos sing,
Cuckoo, to welcome in the spring;
Cuckoo, to welcome in the spring!

HYMN TO APOLLO.

SING to Apollo, god of day,
    Whose golden beams with morning play,
And make her eyes so brightly shine,
Aurora's face is called divine;
Sing to Phœbus and that throne
Of diamonds which he sits upon.
        Io, pæans let us sing
        To Physic's and to Poesy's king!

Crown all his altars with bright fire,
Laurels bind about his lyre,
A Daphnean coronet for his head,
The Muses dance about his bed;
When on his ravishing lute he plays,
Strew his temple round with bays.
      Io, pæans let us sing
      To the glittering Delian king!

FAIRY REVELS.

Omnes. PINCH him, pinch him black and blue;
        Saucy mortals must not view
    What the queen of stars is doing,
    Nor pry into our fairy wooing.
1 Fairy.   Pinch him blue—
2 Fairy.   And pinch him black—
3 Fairy.   Let him not lack
    Sharp nails to pinch him blue and red,
    Till sleep has rocked his addlehead.
4 Fairy. For the trespass he hath done,
    Spots o'er all his flesh shall run.
    Kiss Endymion, kiss his eyes,
    Then to our midnight heydeguyes.

ROBERT GREENE.
(1560?–1592.)

Greene's Lullaby is from his pastoral romance of *Menaphon*, 1589. The second song is from *Pandosto*, 1588, and the last from *Philomela*, 1592. Dyce has edited the *Dramatic and Poetical Works* of Greene, and his *Complete Works*, edited by Dr. Grosart, occupy fifteen volumes in the Huth Library. Selections from his verse occur in Bullen's *Poems from Elizabethan Romances*, and also accompany the last edition of the same editor's *Lyrics from Elizabethan Dramatists*. Additional selections from Greene and other Elizabethan writers of pastoral lyrics may be found in Chambers's *English Pastorals*, in the present series.

SEPHESTIA'S SONG TO HER CHILD.

WEEP not, my wanton, smile upon my knee;
   When thou art old there 's grief enough for thee.
     Mother's wag, pretty boy,
     Father's sorrow, father's joy;
     When thy father first did see
     Such a boy by him and me,
     He was glad, I was woe;
     Fortune changèd made him so,
     When he left his pretty boy,
     Last his sorrow, first his joy.

Weep not, my wanton, smile upon my knee;
When thou art old there 's grief enough for thee.
     Streaming tears that never stint,
     Like pearl drops from a flint,
     Fell by course from his eyes,
     That one another's place supplies;
     Thus he grieved in every part,
     Tears of blood fell from his heart,
     When he left his pretty boy,
     Father's sorrow, father's joy.

Weep not, my wanton, smile upon my knee,
When thou art old there 's grief enough for thee.
     The wanton smiled, father wept,
     Mother cried, baby leapt;

More he crowed, more we cried,
Nature could not sorrow hide:
He must go, he must kiss
Child and mother, baby bless;
For he left his pretty boy,
Father's sorrow, father's joy.
Weep not, my wanton, smile upon my knee;
When thou art old there 's grief enough for thee.

FAWNIA.

AH, were she pitiful as she is fair,
   Or but as mild as she is seeming so,
Then were my hopes greater than my despair,
   Then all the world were heaven, nothing woe.
Ah, were her heart relenting as her hand,
   That seems to melt even with the mildest touch,
Then knew I where to seat me in a land,
   Under wide heavens, but yet I know not such.
So as she shows, she seems the budding rose,
   Yet sweeter far than is an earthly flower,
Sovereign of beauty, like the spray she grows,
   Compassed she is with thorns and cankered flower;
Yet were she willing to be plucked and worn,
She would be gathered, though she grew on thorn.

Ah, when she sings, all music else be still,
   For none must be comparèd to her note;
Ne'er breathed such glee from Philomela's bill,
   Nor from the morning-singer's swelling throat.
Ah, when she riseth from her blissful bed,
   She comforts all the world, as doth the sun,
And at her sight the night's foul vapour 's fled;
   When she is set, the gladsome day is done.
O glorious sun, imagine me the west,
Shine in my arms, and set thou in my breast!

PHILOMELA'S ODE.

SITTING by a river's side,
　　Where a silent stream did glide,
Muse I did of many things,
That the mind in quiet brings.
I 'gan think how some men deem
Gold their god; and some esteem
Honour is the chief content,
That to man in life is lent.
And some others do contend,
Quiet none, like to a friend.
Others hold, there is no wealth
Comparèd to a perfect health.
Some man's mind in quiet stands
When he is lord of many lands:
But I did sigh, and said all this
Was but a shade of perfect bliss;
And in my thoughts I did approve
Nought so sweet as is true love.
Love 'twixt lovers passeth these,
When mouth kisseth and heart 'grees,
With folded arms and lips meeting,
Each soul another sweetly greeting;
For by the breath the soul fleeteth,
And soul with soul in kissing meeteth
If love be so sweet a thing,
That such happy bliss doth bring,
Happy is love's sugared thrall;
But unhappy maidens all,
Who esteem your virgin blisses
Sweeter than a wife's sweet kisses.
No such quiet to the mind
As true love with kisses kind:

But if a kiss prove unchaste,
Then is true love quite disgraced.
Though love be sweet, learn this of me,
No sweet love but honesty.

GEORGE PEELE.

(1558?–1592?.)

The *Song of Paris and Œnone* is from the drama of the *Arraignment of Paris*, 1584 (acted 1581?). The *Song of the Harvesters* occurs in the *Old Wives' Tale*, 1595 (acted 1590?); and the *Farewell to Arms* in *Polyhymnia*, "a Description of a Triumph at Tilt", 1590. In Sir W. Segar's *Honors, Military and Civil*, 1602, it is related that it was actually sung for Sir Henry Lea before Queen Elizabeth as the demission of his office as her champion at tilt on account of age, and as his recommendation of the Earl of Cumberland for the post in his place. Peele's Poems are included in Bullen's edition of Peele's Works (London and Boston, 1888).

SONG OF PARIS AND ŒNONE.

Œnone.   FAIR and fair, and twice so fair,
        As fair as any may be;
    The fairest shepherd on our green,
        A love for any lady.

Paris.   Fair and fair, and twice so fair,
        As fair as any may be;
    Thy love is fair for thee alone,
        And for no other lady.

Œn.   My love is fair, my love is gay,
        As fresh as bin the flowers in May,
    And of my love my roundelay,
        My merry, merry roundelay,
    Concludes with Cupid's curse,—
        They that do change old love for new,
    Pray gods they change for worse!

Ambo simul. They that do change, &c.

Œn.   Fair and fair, &c.
Par.   Fair and fair, &c.
     Thy love is fair, &c.
Œn.   My love can pipe, my love can sing,
     My love can many a pretty thing,
     And of his lovely praises ring
     My merry, merry roundelays,
      Amen to Cupid's curse,—
     They that do change, &c.
Par.   They that do change, &c.
Ambo.   Fair and fair, &c.

HARVESTMEN A-SINGING.

ALL ye that lovely lovers be,
  Pray you for me:
Lo, here we come a-sowing, a-sowing,
And sow sweet fruits of love;
In your sweet hearts well may it prove!

Lo, here we come a-reaping, a-reaping,
To reap our harvest-fruit!
And thus we pass the year so long,
And never be we mute.

FAREWELL TO ARMS.

HIS golden locks time hath to silver turned;
 O time too swift, O swiftness never ceasing!
His youth 'gainst time and age hath ever spurned,
 But spurned in vain; youth waneth by increasing:
Beauty, strength, youth, are flowers but fading seen;
Duty, faith, love, are roots, and ever green.

His helmet now shall make a hive for bees,
 And, lovers' sonnets turned to holy psalms,

A man-at-arms must now serve on his knees,
   And feed on prayers, which are age his alms:
But though from court to cottage he depart,
His saint is sure of his unspotted heart.

And when he saddest sits in homely cell,
   He'll teach his swains this carol for a song,—
"Blessed be the hearts that wish my sovereign well,
   Cursed be the souls that think her any wrong".
Goddess, allow this aged man his right,
To be your beadsman now that was your knight.

THOMAS NASH.

(1567–1601?.)

These songs are from the comedy of *Summer's Last Will and Testament*, 1600 (acted 1592). Nash's works have been edited by Dr. Grosart in the Huth Library.

SPRING, THE SWEET SPRING.

SPRING, the sweet spring, is the year's pleasant king;
   Then blooms each thing, then maids dance in a ring;
Cold doth not sting, the pretty birds do sing,
Cuckoo, jug, jug, pu we, to witta woo.

The palm and may make country houses gay,
Lambs frisk and play, the shepherds pipe all day,
And hear we aye birds tune this merry lay,
Cuckoo, jug, jug, pu we, to witta woo.

The fields breathe sweet, the daisies kiss our feet,
Young lovers meet, old wives a-sunning sit;
In every street these tunes our ears do greet,
Cuckoo, jug, jug, pu we, to witta woo.
      Spring, the sweet spring!

DEATH'S SUMMONS.

ADIEU, farewell, earth's bliss,
    This world uncertain is:
Fond are life's lustful joys,
Death proves them all but toys.
None from his darts can fly:
I am sick, I must die.
        Lord have mercy on us!

Rich men, trust not in wealth,
Gold cannot buy you health;
Physic himself must fade;
All things to end are made;
The plague full swift goes by;
I am sick, I must die.
        Lord have mercy on us!

Beauty is but a flower,
Which wrinkles will devour:
Brightness falls from the air;
Queens have died young and fair;
Dust hath closed Helen's eye;
I am sick, I must die.
        Lord have mercy on us!

Strength stoops unto the grave:
Worms feed on Hector brave;
Swords may not fight with fate:
Earth still holds ope her gate.
Come, come, the bells do cry;
I am sick, I must die.
        Lord have mercy on us!

Wit with his wantonness,
Tasteth death's bitterness.

Hell's executioner
Hath no ears for to hear
What vain art can reply;
I am sick, I must die.
Lord have mercy on us!

Haste therefore each degree
To welcome destiny:
Heaven is our heritage,
Earth but a player's stage.
Mount we unto the sky;
I am sick, I must die.
Lord have mercy on us!

FADING SUMMER.

FAIR summer droops, droop men and beasts therefore;
So fair a summer look for never more:
All good things vanish less than in a day;
Peace, plenty, pleasure, suddenly decay.
Go not yet away, bright soul of the sad year,
The earth is hell when thou leav'st to appear.

What! shall those flowers that decked thy garland erst,
Upon thy grave be wastefully dispersed?
O trees, consume your sap in sorrow's source,
Streams, turn to tears your tributary course.
Go not yet hence, bright soul of the sad year,
The earth is hell when thou leav'st to appear.

THOMAS LODGE.

(1558?–1625.)

The "Song of Rosaline" is in the pastoral romance of *Rosalind*, 1590, the source of *As You Like It*. The second selection is one of the "Sundrie Sweet Sonnets" contained in *Scilla's Metamorphosis*, 1589, written 1577(?). The last selection is found in the *Life of Robert, Second Duke of Normandy*, 1591. Lodge's works are reprinted in the Hunterian Club publications; *Rosalind* in Hazlitt's *Shakespeare's Library*. Many of his lyrics are included among Mr. Bullen's *Lyrics from Elizabethan Romances*.

ROSADER'S DESCRIPTION OF ROSALYND.

LIKE to the clear in highest sphere,
  Where all imperial glory shines,
Of self-same colour is her hair,
  Whether unfolded or in twines;
    Heigh ho, fair Rosalynd!

Her eyes are sapphires set in snow,
  Refining heaven by every wink;
The gods do fear whenas they glow,
  And I do tremble when I think:
    Heigh ho, would she were mine!

Her cheeks are like the blushing cloud
  That beautifies Aurora's face,
Or like the silver-crimson shroud
  That Phœbus' smiling looks doth grace;
    Heigh ho, fair Rosalynd!

Her lips are like two budded roses,
  Whom ranks of lilies neighbour nigh,

Within whose bounds she balm encloses
   Apt to entice a deity.
       Heigh ho, would she were mine!

Her neck like to a stately tower,
   Where Love himself imprisoned lies,
To watch for glances every hour,
   From her divine and sacred eyes;
       Heigh ho, fair Rosalynd!

Her paps are centres of delight,
   Her paps are orbs of heavenly frame,
Where nature moulds the dew of light,
   To feed perfection with the same.
       Heigh ho, would she were mine!

With orient pearl, with ruby red,
   With marble white, with sapphire blue,
Her body every way is fed,
   Yet soft to touch, and sweet in view;
       Heigh ho, fair Rosalynd!

Nature herself her shape admires,
   The gods are wounded in her sight,
And Love forsakes his heavenly fires,
   And at her eyes his brand doth light.
       Heigh ho, would she were mine!

Then muse not, Nymphs, though I bemoan
   The absence of fair Rosalynd;
Since for her fair there is fairer none,
   Nor for her virtues so divine.
       Heigh ho! fair Rosalynd!
Heigh ho! my heart, would God that she were mine!

THE HARMONY OF LOVE.

A VERY phœnix, in her radiant eyes
  I leave mine age, and get my life again;
True Hesperus, I watch her fall and rise,
  And with my tears extinguish all my pain;
My lips for shadows shield her springing roses,
  Mine eyes for watchmen guard her while she sleepeth,
My reasons serve to 'quite her faint supposes;
  Her fancy, mine; my faith her fancy keepeth;
She flowers, I branch; her sweet my sour supporteth,
O happy Love, where such delights consorteth!

WHILST YOUTHFUL SPORTS ARE LASTING.

PLUCK the fruit and taste the pleasure,
    Youthful lordings, of delight;
Whilst occasion gives you seizure,
    Feed your fancies and your sight:
        After death, when you are gone,
        Joy and pleasure is there none.

Here on earth nothing is stable;
    Fortune's changes well are known:
Whilst as youth doth then enable,
    Let your seeds of joy be sown:
        After death, when you are gone,
        Joy and pleasure is there none.

Feast it freely with your lovers,
    Blithe and wanton sports do fade,
Whilst that lovely Cupid hovers
    Round about this lovely shade:
        Sport it freely one to one,
        After death is pleasure none.

Now the pleasant spring allureth,
   And both place and time invites:
But, alas, what heart endureth
   To disclaim his sweet delights?
      After death, when we are gone,
      Joy and pleasure is there none.

JOHN DICKENSON.

(Fl. 1590–1600.)

A PASTORAL CATCH.

From the *Shepherd's Complaint*, circa 1594. Printed also in *England's Helicon*, 1600.

Shepherd.

SWEET thrall, first step to Love's felicity!

Shepherdess.

Sweet thrall, no stop to perfect liberty!
   He. O life!   *She.* What life?
   He. Sweet life.   *She.* No life more sweet.
   He. O love.   *She.* What love?
   He. Sweet love.   *She.* No love more meet.

NICHOLAS BRETON.
(1545?–1626?.)

The "Lullaby" is found in the *Arbor of Amorous Devises*, 1594; "I Would Thou Wert Not Fair" from the *Strange Fortunes of Two Excellent Princes*, 1600; "Lovely Kind and Kindly Loving" from *Melancholic Humours*, 1600; and "What is Love?" from the *Longing of a Blessed Heart*, 1601. Breton's Works, edited by Dr. Grosart, are in the Chertsey Worthies' Library. "Chosen Poems of Nicholas Breton" are appended to Bullen's *Lyrics from Elizabethan Romances*.

A SWEET LULLABY.

COME little babe, come silly soul,
    Thy father's shame, thy mother's grief,
Born as I doubt to all our dole,
And to thyself unhappy chief:
      Sing lullaby and lap it warm,
      Poor soul that thinks no creature harm.

Thou little think'st and less dost know
The cause of this thy mother's moan;
Thou want'st the wit to wail her woe,
And I myself am all alone;
      Why dost thou weep, why dost thou wail,
      And know'st not yet what thou dost ail?

Come little wretch, ah silly heart,
Mine only joy; what can I more?
If there be any wrong, thy smart,
That may the destinies implore;
      'T was I, I say, against my will;
      I wail the time, but be thou still.

And dost thou smile? O, thy sweet face!
Would God himself he might thee see!
No doubt thou soon would'st purchase grace,

I know right well, for thee and me.
>But come to mother, babe, and play;
>For father false is fled away.

Sweet boy, if it by fortune chance
Thy father home again to send,
If death do strike me with his lance,
Yet may'st thou me to him commend;
>If any ask thy mother's name,
>Tell how by love she purchased blame.

Then will his gentle heart soon yield;
I know him of a noble mind;
Although a lion in the field,
A lamb in town thou shalt him find;
>Ask blessing, babe! be not afraid;
>His sugared words have me betrayed.

Then may'st thou joy and be right glad,
Although in woe I seem to moan;
Thy father is no rascal lad,
A noble youth of blood and bone;
>His glancing looks, if once he smile
>Right honest women may beguile.

Come, little boy, and rock asleep;
Sing lullaby and be thou still;
I that can do nought else but weep,
Will sit by thee and wail my fill:
>God bless my babe, and lullaby
>From this thy father's quality!

I WOULD THOU WERT NOT FAIR.

I WOULD thou wert not fair, or I were wise
>I would thou hadst no face, or I no eyes;
I would thou wert not wise, or I not fond;
Or thou not free, or I not so in bond.

But thou art fair, and I cannot be wise:
Thy sunlike face hath blinded both mine eyes;
Thou canst not be but wise, nor I but fond;
Nor thou but free, nor I but still in bond.

Yet am I wise to think that thou art fair;
Mine eyes their pureness in thy face repair;
Nor am I fond, that do thy wisdom see;
Nor yet in bond, because that thou art free.

Then in thy beauty only make me wise,
And in thy face the Graces guide thine eyes;
And in thy wisdom only see me fond;
And in thy freedom keep me still in bond.

So shalt thou still be fair and I be wise;
Thy face shine still upon my clearèd eyes;
Thy wisdom only see how I am fond;
Thy freedom only keep me still in bond.

So would I thou wert fair and I were wise;
So would thou hadst thy face and I mine eyes;
So would I thou wert wise, and I were fond;
And thou wert free, and I were still in bond.

LOVELY KIND, AND KINDLY LOVING.

LOVELY kind, and kindly loving,
    Such a mind were worth the moving:
Truly fair, and fairly true,—
Where are all these, but in you?

Wisely kind, and kindly wise;
Blessed life, where such love lies!
Wise, and kind, and fair, and true,—
Lovely live all these in you.

Sweetly dear, and dearly sweet;
Blessed where these blessings meet!
Sweet, fair, wise, kind, blessed, true,—
Blessed be all these in you!

WHAT IS LOVE?

IT is too clear a brightness for man's eye;
  Too high a wisdom for his wits to find;
Too deep a secret for his sense to try;
And all too heavenly for his earthly mind;
It is a grace of such a glorious kind
  As gives the soul a secret power to know it,
  But gives no heart nor spirit power to show it.

It is of heaven and earth the highest beauty,
The powerful hand of heaven's and earth's creation,
The due commander of all spirits' duty,
The Deity of angels' adoration,
The glorious substance of the soul's salvation:
  The light of truth that all perfection trieth,
  And life that gives the life that never dieth.

It is the height of good and hate of ill,
Triumph of truth, and falsehood's overthrow;
The only worker of the highest will;
And only knowledge that doth knowledge know;
The only ground where it doth only grow:
  It is in sum the substance of all bliss,
  Without whose blessing all thing nothing is.

ANONYMOUS LYRICS.
(1588-1603.)

The writing of lyrics was an art to almost everyone's hand in the days of Elizabeth. Songs sung themselves; the music of words as well as of tones was in the air. The authorship of hundreds of these songs consequently is now unknown,—they came easily, and were easily forgotten.

THE QUIET LIFE.

From William Byrd's *Psalms, Sonnets, and Songs*, 1588.

WHAT pleasure have great princes
　　More dainty to their choice
Than herdsmen wild, who careless
　　In quiet life rejoice,
And fortune's fate not fearing,
Sing sweet in summer morning?

Their dealings plain and rightful,
　　Are void of all deceit;
They never know how spiteful
　　It is to kneel and wait
On favourite presumptuous
Whose pride is vain and sumptuous.

All day their flocks each tendeth;
　　At night, they take their rest;
More quiet than who sendeth
　　His ship into the East,
Where gold and pearl are plenty;
But getting, very dainty.

For lawyers and their pleading,
　　They 'steem it not a straw;
They think that honest meaning
　　Is of itself a law:
Whence conscience judgeth plainly,
They spend no money vainly.

O happy who thus liveth!
Not caring much for gold;
With clothing which sufficeth
To keep him from the cold.
Though poor and plain his diet,
Yet merry it is, and quiet.

LOVE'S PERFECTIONS.

This and the following piece are translations from the Italian, and
appear in Yonge's *Musica Transalpina*, 1588, reprinted in Arber's
Garner, vol. iii.

IN vain he seeks for beauty that excelleth,
   That hath not seen her eyes where Love sojourneth;
How sweetly here and there the same she turneth.
He knows not how Love healeth, and how he quelleth:
That knows not how she sighs, and sweet beguileth;
And how she sweetly speaks, and sweetly smileth.

SWEET LAMENTING.

I SAW my lady weeping, and Love did languish,
   And of their plaint ensued so rare consenting
That never yet was heard more sweet lamenting,
Made all of tender pity and mournful anguish.
The floods forsaking their delightful swelling,
Stayed to attend their plaint.   The winds enraged,
Still and content, to quiet calm assuaged
Their wonted storming and every blast rebelling.

THE TEST.

From *The Phœnix Nest*, 1593.

SET me where Phœbus' heat the flowers slayeth,
   Or where continual snow withstands his forces;
Set me where he his temperate rays displayeth,
   Or where he comes, or where he never courses!

Set me in Fortune's grace, or else dischargèd;
    In sweet and pleasant air, or dark and glooming;
Where days and nights are lesser or enlargèd;
    In years of strength, in failing age, or blooming!

Set me in heaven, or earth, or in the centre;
    Low in a vale, or on a mountain placèd;
Set me to danger, peril, or adventure,
    Gracèd by fame, or infamy disgracèd!

Set me to these, or any other trial
Except my Mistress' anger and denial.

THE SHEPHERD'S PRAISE OF HIS SACRED DIANA.

From *The Phœnix Nest*, 1593.

PRAISED be Diana's fair and harmless light,
    Praised be the dews, wherewith she moists the ground:
Praised be her beams, the glory of the night,
    Praised be her power, by which all powers abound

Praised be her nymphs, with whom she decks the woods,
    Praised be her knights, in whom true honour lives:
Praised be that force by which she moves the floods,
    Let that Diana shine which all these gives.

In heaven Queen she is among the spheres;
    She, mistress-like, makes all things to be pure:
Eternity in her oft change she bears;
    She beauty is, by her the fair endure.

Time wears her not, she doth his chariot guide;
    Mortality below her orb is placed;
By her the virtue of the stars down slide,
    In her is Virtue's perfect image cast.

A knowledge pure it is her worth to know:
With Circes let them dwell that think not so.

THE SHEPHERD TO THE FLOWERS.

From *The Phœnix Nest*, 1593.

SWEET violets, Love's paradise, that spread
    Your gracious odours, which you couchèd bear
      Within your paly faces,
Upon the gentle wing of some calm breathing wind,
      That plays amidst the plain,
      If by the favour of propitious stars you gain
Such grace as in my lady's bosom place to find,
      Be proud to touch those places:
And when her warmth your moisture forth doth wear,
Whereby her dainty parts are sweetly fed,
      You honours of the flow'ry meads, I pray,
      You pretty daughters of the earth and sun,
      With mild and seemly breathing straight display
      My bitter sighs, that have my heart undone.

Vermilion roses, that with new day's rise
Display your crimson folds fresh looking fair,
      Whose radiant bright disgraces
The rich adornèd rays of roseate rising morn;
      Ah, if her virgin's hand
      Do pluck your pure, ere Phœbus view the land,
And veil your gracious pomp, in lovely Nature's scorn;
      If chance my mistress traces
Fast by your flowers to take the summer's air,
Then woful blushing tempt her glorious eyes,
      To spread their tears, Adonis' death reporting,
      And tell Love's torments, sorrowing for her friend,
      Whose drops of blood, within your leaves consorting

Report fair Venus' moans to have no end.
Then may remorse, in pitying of my smart,
Dry up my tears, and dwell within her heart.

TO ZEPHERIA.

From *Zepheria*, 1594, a volume of anonymous poetry, reprinted in
Arber's *Garner*, vol. v.

WHAT! shall I ne'er more see those halcyon days!
  Those sunny Sabbaths! days of jubilee!
Wherein I carolled merry roundelays,
Odes, and love songs? which, being viewed by thee,
Received allowance worthy better writ!
When we, on shepherds' holy days have hied
Down to the flowery pastures (flowers, for thy treading fit!)
Holy the day, when thou it sanctified!
  When thou, Zepheria, wouldst but deign to bless it,
How have I, jealous over Phœbus' rays,
Clouded thy fair! Then, fearing he would guess it
By thy white brow, it have I cinct' with bays!
  But, woe is me! that I have fenced thy beauty!
  Sith other must enjoy it, and not I.

HENCE CARE!

From Thomas Morley's *First Book of Ballets*, 1595.

SING we and chant it
  While love doth grant it
        Fa la la!

Not long youth lasteth
And old age hasteth.
        Fa la la!

Now is best leisure
To take our pleasure.
   Fa la la!

All things invite us
Now to delight us.
   Fa la la!

Hence care be packing,
No mirth be lacking.
   Fa la la!

Let spare no treasure
To live in pleasure.
   Fa la la!

THE MONTH OF MAYING.

NOW is the month of maying,
 When merry lads are playing
Each with his bonny lass
Upon the greeny grass.
   Fa la la!

The spring clad all in gladness
Doth laugh at winter's sadness,
And to the bagpipe's sound
The nymphs tread out their ground.
   Fa la la!

Fie then, why sit we musing,
Youth's sweet delight refusing?
Say, dainty nymphs, and speak,
Shall we play barley-break?
   Fa la la!

BROWN IS MY LOVE.

From the Second Book of *Musica Transalpina*, 1597.

BROWN is my Love, but graceful;
    And each renownèd whiteness
Matched with thy lovely brown loseth its brightness.

    Fair is my Love, but scornful;
    Yet have I seen despisèd
Dainty white lilies, and sad flowers well prizèd.

COME AWAY! COME, SWEET LOVE!

From John Dowland's *First Book of Songs or Airs*, 1597; reprinted
in Arber's *Garner*, vol. iv.

COME away! come, sweet love!
    The golden morning breaks;
All the earth, all the air,
Of love and pleasure speaks!
Teach thine arms then to embrace,
And sweet rosy lips to kiss,
And mix our souls in mutual bliss!
Eyes were made for beauty's grace,
Viewing, ruing, love's long pain,
Procured by beauty's rude disdain.

Come away! come, sweet love!
Do not in vain adorn
Beauty's grace, that should rise
Like to the naked morn!
Lilies on the river's side,
And fair Cyprian flowers new-blown,
Desire no beauties but their own:
Ornament is nurse of pride,
Pleasure, measure love's delight,
Haste then, sweet love, our wishèd flight!

MADRIGAL.

From Wilbye's *Madrigals*, 1598.

LADY, when I behold the roses sprouting,
  Which, clad in damask mantles, deck the arbours,
And then behold your lips, where sweet love harbours,
  My eyes present me with a double doubting:
For viewing both alike, hardly my mind supposes,
Whether the roses be your lips, or your lips the roses.

I SAW MY LADY WEEP.

From Dowland's *Second Book of Songs or Airs*, 1600.

I SAW my lady weep,
And Sorrow proud to be advancèd so
In those fair eyes where all perfections keep.
    Her face was full of woe:
But such a woe, believe me, as wins more hearts
Than Mirth can do with her enticing parts.

    Sorrow was there made fair,
And passion wise; tears a delightful thing;
Silence beyond all speech, a wisdom rare;
    She made her sighs to sing,
And all things with so sweet a sadness move
As made my heart at once both grieve and love.

    O fairer than aught else
The world can show, leave off in time to grieve.
Enough, enough! your joyful look excels;
    Tears kill the heart, believe.
O strive not to be excellent in woe,
Which only breeds your beauty's overthrow.

LOVE AND MAY.

From T. Morley's *Madrigals*, 1600.

NOW is the gentle season, freshly flowering,
    To sing, and play, and dance, while May endureth,
    And woo, and wed too, that sweet delight procureth.

The fields abroad with spangled flowers are gilded,
    The meads are mantled, and closes[1];
    In May each bush arrayèd, and sweet wild roses.

The nightingale her bower hath gaily builded,
    And full of kindly lust and loves inspiring,
    I love, I love, she sings, hark, her mate desiring.

LOVE'S REALITIES.

From Robert Jones' *First Book of Songs and Airs*, 1601.

WHEN love on time and measure makes his ground,
    Time that must end, though love can never die,
'T is love betwixt a shadow and a sound,
    A love not in the heart but in the eye;
A love that ebbs and flows, now up, now down,
A morning's favour and an evening's frown.

Sweet looks show love, yet they are but as beams:
    Fair words seem true, yet they are but as wind;
Eyes shed their tears, yet are but outward streams;
    Sighs paint a shadow in the falsest mind.
Looks, words, tears, sighs show love when love they leave;
False hearts can weep, sigh, swear, and yet deceive.

---

[1] *closes*, gardens. The music in the original text shows that the composer had this apparently defective line before him.

MADRIGAL.

From Davison's *Poetical Rhapsody*, 1602.

M Y love in her attire doth show her wit,
　　It doth so well become her:
For every season she hath dressings fit,
　　For winter, spring, and summer.
　　No beauty she doth miss,
　　When all her robes are on:
　　But Beauty's self she is
　　When all her robes are gone.

THE GRACE OF BEAUTY.

From Dowland's *Third Book of Songs or Airs*, 1603.

B Y a fountain where I lay,
　　(All blessed be that blessed day!)
By the glimmering of the sun,
(O never be her shining done!)
　　When I might see alone
　　My true love, fairest one!
　　　Love's dear light!
　　　Love's clear sight!
No world's eyes can clearer see!
A fairer sight none can be!

Fair with garlands all addrest,
(Was never Nymph more fairly blest!)
Blessed in the highest degree;
(So may she ever blessed be!)
　　Came to this fountain near,
　　With such a smiling cheer!
　　　Such a face!
　　　Such a grace!
Happy! happy eyes! that see
Such a heavenly sight as she!

Then I forthwith took my pipe,
Which I all fair and clean did wipe,
And upon a heavenly ground,
All in the grace of beauty found,
  Played this roundelay,
   "Welcome, fair Queen of May!
    Sing, sweet air!
    Welcome Fair!
Welcome be the Shepherds' Queen!
The glory of all our green!"

LULLABY.

From Dowland's *Third Book of Songs or Airs*, 1603.

WEEP you no more, sad fountains,
   What need you flow so fast?
Look how the snowy mountains
  Heaven's sun doth gently waste.
But my sun's heavenly eyes,
  View not your weeping,
  That now lies sleeping,
Softly, now softly lies
   Sleeping.

Sleep is a reconciling,
  A rest that peace begets;
Doth not the sun rise smiling
  When fair at even he sets?
Rest you, then, rest sad eyes,
  Melt not in weeping,
  While she lies sleeping,
Softly, now softly lies
   Sleeping.

WILLIAM SHAKESPEARE.

(1564–1616.)

There are several convenient modern reprints of Shakespeare's Songs and Sonnets, including Prof. Dowden's, Prof. Palgrave's, and the edition by Mr. William Sharp in the Canterbury Poets. About the sonnets a voluminous literature has grown up. They appeared in 1609. It is conjectured they were written about 1598.

From *Love's Labour's Lost*, Act v. Sc. 2.

WHEN icicles hang by the wall,
   And Dick the shepherd blows his nail,
And Tom bears logs into the hall,
   And milk comes frozen home in pail,
When blood is nipped and ways be foul,
Then nightly sings the staring owl,
      Tu-whit;
Tu-who, a merry note,
While greasy Joan doth keel the pot.

When all aloud the wind doth blow,
   And coughing drowns the parson's saw,
And birds sit brooding in the snow,
   And Marian's nose looks red and raw,
When roasted crabs hiss in the bowl,
Then nightly sings the staring owl,
      Tu-whit;
Tu-who, a merry note,
While greasy Joan doth keel the pot.

From *Midsummer Night's Dream*, Act ii. Sc. 1.

OVER hill, over dale,
   Thorough bush, thorough brier,
Over park, over pale,
   Thorough flood, thorough fire,

I do wander everywhere,
Swifter than the moonës sphere;
And I serve the fairy queen,
To dew her orbs upon the green.
The cowslips tall her pensioners be;
In their gold coats spots you see;
Those be rubies, fairy favours,
In those freckles live their savours:
I must go seek some dewdrops here,
And hang a pearl in every cowslip's ear.

From *Midsummer Night's Dream*, Act ii. Sc. 2.

First Fairy.   YOU spotted snakes with double tongue,
        Thorny hedge-hogs, be not seen;
    Newts and blind-worms, do no wrong;
        Come not near our fairy queen.
Chorus.   Philomel, with melody,
        Sing in our sweet lullaby;
Lulla, lulla, lullaby, lulla, lulla, lullaby;
        Never harm,
        Nor spell, nor charm,
        Come our lovely lady nigh;
        So, good night, with lullaby.
First Fairy. Weaving spiders, come not here:
        Hence, you long-legged spinners, hence!
    Beetles black, approach not near;
        Worm, nor snail, do no offence.
Chorus.   Philomel, with melody, &c.

From *The Two Gentlemen of Verona*, Act iv. Sc. 1.

WHO is Silvia? what is she,
    That all our swains commend her?
Holy, fair, and wise is she;

The heaven such grace did lend her,
That she might admired be.

Is she kind as she is fair?
 For beauty lives with kindness.
Love doth to her eyes repair,
 To help him of his blindness,
And, being helped, inhabits there.

Then to Silvia let us sing,
 That Silvia is excelling;
She excels each mortal thing
 Upon the dull earth dwelling:
To her let us garlands bring.

From *The Merchant of Venice*, Act iii. Sc. 2.

TELL me where is fancy bred,
 Or in the heart, or in the head?
How begot, how nourishèd?
  Reply, reply.

It is engendered in the eyes,
With gazing fed; and fancy dies
In the cradle where it lies:
Let us all ring fancy's knell;
I'll begin it,—Ding-dong, bell.
  Ding, dong, bell.

From *As You Like It*, Act ii. Sc. 5.

UNDER the greenwood tree
 Who loves to lie with me
And turn his merry note
Unto the sweet bird's throat,

Come hither, come hither, come hither:
   Here shall he see
   No enemy
But winter and rough weather.

   Who doth ambition shun
   And loves to live i' the sun,
   Seeking the food he eats,
   And pleased with what he gets,
Come hither, come hither, come hither:
   Here shall he see
   No enemy
But winter and rough weather.

From *As You Like It*, Act ii. Sc. 7.

BLOW, blow, thou winter wind,
   Thou art not so unkind
   As man's ingratitude;
Thy tooth is not so keen,
Because thou art not seen,
   Although thy breath be rude.

Heigh ho! sing, heigh ho! unto the green holly:
Most friendship is feigning, most loving mere folly:
   Then, heigh ho, the holly!
   This life is most jolly.

   Freeze, freeze, thou bitter sky,
   That dost not bite so nigh
     As benefits forgot:
   Though thou the waters warp,
   Thy sting is not so sharp
     As friend remembered not.

Heigh ho! sing, heigh ho! &c.

From *Much Ado about Nothing*, Act ii. Sc. 3.

SIGH no more, ladies, sigh no more,
　　Men were deceivers ever,
One foot in sea and one on shore,
　　To one thing constant never:
Then sigh not so, but let them go,
　　And be you blithe and bonny,
Converting all your sounds of woe
　　Into Hey nonny, nonny.

Sing no more ditties, sing no moe,
　　Of dumps so dull and heavy;
The fraud of men was ever so,
　　Since summer first was leafy:
Then sigh not so, but let them go,
　　And be you blithe and bonny,
Converting all your sounds of woe
　　Into Hey nonny, nonny.

From *Twelfth Night*, Act ii. Sc. 3.

O MISTRESS mine, where are you roaming?
　　O, stay and hear; your true love's coming,
That can sing both high and low:
Trip no further, pretty sweeting;
Journeys end in lovers' meeting
　　Every wise man's son doth know.

What is love? 't is not hereafter;
Present mirth hath present laughter;
　　What's to come is still unsure:
In delay there lies no plenty;
Then come kiss me, sweet and twenty,
　　Youth's a stuff will not endure.

From *Twelfth Night*, Act ii. Sc. 4.

COME away, come away, death,
　　And in sad cypress let me be laid;
Fly away, fly away, breath;
　　I am slain by a fair cruel maid.
My shroud of white, stuck all with yew,
　　O, prepare it!
My part of death, no one so true
　　Did share it.

Not a flower, not a flower sweet,
　　On my black coffin let there be strown;
Not a friend, not a friend greet
　　My poor corpse, where my bones shall be thrown:
A thousand thousand sighs to save,
　　Lay me, O, where
Sad true lover never find my grave,
　　To weep there!

From *Hamlet*, Act iv. Sc. 5.

HOW should I your true love know
　　From another one?
By his cockle hat and staff,
　　And his sandal shoon.

He is dead and gone, lady,
　　He is dead and gone;
At his head a grass-green turf,
　　At his heels a stone.

White his shroud as the mountain snow,
　　Larded with sweet flowers,
Which bewept to the grave did go
　　With true-love showers.

From *Measure for Measure*, Act iv. Sc. 1.

TAKE, O, take those lips away,
    That so sweetly were forsworn;
And those eyes, the break of day,
    Lights that do mislead the morn:
But my kisses bring again,
                Bring again;
Seals of love, but sealed in vain,
                Sealed in vain.

From *Cymbeline*, Act ii. Sc. 3.

HARK, hark! the lark at heaven's gate sings,
    And Phœbus 'gins arise,
His steeds to water at those springs
    On chaliced flowers that lies;
And winking Mary-buds begin
    To ope their golden eyes:
With every thing that pretty is,
    My lady sweet, arise:
        Arise, arise.

From *Cymbeline*, Act iv. Sc. 2.

FEAR no more the heat o' the sun,
    Nor the furious winter's rages;
Thou thy worldly task hast done,
    Home art gone, and ta'en thy wages:
Golden lads and girls all must,
As chimney-sweepers, come to dust.

Fear no more the frown o' the great;
    Thou art past the tyrant's stroke;
Care no more to clothe and eat;
    To thee the reed is as the oak:
The sceptre, learning, physic, must
All follow this, and come to dust.

Fear no more the lightning-flash,
  Nor the all-dreaded thunder-stone;
Fear not slander, censure rash;
  Thou hast finished joy and moan:
All lovers young, all lovers must
Consign to thee, and come to dust.

No exorciser harm thee!
Nor no witchcraft charm thee!
Ghost unlaid forbear thee!
Nothing ill come near thee!
Quiet consummation have;
And renowned be thy grave!

From *The Tempest*, Act i. Sc. 2.

FULL fathom five thy father lies;
  Of his bones are coral made;
Those are pearls that were his eyes:
  Nothing of him that doth fade
But doth suffer a sea-change
Into something rich and strange.
Sea-nymphs hourly ring his knell:
                    Ding-dong.
Hark! now I hear them, Ding-dong, bell.

From *The Tempest*, Act v. Sc. 1.

WHERE the bee sucks, there suck I:
  In a cowslip's bell I lie:
There I couch when owls do cry.
On the bat's back I do fly
After summer merrily.
Merrily, merrily, shall I live now
Under the blossom that hangs on the bough.

SONNETS.

WHEN, in disgrace with fortune and men's eyes,
　　I all alone beweep my outcast state,
And trouble deaf heaven with my bootless cries,
And look upon myself and curse my fate,
Wishing me like to one more rich in hope,
Featured like him, like him with friends possessed,
Desiring this man's art and that man's scope,
With what I most enjoy contented least;
Yet in these thoughts myself almost despising,
Haply I think on thee, and then my state,
Like to the lark at break of day arising
From sullen earth, sings hymns at heaven's gate;
　　For thy sweet love remembered such wealth brings
　　That then I scorn to change my state with kings.

———

WHEN to the sessions of sweet silent thought
　　I summon up remembrance of things past,
I sigh the lack of many a thing I sought,
And with old woes new wail my dear time's waste:
Then can I drown an eye, unused to flow,
For precious friends hid in death's dateless night,
And weep afresh love's long since cancelled woe,
And moan the expense of many a vanished sight:
Then can I grieve at grievances foregone,
And heavily from woe to woe tell o'er
The sad account of fore-bemoaned moan,
Which I new pay as if not paid before.
　　But if the while I think on thee, dear friend,
　　All losses are restored and sorrows end.

———

FULL many a glorious morning have I seen
    Flatter the mountain-tops with sovran eye,
Kissing with golden face the meadows green,
Gilding pale streams with heavenly alchemy;
Anon permit the basest clouds to ride
With ugly rack on his celestial face,
And from the forlorn world his visage hide,
Stealing unseen to west with this disgrace:
Even so my sun one early morn did shine
With all-triumphant splendour on my brow;
But out, alack! he was but one hour mine;
The region cloud hath masked him from me now.
    Yet him for this my love no whit disdaineth;
    Suns of the world may stain when heaven's sun staineth.

LIKE as the waves make towards the pebbled shore,
    So do our minutes hasten to their end;
Each changing place with that which goes before,
In sequent toil all forwards do contend.
Nativity, once in the main of light,
Crawls to maturity, wherewith being crowned,
Crookéd eclipses 'gainst his glory fight,
And Time that gave doth now his gift confound.
Time doth transfix the flourish set on youth,
And delves the parallels in beauty's brow;
Feeds on the rarities of nature's truth,
And nothing stands but for his scythe to mow:
    And yet to times in hope my verse shall stand,
    Praising thy worth, despite his cruel hand.

TIRED with all these, for restful death I cry,
    As, to behold desert a beggar born,
And needy nothing trimmed in jollity,
And purest faith unhappily forsworn,

And gilded honour shamefully misplaced,
And maiden virtue rudely strumpeted,
And right perfection wrongfully disgraced,
And strength by limping sway disabled,
And art made tongue-tied by authority,
And folly doctor-like controlling skill,
And simple truth miscalled simplicity,
And captive good attending captain ill.
   Tired with all these, from these would I be gone,
   Save that, to die, I leave my love alone.

N O longer mourn for me when I am dead
   Than you shall hear the surly sullen bell
Give warning to the world that I am fled
From this vile world, with vilest worms to dwell:
Nay, if you read this line, remember not
The hand that writ it; for I love you so
That I in your sweet thoughts would be forgot
If thinking on me then should make you woe.
Oh, if, I say, you look upon this verse
When I perhaps compounded am with clay,
Do not so much as my poor name rehearse;
But let your love even with my life decay;
   Lest the wise world should look into your moan,
   And mock you with me after I am gone.

T HAT time of year thou mayst in me behold
   When yellow leaves, or none, or few, do hang
Upon those boughs which shake against the cold,
Bare ruin'd choirs, where late the sweet birds sang.
In me thou see'st the twilight of such day
As after sunset fadeth in the west,
Which by and by black night doth take away,
Death's second self, that seals up all in rest.

In me thou see'st the glowing of such fire
That on the ashes of his youth doth lie,
As the death-bed whereon it must expire,
Consumed with that which it was nourished by.
This thou perceivest, which makes thy love more strong,
To love that well which thou must leave ere long.

———

To me, fair friend, you never can be old,
For as you were when first your eye I eyed,
Such seems your beauty still.   Three winters cold
Have from the forests shook three summers' pride,
Three beauteous springs to yellow autumn turned
In process of the seasons have I seen,
Three April perfumes in three hot Junes burned,
Since first I saw you fresh, which yet are green.
Ah! yet doth beauty, like a dial-hand,
Steal from his figure and no pace perceived;
So your sweet hue, which methinks still doth stand,
Hath motion and mine eye may be deceived:
For fear of which, hear this, thou age unbred;
Ere you were born was beauty's summer dead.

———

When in the chronicle of wasted time
I see descriptions of the fairest wights,
And beauty making beautiful old rhyme
In praise of ladies dead and lovely knights,
Then, in the blazon of sweet beauty's best,
Of hand, of foot, of lip, of eye, of brow,
I see their antique pen would have expressed
Even such a beauty as you master now.
So all their praises are but prophecies
Of this our time, all you prefiguring;

And, for they looked but with divining eyes,
They had not skill enough your worth to sing:
    For we, which now behold these present days,
    Have eyes to wonder, but lack tongues to praise.

———

NOT mine own fears, nor the prophetic soul
    Of the wide world dreaming on things to come,
Can yet the lease of my true love control,
Supposed as forfeit to a confined doom.
The mortal moon hath her eclipse endured
And the sad augurs mock their own presage;
Incertainties now crown themselves assured,
And peace proclaims olives of endless age.
Now with the drops of this most balmy time
My love looks fresh, and Death to me subscribes,
Since, spite of him, I'll live in this poor rhyme,
While he insults o'er dull and speechless tribes:
    And thou in this shalt find thy monument,
    When tyrants' crests and tombs of brass are spent.

———

OH, never say that I was false of heart,
    Though absence seemed my flame to qualify.
As easy might I from myself depart
As from my soul, which in thy breast doth lie:
That is my home of love: if I have ranged
Like him that travels, I return again,
Just to the time, not with the time exchanged,—
So that myself bring water for my stain.
Never believe, though in my nature reigned
All frailties that besiege all kinds of blood,
That it could so preposterously be stained,
To leave for nothing all thy sum of good;
    For nothing this wide universe I call,
    Save thou, my rose; in it thou art my all.

LET me not to the marriage of true minds
Admit impediments.   Love is not love
Which alters when it alteration finds,
Or bends with the remover to remove:
Oh no! it is an ever-fixèd mark,
That looks on tempests, and is never shaken;
It is the star to every wandering bark,
Whose worth's unknown, although his height be taken.
Love's not Time's fool, though rosy lips and cheeks
Within his bending sickle's compass come;
Love alters not with his brief hours and weeks,
But bears it out even to the edge of doom.
    If this be error, and upon me proved,
    I never writ, nor no man ever loved.

THE expense of spirit in a waste of shame
Is lust in action; and till action, lust
Is perjured, murderous, bloody, full of blame,
Savage, extreme, rude, cruel, not to trust;
Enjoyed no sooner but despisèd straight;
Past reason hunted; and no sooner had,
Past reason hated, as a swallowed bait,
On purpose laid to make the taker mad:
Mad in pursuit, and in possession so;
Had, having, and in quest to have, extreme;
A bliss in proof,—and proved, a very woe;
Before, a joy proposed; behind, a dream.
    All this the world well knows; yet none knows well
    To shun the heaven that leads men to this hell.

POOR soul, the centre of my sinful earth,
    [Foiled by] these rebel powers that thee array,
Why dost thou pine within and suffer dearth,
Painting thy outward walls so costly gay?

Why so large cost, having so short a lease,
Dost thou upon thy fading mansion spend?
Shall worms, inheritors of this excess,
Eat up thy charge? is this thy body's end?
Then, soul, live thou upon thy servant's loss,
And let that pine to aggravate thy store;
Buy terms divine in selling hours of dross;
Within be fed, without be rich no more:
 So shalt thou feed on Death, that feeds on men,
 And Death once dead, there's no more dying then.

———

SAMUEL DANIEL.
(1562?–1619.)

The Sonnets are from *Delia, containing Certain Sonnets*, 1592. The Shadow-Song is from *Thetys' Festival*, a masque presented in 1610. The last selection is a lyric passage occurring in *Hymen's Triumph*, "A Pastoral Tragicomedy", 1614. Daniel's Works are edited by Dr. Grosart (Spenser Society, 1885), and his poems are to be found in Chalmer's *Poets*, vol. iii. *Delia* is reprinted in Arber's *Garner*, vol. iii.

SONNET TO DELIA.

BEAUTY, sweet love, is like the morning dew,
 Whose short refresh upon the tender green
Cheers for a time, but till the Sun doth shew,
And straight 't is gone, as it had never been.
Soon doth it fade that makes the fairest flourish;
Short is the glory of the blushing rose:
The hue which thou so carefully dost nourish,
Yet which at length thou must be forced to lose.
When thou, surcharged with burthen of thy years,
Shalt bend thy wrinkles homeward to the earth;
And that in beauty's lease expired, appears
The date of age, the calends of our death.
 But ah! no more; this must not be foretold:
 For women grieve to think they must be old.

CARE-CHARMER SLEEP.

CARE-CHARMER Sleep, son of the sable Night,
    Brother to Death, in silent darkness born:
Relieve my languish and restore the light;
With dark forgetting of my care, return,
And let the day be time enough to mourn
The shipwreck of my ill-adventured youth:
Let waking eyes suffice to wail their scorn
Without the torment of the night's untruth.
Cease dreams, the images of day desires,
To model forth the passions of the morrow;
Never let rising sun approve you liars,
To add more grief to aggravate my sorrow.
    Still let me sleep, embracing clouds in vain,
    And never wake to feel the day's disdain.

SONG.

ARE they shadows that we see?
    And can shadows pleasure give?
Pleasures only shadows be
Cast by bodies we conceive,
And are made the things we deem,
In those figures which they seem.
But these pleasures vanish fast,
Which by shadows are exprest:
Pleasures are not if they last,
In their passing is their best.
Glory is most bright and gay
In a flash, and so away.
Feed apace then, greedy eyes,
On the wonder you behold.
Take it sudden as it flies,
Though you take it not to hold:

When your eyes have done their part,
Thought must length it in the heart.

LOVE'S BIRTH AND BECOMING.

From *Hymen's Triumph.*

Thyrsis.

AH I remember well (and how can I
But evermore remember well) when first
Our flame began, when scarce we knew what was
The flame we felt, when as we sat and sighed
And looked upon each other, and conceived
Not what we ailed; yet something we did ail,
And yet were well, and yet we were not well;
And what was our disease we could not tell.
Then would we kiss, then sigh, then look; and thus
In that first garden of our simpleness
We spent our childhood; but when years began
To reap the fruit of knowledge, ah, how then
Would she with graver looks, with sweet stern brow
Check my presumption and my forwardness;
Yet still would give me flowers, still would me show
What she would have me, yet not have me know.

Palæmon.

Alas with what poor coin are lovers paid,
And taken with the smallest bait is laid!

Thyrsis.

And when in sport with other company,
Of nymphs and shepherds we have met abroad
How would she steal a look: and watch mine eye
Which way it went! and when at barley-break
It came unto my turn to rescue her,
With what an earnest, swift, and nimble pace

Would her affection make her feet to run,
Nor farther run than to my hand! her race
Had no stop but my bosom, where no end.
And when we were to break again, how late
And loath her trembling hand would part with mine,
And with how slow a pace would she set forth
To meet th' encountering party, who contends
T' attain her, scarce affording him her fingers' ends!

MICHAEL DRAYTON.

(1563–1631.)

The first two sonnets occur in Drayton's *Poems*, 1605; "Since there's no help" in the *Poems*, 1619; and the "Ballad of Agincourt" in the *Poems, Lyric and Pastoral*, 1606(?). There is no satisfactory modern edition of Drayton. Most of his poems are reprinted in Chalmer's *Poets*, vol. iv. Mr. Oliver Elton has written an "Introduction to Michael Drayton", 1895, containing a sketch of the poet's life and a bibliography of his works, to accompany the reprint of the Poems by the Spenser Society.

SONNET: TO THE LADY L. S.

BRIGHT star of beauty, on whose eyelids sit
    A thousand nymph-like and enamoured graces,
The goddesses of memory and wit,
Which in due order take their several places;
In whose dear bosom, sweet delicious Love
Lays down his quiver, that he once did bear,
Since he that blessed Paradise did prove,
Forsook his mother's lap to sport him there.
Let others strive to entertain with words,
My soul is of another temper made;
I hold it vile that vulgar wit affords,
Devouring time my faith shall not invade:
    Still let my praise be honoured thus by you,
    Be you most worthy, whilst I be most true.

TO THE RIVER ANKOR.

CLEAR Ankor, on whose silver-sanded shore,
  My soul-shrined saint, my fair Idea lies,
O blessed brook, whose milk-white swans adore
Thy crystal stream refinèd by her eyes,
Where sweet myrrh-breathing Zephyr in the spring
Gently distils his nectar-dropping showers,
Where nightingales in Arden sit and sing,
Amongst the dainty dew-impearlèd flowers;
Say thus, fair brook, when thou shalt see thy queen,
Lo, here thy shepherd spent his wandering years,
And in these shades, dear nymph, he oft had been,
And here to thee he sacrificed his tears:
  Fair Arden, thou my Tempe art alone,
  And thou, sweet Ankor, art my Helicon.

SONNET.

SINCE there's no help, come, let us kiss and part,—
  Nay I have done, you get no more of me;
And I am glad, yea glad with all my heart,
That thus so cleanly I myself can free;
Shake hands for ever, cancel all our vows,
And when we meet at any time again,
Be it not seen in either of our brows
That we one jot of former love retain.
Now at the last gasp of Love's latest breath,
When his pulse failing, Passion speechless lies,
When Faith is kneeling by his bed of death,
And Innocence is closing up his eyes,—
  Now if thou would'st, when all have given him over,
  From death to life thou might'st him yet recover!

TO THE CAMBRO-BRITONS AND THEIR HARP:
HIS BALLAD OF AGINCOURT.

FAIR stood the wind for France,
 When we our sails advance,
Nor now to prove our chance
 Longer will tarry;
But putting to the main,
At Caux, the mouth of Seine,
With all his martial train,
 Landed King Harry.

And taking many a fort,
Furnished in warlike sort,
Marcheth towards Agincourt
 In happy hour;
Skirmishing day by day,
With those that stopped his way
Where the French general lay
 With all his power;

Which in his height of pride,
King Henry to deride,
His ransom to provide
 To the king sending.
Which he neglects the while,
As from a nation vile,
Yet with an angry smile
 Their fall portending.

And turning to his men,
Quoth our brave Henry then,
Though they to one be ten,
 Be not amazed.

Yet have we well begun,
Battles so bravely won,
Have ever to the sun
    By fame been raised.

And for myself (quoth he),
This my full rest shall be:
England ne'er mourn for me,
    Nor more esteem me;
Victor I will remain,
Or on this earth lie slain,
Never shall she sustain
    Loss to redeem me.

Poitiers and Cressy tell,
When most their pride did swell,
Under our swords they fell;
    No less our skill is,
Than when our grandsire-great,
Claiming the regal seat,
By many a warlike feat
    Lopped the French lilies.

The Duke of York so dread
The eager vaward led,
With the main, Henry sped,
    Amongst his henchmen;
Exeter had the rear,
A braver man not there:
O Lord, how hot they were
    On the false Frenchmen!

They now to fight are gone,
Armour on armour shone,
Drum now to drum did groan,
    To hear was wonder;

That with the cries they make,
The very earth did shake,
Trumpet to trumpet spake,
    Thunder to thunder.

Well it thine age became,
O noble Erpingham,
Which didst the signal aim
    To our hid forces!
When from a meadow by,
Like a storm suddenly,
The English archery
    Struck the French horses.

With Spanish yew so strong,
Arrows a cloth-yard long,
That like to serpents stung,
    Piercing the weather;
None from his fellow starts,
But playing manly parts,
And like true English hearts
    Stuck close together.

When down their bows they threw,
And forth their bilbos drew,
And on the French they flew,
    Not one was tardy;
Arms were from shoulders sent,
Scalps to the teeth were rent,
Down the French peasants went,
    Our men were hardy.

This while our noble king,
His broadsword brandishing,
Down the French host did ding,
    As to o'erwhelm it.

And many a deep wound lent,
His arms with blood besprent,
And many a cruel dent
    Bruisèd his helmet.

Gloucester, that duke so good,
Next of the royal blood,
For famous England stood,
    With his brave brother;
Clarence, in steel so bright,
Though but a maiden knight,
Yet in that furious fight
    Scarce such another!

Warwick in blood did wade.
Oxford the foe invade,
And cruel slaughter made,
Still as they ran up;
Suffolk his axe did fly,
Beaumont and Willoughby
Bear them right doughtily,
    Ferrers and Fanhope.

Upon Saint Crispin's day
Fought was this noble fray,
Which fame did not delay
    To England to carry;
O when shall Englishmen
With such acts fill a pen,
Or England breed again
    Such a King Harry?

ROBERT SOUTHWELL.

(1562?–1595.)

THE BURNING BABE.

In *St. Peter's Complaint, with other Poems,* 1595. Ben Jonson greatly admired this poem. Southwell's *Poetical Works,* edited by Mr. W. B. Turnbull, were issued in 1856.

AS I in hoary winter's night stood shivering in the snow,
    Surprised I was with sudden heat which made my
       heart to glow;
And lifting up a fearful eye to view what fire was near,
A pretty babe all burning bright did in the air appear,
Who scorchèd with exceeding heat such floods of tears
    did shed,
As though His floods should quench His flames with what
    His tears were fed;
Alas! quoth He, but newly born, in fiery heats I fry,
Yet none approach to warm their hearts or feel my fire
    but I!
My faultless breast the furnace is, the fuel wounding
    thorns;
Love is the fire and sighs the smoke, the ashes shame
    and scorns;
The fuel Justice layeth on, and Mercy blows the coals,
The metal in this furnace wrought are men's defilèd souls
For which, as now on fire I am, to work them to their
    good,
So will I melt into a bath, to wash them in my blood.
With this He vanished out of sight, and swiftly shrunk
    away,
And straight I callèd unto mind that it was Christmas-day.

GEORGE CHAPMAN.
(1557?–1634.)

HER COMING.

Ascribed to Chapman in *England's Parnassus*, 1600. Chapman's
Minor Poems and Translations have been reprinted (London, 1875).

SEE where she issues in her beauty's pomp,
    As Flora to salute the morning sun;
Who when she shakes her tresses in the air,
Rains on the earth dissolvèd pearl in showers,
Which with his beams the sun exhales to heaven:
She holds the spring and summer in her arms,
And every plant puts on his freshest robes,
To dance attendance on her princely steps,
Springing and fading as she comes and goes.

OF CIRCUMSPECTION.

IN hope to 'scape the law, do naught amiss,
    The penance ever in the action is.

SIR JOHN DAVIES.
(1569–1626.)

From the *Hymns to Astræa*, 1599,—in acrostics! Davies' Poems may
be read in volume v. of Chalmer's *Poets*, or in Dr. Grosart's edition
(2 vols., London, 1876), or in Arber's *Garner*, vol. v.

TO THE ROSE.

EYE of the garden, queen of flowers,
    Love's cup wherein he nectar pours,
Ingendered first of nectar:
Sweet nurse-child of the spring's young hours,
And beauty's fair character.

Best jewel that the earth doth wear!
Even when the brave young sun draws near,
To her hot love pretending;
Himself likewise like form doth bear,
At rising and descending.

Rose, of the queen of love beloved;
England's great kings divinely moved
Gave roses in their banner;
It showed that beauty's rose indeed,
Now in this age should them succeed,
And reign in more sweet manner.

BARNABE BARNES.

(1569?–1609.)

Ode 9 and Sonnet lxvi. of *Parthenophil and Parthenope*, 1593.
Reprinted in Arber's *Garner*, vol. v.

ODE.

BEHOLD, out walking in these valleys,
    When fair PARTHENOPE doth tread,
  How joysome FLORA with her dallies!
  And, at her steps, sweet flowers bred!
        Narcissus yellow,
  And Amaranthus ever red,
    Which all her footsteps overspread;
With Hyacinth that finds no fellow.

Behold, within that shady thick,
    Where my PARTHENOPE doth walk,
  Her beauty makes trees moving quick,
  Which of her grace in murmur talk!
        The Poplar trees shed tears;

The blossomed Hawthorn, white as chalk;
And Aspen trembling on his stalk;
The tree which sweet frankincense bears;

The barren Hebene coaly black;
Green Ivy, with his strange embraces;
Daphne,[1] which scorns JOVE'S thundercrack;
Sweet Cypress, set in sundry places;
And singing Atys[2] tells
Unto the rest, my Mistress' graces!
From them, the wind her glory chases
Throughout the West, where it excels.

SONNET.

AH, sweet Content! where is thy mild abode?
Is it with shepherds, and light-hearted swains,
Which sing upon the downs, and pipe abroad,
Tending their flocks and cattle on the plains?
Ah, sweet Content! where dost thou safely rest?
In heaven, with angels, which the praises sing
Of Him that made, and rules at His behest,
The minds and hearts of every living thing?
Ah, sweet Content! where doth thine harbour hold?
Is it in churches, with religious men,
Which please the gods with prayers manifold,
And in their studies meditate it then?
Whether thou dost in heaven, or earth appear;
Be where thou wilt! Thou wilt not harbour here!

[1] the laurel.   [2] the pine-tree.

"J. C."

BEAUTY AND TIME.

From *Alcilia: Philoparthen's Loving Folly*, 1595.
Reprinted in Arber's *Garner*, vol. iv.

WHAT thing is Beauty? "Nature's dearest Minion!"
    "The Snare of Youth! like the inconstant moon
Waxing and waning!"   "Error of Opinion!"
"A Morning's Flower, that withereth ere noon!"
"A swelling Fruit! no sooner ripe, than rotten!"
"Which sickness makes forlorn, and time forgotten!"

.   .   .   .

The time will come when, looking in a glass,
Thy rivelled face with sorrow thou shalt see!
And sighing, say, "It is not as it was!
These cheeks were wont more fresh and fair to be!
But now, what once made me so much admired
Is least regarded, and of none desired!"

Though thou be fair, think Beauty but a blast!
A morning's dew! a shadow quickly gone!
A painted flower, whose colour will not last!
Time steals away, when least we think thereon.
Most precious time! too wastefully expended;
Of which alone the sparing is commended.

.   .   .   .   .   .

Thy large smooth forehead, wrinkled shall appear!
Vermilion hue, to pale and wan shall turn!
Time shall deface what Youth has held most dear!
Yea, those clear Eyes (which once my heart did burn)
Shall, in their hollow circles, lodge the night;
And yield more cause of terror than delight!

THOMAS HEYWOOD.

(1575?–1650?)

These are songs in the drama of the *Rape of Lucrece*, 1608 (acted 1605), accessible in the Mermaid edition of Heywood's *Best Plays*, or in the collected edition of his *Dramatic Works* (in six volumes, London, 1874).

PACK CLOUDS AWAY.

PACK clouds away, and welcome day,
　　With night we banish sorrow;
Sweet air, blow soft; mount, lark, aloft,
　　To give my love good-morrow.
Wings from the wind to please her mind,
　　Notes from the lark I 'll borrow:
Bird, prune thy wing; nightingale, sing,
　　To give my love good-morrow.
　　To give my love good-morrow,
　　Notes from them all I 'll borrow.

Wake, from thy nest, robin redbreast,
　　Sing, birds, in every furrow;
And from each bill let music shrill
　　Give my fair love good-morrow.
Blackbird and thrush in every bush,
　　Stare, linnet, and cock-sparrow,
You pretty elves, amongst yourselves,
　　Sing my fair love good-morrow.
　　To give my love good-morrow,
　　Sing, birds, in every furrow.

SONG OF THE BELL.

COME, list and hark;
　　The bell doth toll,
For some but now
　　Departing soul.

And was not that
   Some ominous fowl
The bat, the night-
   Crow, or screech owl?
To these I hear
   The wild wolf howl
In this black night
   That seems to scowl.
All these my black-
   Book shall enroll;
For hark! still, still
   The bell doth toll
For some but now
   Departing soul.

THOMAS DEKKER.

(1570?–1641.)

The first two songs are from the *Shoemaker's Holiday*, acted 1599.
The next two occur in the *Pleasant Comedy of Patient Grissell*, acted 1599,
which was only written in part by Dekker, and possibly they are not by
Dekker. The music of the first and fourth is given in Chappell's *Old
English Popular Music*, and in *Hullah's Golden Treasury Song Book*.
"The Gifts of Fortune and Cupid" is found in the *Sun's Darling*, a *Moral
Masque*, by Ford and Dekker, acted 1624, which however is probably
an adaptation of Dekker's *Phaeton*, a play of much earlier date. Dekker
probably wrote the song. Dekker's *Dramatic Works* were collected
into four volumes in 1873; they were also edited by Mr. Bullen in 1887.

TROLL THE BOWL!

COLD'S the wind, and wet's the rain,
   Saint Hugh be our good speed!
Ill is the weather that bringeth no gain,
   Nor helps good hearts in need.

Troll the bowl, the jolly nut-brown bowl,
   And here, kind mate, to thee!

Let 's sing a dirge for Saint Hugh's soul,
 And down it merrily.

Down-a-down, hey, down-a-down,
 Hey derry derry down-a-down!
Ho! well done, to me let come,
 Ring compass, gentle joy!

Troll the bowl, the nut-brown bowl,
 And here kind, &c. (*as often as there be men to* drink). *At last, when all have drunk, this verse.*

Cold 's the wind, and wet 's the rain,
 Saint Hugh be our good speed!
Ill is the weather that bringeth no gain,
 Nor helps good hearts in need.

THE MERRY MONTH OF MAY.

O, THE month of May, the merry month of May,
 So frolic, so gay, and so green, so green, so green!
O, and then did I unto my true love say,
Sweet Peg, thou shalt be my summer's queen.

Now the nightingale, the pretty nightingale,
The sweetest singer in all the forest quire,
Entreats thee, sweet Peggy, to hear thy true love's tale;
Lo, yonder she sitteth, her breast against a brier.

But O, I spy the cuckoo, the cuckoo, the cuckoo;
See where she sitteth; come away, my joy:
Come away, I prithee, I do not like the cuckoo
Should sing where my Peggy and I kiss and toy.

O, the month of May, the merry month of May,
So frolic, so gay, and so green, so green, so green;
And then did I unto my true love say,
Sweet Peg, thou shalt be my summer's queen.

CONTENT.

ART thou poor, yet hast thou golden slumbers?
      O sweet Content!
Art thou rich, yet is thy mind perplexed?
      O Punishment!
Dost laugh to see how fools are vexed
To add to golden numbers golden numbers?
  O sweet Content, O sweet, O sweet Content!

    Work apace, apace, apace, apace;
    Honest labour bears a lovely face.
    Then hey noney, noney; hey noney, noney.

Canst drink the waters of the crispèd spring?
      O sweet Content!
Swim'st thou in wealth, yet sink'st in thine own tears?
      O Punishment!
Then he that patiently Want's burden bears
No burden bears, but is a king, a king.
  O sweet Content, O sweet, O sweet Content!

    Work apace, apace, &c.

LULLABY.

GOLDEN slumbers kiss your eyes,
    Smiles awake you when you rise.
Sleep, pretty wantons, do not cry,
And I will sing a lullaby.
Rock them, rock them, lullaby.

Care is heavy, therefore sleep you.
You are care, and care must keep you.
Sleep, pretty wantons, do not cry,
And I will sing a lullaby,
Rock them, rock them, lullaby.

THE GIFTS OF FORTUNE AND CUPID.

Fortune. BE a merchant, I will freight thee
    With all store that time is bought for.

Cupid. Be a lover, I will wait thee
    With success in life most sought for.

Fortune. Be enamoured on bright honour,
    And thy greatness shall shine glorious.

Cupid. Chastity, if thou smile on her,
    Shall grow servile, thou victorious.

Fortune. Be a warrior, conquest ever
    Shall triumphantly renown thee.

Cupid. Be a courtier, beauty never
    Shall but with her duty crown thee.

Fortune. Fortune's wheel is thine, depose me;
    I'm thy slave, thy power hath bound me.

Cupid. Cupid's shafts are thine, dispose me;
    Love loves love; thy graces wound me.

Both. Live, reign! pity is fame's jewel;
    We obey; O, be not cruel!

ROBERT DEVEREUX, EARL OF ESSEX.
(1567–1601.)

"A PASSION OF MY LORD OF ESSEX."

From *Ashm. MS.* 781. In Grosart's edition of Essex in vol. iv. of the
Miscellanies of the Fuller Worthies' Library. It is said to have been
inclosed in a letter to the queen from Ireland, in 1599.

HAPPY were he could finish forth his fate
 In some unhaunted desert, most obscure
From all societies, from love and hate
 Of worldly folk; then might he sleep secure;
Then wake again, and ever give God praise,
 Content with hips and haws and bramble-berry;

In contemplation spending all his days,
    And change of holy thoughts to make him merry;
Where, when he dies, his tomb may be a bush,
Where harmless robin dwells with gentle thrush.

JOHN DONNE.

(1573-1631.)

From *Poems*, 1633. Although not published till after the author's death, almost all of Donne's poetry was written in his youth, before 1600. The Ode to Absence appeared in Davison's *Poetical Rhapsody*, 1602. Donne's poems are reprinted in Chalmer's *Poets*; in Grosart s edition, two vols., 1872; and in the Muses' Library, edited by Mr. E. K. Chambers, two vols., 1895. The Sonnet to Death was written before 1607, and the Hymn to God the Father in 1627.

A VALEDICTION FORBIDDING MOURNING.

AS virtuous men pass mildly away,
    And whisper to their souls to go,
Whilst some of their sad friends do say,
    "Now his breath goes", and some say "No";

So let us melt and make no noise,
    No tear-floods, nor sigh-tempests move,
'T were profanation of our joys,
    To tell the laity our love.

Moving of th' earth brings harm and fears,
    Men reckon what it did and meant;
But trepidation of the spheres,
    Though greater far, is innocent.

Dull sublunary lovers' love,
    Whose soul is sense, cannot admit
Absence, for that it doth remove
    Those things which elemented it

But we by a love so far refined,
　　That ourselves know not what it is,
Inter-assurèd of the mind,
　　Careless eyes, lips, and hands, to miss;

Our two souls therefore, which are one,
　　Though I must go, endure not yet
A breach, but an expansion,
　　Like gold to airy thinness beat.

If they be two, they are two so
　　As stiff twin compasses are two;
Thy soul, the fixed foot, makes no show
　　To move, but doth, if the other do.

And though it in the centre sit,
　　Yet when the other far doth roam,
It leans and hearkens after it,
　　And grows erect as that comes home.

Such wilt thou be to me, who must,
　　Like the other foot, obliquely run;
Thy firmness makes my circle just,
　　And makes me end where I begun.

THE FUNERAL.

WHOEVER comes to shroud me, do not harm
　　　　　Nor question much
That subtle wreath of hair about mine arm;
The mystery, the sign, you must not touch,
　　　　　For 't is my outward soul,
Viceroy to that which, unto heaven being gone,
　　　　　Will leave this to control
And keep these limbs, her provinces, from dissolution.

For if the sinewy thread my brain lets fall
        Through every part,
Can tie those parts, and make me one of all;
The hairs, which upward grew and strength and art
        Have from a better brain,
Can better do it: except she meant that I
        By this should know my pain,
As prisoners then are manacled, when they're con-
    demned to die.

Whate'er she meant by 't, bury it with me;
        For since I am
Love's martyr, it might breed idolatry,
If into others' hands these relics came.
        As 't was humility
To afford to it all that a soul can do;
        So 't is some bravery,
That, since you would have none of me, I bury some
    of you.

ODE.

*"That time and absence proves
Rather helps than hurts to loves."*

ABSENCE, hear thou my protestation
        Against thy strength,
        Distance and length:
Do what thou canst for alteration,
        For hearts of truest mettle
Absence doth join, and time doth settle.

Who loves a mistress of such quality,
        He soon hath found
        Affection's ground
Beyond time, place, and all mortality.
        To hearts that cannot vary
Absence is present, Time doth tarry.

My senses want their outward motiòns,
Which now within
Reason doth win,
Redoubled in her secret notiòns:
Like rich men that take pleasure
In hiding more than handling treasure.

By absence this good means I gain,
That I can catch her,
Where none can watch her,
In some close corner of my brain:
There I embrace and kiss her;
And so I both enjoy and miss her.

SONG.

SWEETEST love, I do not go
For weariness of thee,
Nor in hope the world can show
A fitter love for me;
But since that I
Must die at last, 't is best
Thus to use myself in jest
By feignèd deaths to die.

Yesternight the sun went hence,
And yet is here to-day;
He hath no desire nor sense,
Nor half so short a way;
Then fear not me,
But believe that I shall make
Hastier journeys, since I take
More wings and spurs than he.

O how feeble is man's power,
That if good fortune fall,

Cannot undo another hour,
    Nor a lost hour recall!
       But come bad chance,
And we join to it our strength,
And we teach it art and length,
       Itself o'er us to advance.

When thou sigh'st thou sigh'st no wind,
    But sigh'st my soul away;
When thou weep'st, unkindly kind,
    My life's blood doth decay.
      It cannot be
That thou lov'st me, as thou say'st;
If in thine my life thou waste,
      Thou art the best of me.

Let not thy divining heart
    Forethink me any ill,
Destiny may take my part
    And may thy fears fulfil;
      But think that we
Are but turned aside to sleep:
They who one another keep
      Alive, ne'er parted be.

THE UNDERTAKING.

I HAVE done one braver thing,
    Than all the worthies did;
And yet a braver thence doth spring,
    Which is, to keep that hid.

It were but madness now to impart
    The skill of specular stone,
When he, which can have learned the art
    To cut it, can find none.

So, if I now should utter this,
　　Others (because no more
Such stuff to work upon there is)
　　Would love but as before.

Be he, who loveliness within
　　Hath found, all outward loathes;
For he, who colour loves and skin,
　　Loves but their oldest clothes.

If, as I have, you also do
　　Virtue in woman see,
And dare love that, and say so too,
　　And forget the he and she;

And if this love, though placèd so,
　　From profane men you hide,
Which will no faith on this bestow,
　　Or, if they do, deride:

Then you have done a braver thing,
　　Than all the worthies did,
And a braver thence will spring,
　　Which is, to keep that hid.

THE BLOSSOM.

LITTLE think'st thou, poor flower,
　　Whom I have watched six or seven days,
And seen thy birth, and seen what every hour
　　Gave to thy growth, thee to this height to raise,
And now dost laugh and triumph on this bough,—
　　　　Little think'st thou
That it will freeze anon, and that I shall
To-morrow find thee fallen, or not at all.

Little think'st thou, poor heart,
　　That labourest yet to nestle thee,
And think'st by hovering here to get a part
　　In a forbidden or forbidding tree,
And hop'st her stiffness by long siege to bow,—
　　　　Little think'st thou
That thou to-morrow, ere the sun doth wake,
Must with this sun and me a journey take.

SONNET.

DEATH, be not proud, though some have calléd thee
　　Mighty and dreadful, for thou art not so;
For those whom thou think'st thou dost overthrow
Die not, poor Death; nor yet canst thou kill me.
From rest and sleep, which but thy picture be,
Much pleasure, then from thee much more must flow:
And soonest our best men with thee do go,
Rest of their bones, and souls' delivery.
Thou art slave to fate, chance, kings and desperate men,
And dost with poison, war, and sickness dwell,
And poppy or charms can make us sleep as well,
And better than thy stroke; why swell'st thou then?
　　One short sleep past, we wake eternally,
　　And Death shall be no more; Death, thou shalt die!

HYMN TO GOD THE FATHER.

WILT Thou forgive that sin, where I begun,
　　Which was my sin, though it were done before?
Wilt Thou forgive that sin, through which I run,
　　And do run still, though still I do deplore?
When Thou hast done, Thou hast not done;
　　　　For I have more.

Wilt Thou forgive that sin, which I have won
    Others to sin, and made my sins their door?
Wilt Thou forgive that sin, which I did shun
    A year or two, but wallowed in a score?
When Thou hast done, Thou hast not done;
        For I have more.

I have a sin of fear, that when I've spun
    My last thread, I shall perish on the shore;
But swear by Thyself, that at my death Thy Son
    Shall shine, as He shines now and heretofore:
And having done that, Thou hast done;
        I fear no more.

BEN JONSON.

(1573 1637.)

The Works of Ben Jonson, edited by Gifford and Cunningham, 3 vols.,
London, 1874, is a convenient modern edition. The third volume con-
tains the masques and poems.

ECHO'S LAMENT OF NARCISSUS.

From *Cynthia's Revels* (acted 1600), Act i. Sc. 1.

SLOW, slow, fresh fount, keep time with my salt tears;
    Yet slower, yet; O faintly, gentle springs:
List to the heavy part the music bears,
    Woe weeps out her division, when she sings.
        Droop herbs and flowers,
        Fall grief in showers,
        Our beauties are not ours;
        O, I could still,
Like melting snow upon some craggy hill,
        Drop, drop, drop, drop,
Since nature's pride is now a withered daffodil.

HYMN TO DIANA.

From Cynthia's Revels, 1600.

QUEEN and huntress, chaste and fair,
   Now the sun is laid to sleep,
Seated in thy silver chair,
    State in wonted manner keep:
      Hesperus entreats thy light,
      Goddess excellently bright.

Earth, let not thy envious shade
   Dare itself to interpose;
Cynthia's shining orb was made
    Heaven to clear when day did close:
      Bless us then with wishèd sight,
      Goddess excellently bright.

Lay thy bow of pearl apart,
   And thy crystal shining quiver;
Give unto the flying hart
    Space to breathe, how short soever:
      Thou that mak'st a day of night,
      Goddess excellently bright.

HYMN TO PAN.

From Pan's Anniversary, a masque presented at court in 1625.

1 Nymph.   OF Pan we sing, the best of singers, Pan,
          That taught us swains how first to tune
            our lays,
        And on the pipe more airs than Phœbus can.
Chorus.   Hear, O you groves, and hills resound his
          praise.

2 Nymph. Of Pan we sing, the best of leaders, Pan,
          That leads the Naiads and the Dryads forth;
        And to their dances more than Hermes can.
Chorus.   Hear, O you groves, and hills resound his
          worth.

3 Nymph. Of Pan we sing, the best of hunters, Pan,
              That drives the hart to seek unused ways,
          And in the chase more than Sylvanus can.
Chorus.   Hear, O you groves, and hills resound his
                  praise.

2 Nymph. Of Pan we sing, the best of shepherds, Pan,
              That keeps our flocks and us, and both
                  leads forth
          To better pastures than great Pales can.
Chorus.   Hear, O you groves, and hills resound his
                  worth.
          And while his powers and praises thus we sing,
          The valleys let rebound and all the rivers ring.

SONG,—TO CELIA.

From *The Forest*, 1616 (written 1605). See the music in
Hullah's *Song Book*, p. 47.

DRINK to me only with thine eyes,
    And I will pledge with mine :
Or leave a kiss but in the cup,
    And I 'll not look for wine.
The thirst that from the soul doth rise,
    Doth ask a drink divine :
But might I of Jove's nectar sup,
    I would not change for thine.

I sent thee late a rosy wreath,
    Not so much honouring thee,
As giving it a hope, that there
    It could not withered be.
But thou thereon didst only breathe,
    And sent'st it back to me :
Since when it grows, and smells, I swear,
    Not of itself, but thee.

From *Love Freed from Ignorance and Folly*, a masque
presented in 1610.

HOW near to good is what is fair!
   Which we no sooner see,
But with the lines and outward air
   Our senses taken be.
We wish to see it still, and prove
   What ways we may deserve;
We court, we praise, we more than love:
   We are not grieved to serve.

From *The Masque of Oberon*, 1611.

BUZZ! quoth the Blue-fly,
   Hum! quoth the Bee;
Buzz and hum! they cry,
   And so do we.
In his ear! in his nose!
   Thus,—do you see?
He eat the Dormouse—
   Else it was he.

From *The Gipsies Metamorphosed*, a masque presented in 1621.

THE fairy beam upon you,
   The stars to glister on you;
      A moon of light,
      In the noon of night,
Till the fire-drake hath o'ergone you!
The wheel of fortune guide you,
The boy with the bow beside you;
      Run aye in the way,
      Till the bird of day,
And the luckier lot betide you!

CHARIS' TRIUMPH.

One of the ten pieces forming *A Celebration of Charis*, in *Underwoods*.
The last two stanzas are sung or said by Wittipol in *The Devil is an
Ass* (acted 1616), Act ii. Sc. 2.

SEE the chariot at hand here of Love,
    Wherein my lady rideth!
Each that draws is a swan or a dove,
    And well the car Love guideth.
As she goes, all hearts do duty
Unto her beauty;
And enamoured do wish, so they might
And enjoy such a sight,
That they still were to run by her side,
Thorough swords, thorough seas, whither she would ride.

But look on her eyes, they do light
    All that Love's world compriseth!
Do but look on her hair, it is bright
    As Love's star when it riseth!
Do but mark, her forehead's smoother
Than words that soothe her;
And from her arched brows, such a grace
Sheds itself through the face,
As alone there triumphs to the life
All the gain, all the good of the elements' strife.

Have you seen but a bright lily grow
    Before rude hands have touched it?
Have you marked but the fall o' the snow
    Before the soil hath smutched it?
Have you felt the wool of beaver?
Or swan's down ever?
Or have smelt o' the bud o' the briar?
Or the nard in the fire?
Or have tasted the bag of the bee?
O so white,—O so soft,—O so sweet is she!

THE MEASURE OF THE PERFECT LIFE.

From *A Pindaric Ode on the Death of Sir H. Morison,* in *Underwoods.*

IT is not growing like a tree
    In bulk, doth make man better be;
Or standing long an oak, three hundred year,
To fall a log at last, dry, bald, and sear:
      A lily of a day,
      Is fairer far, in May,
Although it fall and die that night;
It was the plant and flower of light.
In small proportions we just beauties see;
And in short measures life may perfect be.

A HYMN.

From *Underwoods.*

HEAR me, O God!
    A broken heart
  Is my best part:
Use still Thy rod,
    That I may prove
    Therein, Thy love.

If Thou hadst not
    Been stern to me,
    But left me free,
I had forgot
    Myself and Thee.

For, sin 's so sweet,
    As minds ill bent
    Rarely repent,
Until they meet
    Their punishment.

Who more can crave
    Than Thou hast done?
    That gav'st a Son
To free a slave:
    First made of nought;
    With all since bought.

Sin, death, and hell
    His glorious name
    Quite overcame;
Yet I rebel,
    And slight the same.

But, I'll come in,
    Before my loss
    Me further toss,
As sure to win
    Under His cross.

THOMAS CAMPION.

(1567?–1623.)

Campion's works have been edited by Mr. Bullen (London, 1889); selections from Campion are edited by Mr. Ernest Rhys in the Lyric Poets Series (London, 1896); in Arber's *Garner*, vol. iii.; and in Bullen's *Lyrics from Elizabethan Song-Books.*

TO LESBIA.

From Campion and Rosseter's *Book of Airs*, 1601.

Vivamus, mea Lesbia, atque amemus.

MY sweetest Lesbia, let us live and love,
    And though the sager sort our deeds reprove
Let us not weigh them. Heaven's great lamps do dive
Into their west, and straight again revive;

But soon as once set is our little light,
Then must we sleep one ever-during night.

If all would lead their lives in love like me,
Then bloody swords and armour should not be;
No drum nor trumpet peaceful sleeps should move,
Unless alarm came from the camp of love:
But fools do live and waste their little light,
And seek with pain their ever-during night.

When timely death my life and fortune ends,
Let not my hearse be vext with mourning friends;
But let all lovers, rich in triumph, come
And with sweet pastimes grace my happy tomb:
And, Lesbia, close up thou my little light,
And crown with love my ever-during night.

COME AWAY!

WHAT then is love but mourning?
      What desire, but a self-burning?
Till she, that hates, doth love return,
Thus will I mourn, thus will I sing,
"Come away! come away, my darling!"

Beauty is but a blooming,
Youth in his glory entombing;
Time hath a while, which none can stay:
Then come away, while thus I sing,
"Come away! come away, my darling!"

Summer in winter fadeth;
Gloomy night heavenly light shadeth;
Like to the morn are Venus' flowers;
Such are her hours: then will I sing,
"Come away! come away, my darling!"

THE MEASURE OF BEAUTY.

From Thomas Campion's *Two Books of Airs* (circ. 1613).

GIVE Beauty all her right,
  She 's not to one form tied;
Each shape yields fair delight,
  Where her perfections bide:
Helen, I grant, might pleasing be,
And Ros'mond was as sweet as she.

Some the quick eye commends,
  Some swelling lips and red;
Pale looks have many friends,
  Through sacred sweetness bred:
Meadows have flowers that pleasure move,
Though roses are the flowers of love.

Free beauty is not bound
  To one unmoved clime;
She visits every ground
  And favours every time.
Let the old loves with mine compare,
My sovereign is as sweet and fair.

THE SHADOW.

From Campion and Rosseter's *Book of Airs*, 1601.

FOLLOW thy fair sun, unhappy shadow!
  Though thou be black as night,
And she made all of light,
Yet follow thy fair sun, unhappy shadow!

Follow her whose light thy light depriveth;
Though here thou livest disgraced,

And she in heaven is placed,
Yet follow her whose light the world reviveth!

Follow those pure beams whose beauty burneth,
That so have scorched thee,
As thou still black must be,
Till her kind beams thy black to brightness turneth.

Follow her! while yet her glory shineth:
There comes a luckless night,
That will dim all her light;
And this the black unhappy shade divineth.

Follow still! since so thy fates ordained;
The sun must have his shade,
Till both at once do fade;
The sun still proved, the shadow still disdained.

WHEN THOU MUST HOME.

From Campion and Rosseter's *Book of Airs*, 1601.

WHEN thou must home to shades of underground,
  And there arrived, a new admired guest
The beauteous spirits do engirt thee round,
White Iope, blithe Helen, and the rest,
To hear the stories of thy finished love
From that smooth tongue whose music hell can move;

Then wilt thou speak of banqueting delights,
Of masques and revels which sweet youth did make,
Of tourneys and great challenges of knights,
And all these triumphs for thy beauty's sake:
When thou hast told these honours done to thee,
Then tell, O tell, how thou didst murder me.

DAY AND NIGHT.

From Campion's *Two Books of Airs*, 1613.

COME, cheerful day, part of my life to me.
    For while thou view'st me with thy fading light,
Part of my life doth still depart with thee,
And I still onward haste to my last night.
Time's fatal wings do ever forward fly:
So every day we live a day we die.

But, O ye nights, ordained for barren rest,
How are my days deprived of life in you,
When heavy sleep my soul hath dispossest,
By feignèd death life sweetly to renew!
Part of my life in that, you life deny:
So every day we live a day we die.

THE MAN OF LIFE UPRIGHT.

From Campion and Rosseter's *Book of Airs*, 1601.

THE man of life upright,
    Whose guiltless heart is free
From all dishonest deeds,
    Or thought of vanity;

The man whose silent days
    In harmless joys are spent,
Whom hopes cannot delude
    Nor sorrow discontent:

That man needs neither towers
    Nor armour for defence,
Nor secret vaults to fly
    From thunder's violence:

He only can behold
    With unaffrighted eyes

The horrors of the deep
    And terrors of the skies.

Thus scorning all the cares
    That fate or fortune brings,
He makes the heaven his book,
    His wisdom heavenly things;

Good thoughts his only friends,
    His wealth a well-spent age,
The earth his sober inn
    And quiet pilgrimage.

A HYMN IN PRAISE OF NEPTUNE.

From *Gesta Graiorum: Gray's Inn Masque*, 1594.

OF Neptune's empire let us sing,
    At whose command the waves obey;
To whom the rivers tribute pay,
Down the high mountains sliding:
To whom the scaly nation yields
Homage for the crystal fields
        Wherein they dwell:
And every sea-god pays a gem
Yearly out of his watery cell
To deck great Neptune's diadem.

The Tritons dancing in a ring,
Before his palace-gates do make
The water with their echoes quake,
Like the great thunder sounding:
The sea-nymphs chant their accents shrill,
And the sirens, taught to kill
        With their sweet voice,
Make every echoing rock reply,
Unto their gentle murmuring noise,
The praise of Neptune's empery.

WINTER NIGHTS.

From Campion's *Third Book of Airs*, about 1617.

NOW winter nights enlarge
      The number of their hours;
And clouds their storms discharge
Upon the airy towers.
Let now the chimneys blaze
And cups o'erflow with wine,
Let well-tuned words amaze
With harmony divine!
Now yellow waxen lights
Shall wait on honey love
While youthful revels, masques, and courtly sights.
Sleep's leaden spells remove.

This time doth well dispense
With lovers' long discourse;
Much speech hath some defence,
Though beauty no remorse.
All do not all things well:
Some measures comely tread,
Some knotted riddles tell,
Some poems smoothly read.
The summer hath his joys,
And winter his delights;
Though love and all his pleasures are but toys,
They shorten tedious nights.

THE CHARM.

From Campion's *Third Book of Airs*.

THRICE toss these oaken ashes in the air,
      Thrice sit thou mute in this enchanted chair,
Then thrice-three times tie up this true love's knot,
And murmur soft " She will or she will not ".

Go, burn these poisonous weeds in yon blue fire,
These screech-owl's feathers and this prickling briar,
This cypress gathered at a dead man's grave,
That all thy fears and cares an end may have.

Then come, you Fairies! dance with me a round!
Melt her hard heart with your melodious sound!
In vain are all the charms I can devise:
She hath an art to break them with her eyes.

THERE IS NONE, O, NONE BUT YOU.

From Campion's *Two Books of Airs*.

THERE is none, O none but you,
    That from me estrange your sight,
Whom mine eyes affect to view
    Or chained ears hear with delight.

Other beauties others move,
    In you I all graces find;
Such is the effect of Love,
    To make them happy that are kind.

Women in frail beauty trust,
    Only seem you fair to me;
Yet prove truly kind and just,
    For that may not dissembled be.

Sweet, afford me then your sight,
    That, surveying all your looks,
Endless volumes I may write
    And fill the world with envied books:

Which when after-ages view,
    All shall wonder and despair,
Woman to find man so true,
    Or man a woman half so fair.

FOLLOW YOUR SAINT!

From Campion and Rosseter's *Book of Airs*, 1601.

FOLLOW your saint, follow with accents sweet!
    Haste you, sad notes, fall at her flying feet!
There, wrapped in cloud of sorrow, pity move,
And tell the ravisher of my soul I perish for her love:
But, if she scorns my never-ceasing pain,
Then burst with sighing in her sight and ne'er return
    again.

All that I sang still to her praise did tend,
Still she was first, still she my songs did end,
Yet she my love and music both doth fly,
The music that her echo is and beauty's sympathy:
Then let my notes pursue her scornful flight!
It shall suffice that they were breathed and died for her
    delight.

ROSE-CHEEKED LAURA.

From Campion's *Observations on the Art of English Poesy*, 1602.

ROSE-CHEEKED Laura, come;
    Sing thou smoothly with thy beauty's
Silent music, either other
        Sweetly gracing.

Lovely forms do flow
From concent divinely framed;
Heaven is music, and thy beauty's
        Birth is heavenly.

These dull notes we sing
Discords need for helps to grace them,
Only beauty purely loving
        Knows only discord;

But still moves delight,
Like clear springs renewed by flowing,
Ever perfect, ever in them-
      selves eternal.

WILLIAM BROWNE.
(1590?–1645?.)

Browne's Poems are published in the Roxburghe Library, edited by
Mr. W. C. Hazlitt, and in the Muses' Library, edited by Mr. Gordon
Goodwin, 1894.

CARPE DIEM.

From *Britannia's Pastorals*, Book i., 1613.

GENTLE nymphs, be not refusing,
   Love's neglect is time's abusing,
They and beauty are but lent you,
Take the one and keep the other:
Love keeps fresh what age doth smother:
   Beauty gone you will repent you.

'T will be said when ye have proved,
Never swains more truly loved:
   O then fly all nice behaviour.
Pity fain would, as her duty,
Be attending still on beauty,
   Let her not be out of favour.

THE SONG IN THE WOOD.

From the *Inner Temple Masque*, 1614–15.

WHAT sing the sweet birds in each grove?
   Nought but love.
What sound our echoes day and night?
   All delight.

What doth each wind breathe as it fleets?
Endless sweets.

Chorus.

Is there a place on earth this Isle excels,
Or any nymphs more happy live than we?
When all our songs, our sounds, and breathings be,
That here all love, delight, and sweetness dwells.

THE SIREN'S SONG.

From the *Inner Temple Masque.*

STEER hither, steer your wingèd pines,
   All beaten mariners,
Here lie Love's undiscovered mines,
   A prey to passengers;
Perfumes far sweeter than the best
Which make the Phœnix' urn and nest.
   Fear not your ships,
Nor any to oppose you save our lips,
   But come on shore,
Where no joy dies till love hath gotten more.

For swelling waves our panting breasts,
   Where never storms arise,
Exchange; and be awhile our guests:
   For stars gaze on our eyes.
The compass love shall hourly sing,
And as he goes about the ring,
   We will not miss
To tell each point he nameth with a kiss

Chorus.

Then come on shore,
Where no joy dies till love hath gotten more.

LOVE'S REASONS.

From *Lansdowne MS. 777*, first printed 1815.

FOR her gait if she be walking,
  Be she sitting I desire her
For her state's sake, and admire her
For her wit if she be talking.
    Gait and state and wit approve her;
    For which all and each I love her.

Be she sullen, I commend her
For a modest.   Be she merry,
For a kind one her prefer I.
Briefly everything doth lend her
    So much grace and so approve her,
    That for everything I love her.

EPITAPH ON THE COUNTESS OF PEMBROKE

From *Lansdowne MS. 777*, first published in Osborne's *Memoirs of the Reign of King James*, 1658; often, but erroneously, ascribed to Ben Jonson.

UNDERNEATH this sable hearse,
  Lies the subject of all verse,
SIDNEY'S sister, PEMBROKE'S mother;
Death! ere thou hast slain another,
Fair and learn'd, and good as she,
Time shall throw a dart at thee

EPITAPH.

From *Lansdowne MS. 777*

MAY! be thou never graced with birds that sing,
  Nor Flora's pride!
In thee all flowers and roses spring;
  Mine only died.

WELCOME.

From *Lansdowne MS.* 777.

WELCOME, welcome do I sing,
        Far more welcome than the spring:
He that parteth from you never
        Shall enjoy a spring for ever.

Love, that to the voice is near
        Breaking from your ivory pale,
Need not walk abroad to hear
        The delightful nightingale.
                Welcome, welcome then I sing,
                        Far more welcome than the spring:
                He that parteth from you never
                        Shall enjoy a spring for ever.

Love, that looks still on your eyes
        Though the winter have begun
To benumb our arteries,
        Shall not want the summer's sun.
                Welcome, welcome, &c.

Love, that still may see your cheeks,
        Where all rareness still reposes,
Is a fool if e'er he seeks
        Other lilies, other roses.
                Welcome, welcome, &c.

Love, to whom your soft lip yields,
        And perceives your breath in kissing,
All the odours of the fields
        Never, never shall be missing.
                Welcome, welcome, &c.

Love, that question would anew
        What fair Eden was of old,
Let him rightly study you,
        And a brief of that behold.
                Welcome, welcome, &c.

VISION OF THE ROSE.

From *Lansdowne MS. 777*.

A ROSE, as fair as ever saw the North,
　　Grew in a little garden all alone;
A sweeter flower did Nature ne'er put forth,
Nor fairer garden yet was never known;
The maidens danced about it morn and noon,
And learned bards of it their ditties made;
The nimble fairies by the pale-faced moon
Watered the root and kissed her pretty shade.
But well-a-day, the gardener careless grew;
The maids and fairies both were kept away,
And in a drought the caterpillars threw
Themselves upon the bud and every spray.
　　　God shield the stock! if heaven send no supplies
　　　The fairest blossom of the garden dies.

WILLIAM DRUMMOND
OF HAWTHORNDEN.
(1585–1649.)

Drummond's Poems are reprinted in Chalmers' *Poets*; and are also edited by Mr. W. B. Turnbull in the Library of Old Authors, 1856, and by Mr. W. C. Ward in the Muses' Library, 1895. The first sonnet and the three madrigals are from Drummond's *Poems, Amorous, Funeral, &c.*, Part i. 1616; the other sonnets are from the *Flowers of Sion*, 1623.

SONNET: TO THE NIGHTINGALE.

DEAR chorister, who from those shadows sends,
　　Ere that the blushing morn dare show her light,
Such sad lamenting strains, that night attends,
Become all ear, stars stay to hear thy plight:
If one whose grief even reach of thought transcends,
Who ne'er, not in a dream, did taste delight,

May thee importune who like case pretends,
And seems to joy in woe, in woe's despite;
Tell me (so may thou fortune milder try,
And long, long sing) for what thou thus complains,
Sith, winter gone, the sun in dappled sky
Now smiles on meadows, mountains, woods, and plains?
  The bird, as if my question did her move,
  With trembling wings sobbed forth, " I love, I love ".

SONNET: SPRING.

SWEET Spring, thou turn'st with all thy goodly train,
  Thy head with flames, thy mantle bright with flowers;
The zephyrs curl the green locks of the plain,
The clouds for joy in pearls weep down their showers;
Thou turn'st, sweet Youth—but, ah! my pleasant hours,
And happy days, with thee come not again;
The sad memorials only of my pain
Do with thee turn, which turn my sweets in sours.
Thou art the same which still thou wast before,
Delicious, wanton, amiable, fair;
But she whose breath embalmed thy wholesome air
Is gone; nor gold, nor gems can her restore.
  Neglected virtue, seasons go and come,
  While thine forgot lie closèd in a tomb.

SONNET: POSTING TIME.

LOOK how the flower which lingeringly doth fade,
  The morning's darling late, the summer's queen,
Spoiled of that juice which kept it fresh and green,
As high as it did raise, bows low the head:
Right so my life, contentments being dead,
Or in their contraries but only seen,
With swifter speed declines than erst it spread,
And, blasted, scarce now shows what it hath been.

As doth the pilgrim therefore, whom the night
By darkness would imprison on his way,
Think on thy home, my soul, and think aright
Of what yet rests thee of life's wasting day:
 Thy sun posts westward, passèd is thy morn,
 And twice it is not given thee to be born.

SONNET: SWEET BIRD

SWEET bird, that sing'st away the early hours,
 Of winters past or coming void of care,
Well pleasèd with delights which present are,
Fair seasons, budding sprays, sweet-smelling flowers;
To rocks, to springs, to rills, from leafy bowers,
Thou thy Creator's goodness dost declare,
And what dear gifts on thee he did not spare,
A stain to human sense in sin that lowers.
What soul can be so sick which by thy songs,
Attired in sweetness, sweetly is not driven
Quite to forget earth's turmoils, spites, and wrongs,
And lift a reverent eye and thought to heaven?
 Sweet artless songster, thou my mind dost raise
 To airs of spheres, yes, and to angel's lays.

SONNET: ON SOLITUDE.

THRICE happy he who by some shady grove,
 Far from the clamorous world, doth live his own;
Though solitary, who is not alone,
But doth converse with that eternal love.
O! how more sweet is birds' harmonious moan,
Or the hoarse sobbings of the widowed dove,
Than those smooth whisperings near a prince's throne,
Which good make doubtful, do the evil approve!
O! how more sweet is zephyr's wholesome breath,
And sighs embalmed, which new born flowers unfold,

Than that applause vain honour doth bequeath!
How sweet are streams, to poison drunk in gold!
  The world is full of horrors, troubles, slights:
  Woods' harmless shades have only true delights.

SONNET: REPENT, REPENT!

THE last and greatest herald of heaven's King,
    Girt with rough skins, hies to the deserts wild,
Among that savage brood the woods forth bring,
Which he than man more harmless found and mild:
His food was locusts, and what young doth spring,
With honey that from virgin hives distilled;
Parched body, hollow eyes, some uncouth thing
Made him appear, long since from earth exiled.
There burst he forth: "All ye, whose hopes rely
On God, with me amidst these deserts mourn;
Repent, repent, and from old errors turn".
Who listened to his voice, obeyed his cry?
    Only the echoes, which he made relent,
    Rung from their marble caves, "Repent, repent".

SONNET TO SIR WILLIAM ALEXANDER.

THOUGH I have twice been at the doors of death,
    And twice found shut those gates which ever mourn,
This but a lightening is, truce ta'en to breath,
For late-born sorrows augur fleet return.
Amidst thy sacred cares and courtly toils,
Alexis, when thou shalt hear wandering Fame
Tell Death hath triumphed o'er my mortal spoils,
And that on earth I am but a sad name;
If thou e'er held me dear, by all our love,
By all that bliss, those joys Heaven here us gave,
I conjure thee, and by the maids of Jove,
To grave this short remembrance on my grave:
    Here Damon lies, whose songs did sometime grace
    The murmuring Esk; may roses shade the place!

MADRIGAL.

THIS Life, which seems so fair,
  Is like a bubble blown up in the air
By sporting children's breath,
Who chase it everywhere
And strive who can most motion it bequeath;
And though it sometime seem of its own might,
Like to an eye of gold, to be fixed there,
And firm to hover in that empty height;
That only is because it is so light.
But in that pomp it doth not long appear;
For when 't is most admirèd, in a thought,
Because it erst was naught, it turns to naught.

SONG.

PHŒBUS, arise,
  And paint the sable skies
With azure, white, and red;
Rouse Memnon's mother from her Tithon's bed,
That she thy career may with roses spread;
The nightingales thy coming each where sing;
Make an eternal spring,
Give life to this dark world which lieth dead;
Spread forth thy golden hair
In larger locks than thou wast wont before,
And, emperor-like, decore
With diadem of pearl thy temples fair:
Chase hence the ugly night,
Which serves but to make dear thy glorious light.
This is that happy morn
That day, long-wishèd day,
Of all my life so dark
(If cruel stars have not my ruin sworn,

And fates not hope betray),
Which, only white, deserves
A diamond for ever should it mark:
This is the morn should bring unto this grove
My love, to hear and recompense my love.
Fair king, who all preserves,
But show thy blushing beams,
And thou two sweeter eyes
Shalt see, than those which by Peneus' streams
Did once thy heart surprise;
Nay, suns, which shine as clear
As thou when two thou did to Rome appear.
Now, Flora, deck thyself in fairest guise;
If that ye, winds, would hear
A voice surpassing far Amphion's lyre,
Your stormy chiding stay;
Let zephyr only breathe,
And with her tresses play,
Kissing sometimes these purple ports of death.
The winds all silent are,
And Phœbus in his chair,
Ensaffroning sea and air,
Makes vanish every star:
Night like a drunkard reels
Beyond the hills to shun his flaming wheels;
The fields with flowers are deckèd in every hue,
The clouds bespangle with bright gold their blue:
Here is the pleasant place,
And every thing, save her, who all should grace.

MADRIGAL.

SWEET rose, whence is this hue
Which doth all hues excel?
Whence this most fragrant smell?
And whence this form and gracing grace in you?

In fair Pæstana's fields perhaps you grew,
   Or Hybla's hills you bred,
Or odoriferous Enna's plains you fed,
Or Tmolus, or where boar young Adon slew;
Or hath the queen of love you dyed of new,
In that dear blood, which makes you look so red?
   No, none of those, but cause more high you blissed,
   My lady's breast you bore, her lips you kissed.

SIMON WASTELL.

(Fl. circa 1625.)

OF MAN'S MORTALITY.

From *Microbiblion*, 1629.

LIKE as the damask rose you see,
   Or like the blossom on the tree,
Or like the dainty flower of May,
Or like the morning to the day,
Or like the sun, or like the shade,
Or like the gourd which Jonas had,
E'en such is man;—whose thread is spun,
Drawn out, and cut, and so is done.—
The rose withers, the blossom blasteth,
The flower fades, the morning hasteth,
The sun sets, the shadow flies,
The gourd consumes—and man he dies!

Like to the grass that's newly sprung,
Or like a tale that's new begun,
Or like a bird that's here to-day,
Or like the pearled dew of May,
Or like an hour, or like a span,
Or like the singing of a swan,

E'en such is man;—who lives by breath,
Is here, now there, in life and death.—
The grass withers, the tale is ended,
The bird is flown, the dew's ascended,
The hour is short, the span not long,
The swan's near death,—man's life is done!

JOHN WEBSTER.

(?–1625?.)

These are dirges from Webster's sombre dramas; the first is from
Vittoria Corombona, or the White Devil, 1612 (acted 1608?),—Lamb
compares and constrasts it with "the ditty which reminds Ferdinand of
his drowned father in *The Tempest*". The second is from the *Duchess
of Malfi,* 1623 (acted about 1612); and the last from the *Devil's Law-
Case,* a tragi-comedy, 1623. Dyce has edited Webster's Dramas.

A DIRGE.

CALL for the robin redbreast and the wren,
    Since o'er shady groves they hover,
And with leaves and flowers do cover
The friendless bodies of unburied men.
Call unto his funeral dole
The ant, the field-mouse, and the mole,
To rear him hillocks that shall keep him warm,
And, when gay tombs are robbed, sustain no harm;
But keep the wolf far thence, that's foe to men,
For with his nails he'll dig them up again.

HARK, NOW EVERYTHING IS STILL.

HARK, now everything is still,
    The screech-owl and the whistler shrill,
Call upon our dame aloud,
And bid her quickly don her shroud!

Much you had of land and rent;
Your length in clay's now competent:
A long war disturbed your mind;
Here your perfect peace is signed.
Of what is't fools make such vain keeping?
Sin their conception, their birth weeping,
Their life a general mist of error,
Their death a hideous storm of terror.
Strew your hair with powders sweet,
Don clean linen, bathe your feet,
And (the foul fiend more to check)
A crucifix let bless your neck;
'T is now full tide 'tween night and day;
End your groan, and come away.

VANITAS VANITATUM

ALL the flowers of the spring
    Meet to perfume our burying;
These have but their growing prime,
And man does flourish but his time:
Survey our progress from our birth;
We are set, we grow, we turn to earth.
Courts adieu, and all delights,
All bewitching appetites!
Sweetest breath and clearest eye,
Like perfumes, go out and die;
And consequently this is done
As shadows wait upon the sun.
Vain the ambition of kings
Who seek by trophies and dead things
To leave a living name behind,
And weave but nets to catch the wind.

FRANCIS BACON (?).

(1561–1626.)

THE WORLD.

This is a paraphrase of a poem in the Greek Anthology. There is a
similar paraphrase by Sir John Beaumont. From *Reliquiæ Wottonianæ*,
1651 (written about 1625?). It has been ascribed also to Raleigh, Donne,
and others.

THE world 's a bubble, and the life of man
      Less than a span;
In his conception wretched, from the womb,
      So to the tomb;
Curst from his cradle, and brought up to years
      With cares and fears.
Who then to frail mortality shall trust
But limns on water, or but writes in dust.

Yet, whilst with sorrow here we live oppressed,
      What life is best?
Courts are but only superficial schools,
      To dandle fools;
The rural part is turned into a den
      Of savage men;
And where 's a city from foul vice so free
But may be termed the worst of all the three?

Domestic cares afflict the husband's bed,
      Or pains his head:
Those that live single take it for a curse,
      Or do things worse:
These would have children; those that have them moan,
      Or wish them gone;
What is it, then, to have or have no wife,
But single thraldom or a double strife?

Our own affections still at home to please
      Is a disease;
To cross the seas to any foreign soil,
      Peril and toil;
Wars with their noise affright us; when they cease,
      We 're worse in peace:
What then remains, but that we still should cry
For being born, and, being born, to die?

SIR HENRY WOTTON.
(1568–1639.)

THE CHARACTER OF A HAPPY LIFE.

This was first printed in Overbury's *Wife and Characters*, 1614.   Note
its similarity to the verses by Essex, above, and to a poem by John
Davies of Hereford, beginning:
      " How blessed is he, though ever crossed,
        That can all crosses blessings make ".
The second poem first appeared in Este's *Sixth Set of Books*, 1624.
Others of Wotton's poems may be found in Hannah's *Courtly Poets*.

HOW happy is he born and taught
    That serveth not another's will;
Whose armour is his honest thought,
    And simple truth his utmost skill;

Whose passions not his masters are;
    Whose soul is still prepared for death,
Untied unto the world by care
    Of public fame or private breath;

Who envies none that chance doth raise,
    Nor vice; who never understood
How deepest wounds are given by praise;
    Nor rules of state, but rules of good;

Who hath his life from rumours freed;
    Whose conscience is his strong retreat;

Whose state can neither flatterers feed,
　　Nor ruin make oppressors great;

Who God doth late and early pray
　　More of his grace than gifts to lend;
And entertains the harmless day
　　With a religious book or friend.

This man is freed from servile bands
　　Of hope to rise or fear to fall:
Lord of himself, though not of lands,
　　And, having nothing, yet hath all.

ON HIS MISTRESS, THE QUEEN OF BOHEMIA.

YOU meaner beauties of the night,
　　That poorly satisfy our eyes
More by your number than your light,
You common people of the skies;
What are you when the moon shall rise?

You curious chanters of the wood,
That warble forth Dame Nature's lays,
Thinking your passions understood
By your weak accents; what's your praise,
When Philomel her voice shall raise?

You violets that first appear,
By your pure purple mantles known
Like the proud virgins of the year,
As if the spring were all your own;
What are you when the rose is blown?

So, when my mistress shall be seen
In form and beauty of her mind,
By virtue first, then choice, a Queen,
Tell me if she were not designed
The eclipse and glory of her kind?

SIR JOHN WOTTON(?).

(Fl. circa 1600.)

Conjectured to be the half-brother of Sir Henry Wotton. The following poem appears in *England's Helicon*, 1600.

DAMÆTAS' JIG IN PRAISE OF HIS LOVE.

JOLLY shepherd, shepherd on a hill,
   On a hill so merrily,
   On a hill so cheerily,
Fear not, shepherd, there to pipe thy fill;
   Fill every dale, fill every plain;
   Both sing and say; Love feels no pain.

Jolly shepherd, shepherd on a green,
   On a green so merrily,
   On a green so cheerily,
Be thy voice shrill, be thy mirth seen,
   Heard to each swain, seen to each trull:
   Both sing and say; Love's joy is full.

Jolly shepherd, shepherd in the sun,
   In the sun so merrily,
   In the sun so cheerily,
Sing forth thy songs, and let thy rimes run
   Down to the dales from the hills above:
   Both sing and say; No life to love.

Jolly shepherd, shepherd in the shade,
   In the shade so merrily,
   In the shade so cheerily,
Joy in thy life, life of shepherd's trade,
Joy in thy love, love full of glee,
   Both sing and say; Sweet Love for me.

Jolly shepherd, shepherd here or there,
　　Here or there so merrily,
　　Here or there so cheerily,
Or in thy chat, either at thy cheer,
In every jig, in every lay,
　　Both sing and say; Love lasts for aye.

Jolly shepherd, shepherd Daphne's love,
　　Daphne's love so merrily,
　　Daphne's love so cheerily,
Let thy fancy never more remove,
Fancy be fixed, fixed not to fleet,
　　Still sing and say; Love's yoke is sweet.

FRANCIS BEAUMONT.

(1584–1616.)

ON THE LIFE OF MAN.

From *Poems*, 1640 and 1653; written before 1616.

LIKE to the falling of a star,
　　Or as the flights of eagles are,
Or like the fresh spring's gaudy hue,
Or silver drops of morning dew,
Or like a wind that chafes the flood,
Or bubbles which on water stood:
Even such is man, whose borrowed light
Is straight called in and paid to night:
The wind blows out, the bubble dies,
The spring intombed in autumn lies:
The dew 's dried up, the star is shot,
The flight is past, and man forgot.

LINES ON THE TOMBS IN WESTMINSTER.

MORTALITY, behold and fear!
　　What a change of flesh is here!
Think how many royal bones
Sleep within this heap of stones;
Here they lie had realms and lands,
Who now want strength to stir their hands;
Where from their pulpits sealed with dust
They preach, "In greatness is no trust".
Here's an acre sown indeed
With the richest royal'st seed
That the earth did e'er suck in,
Since the first man died for sin:
Here the bones of birth have cried,
"Though gods they were, as men they died":
Here are sands, ignoble things,
Dropt from the ruined sides of kings:
Here's a world of pomp and state,
Buried in dust, once dead by fate.

JOHN FLETCHER.

(1579–1625.)

OR, BEAUMONT AND FLETCHER.

Dyce's is the standard modern edition of the works of Beaumont and
Fletcher. Most of the lyrics occur in plays in which Beaumont doubt-
less had no share.

SWEETEST MELANCHOLY.

From the *Nice Valour*, in the folio of 1647 (acted 1613?). Compare
Burton's verses introductory to his *Anatomy of Melancholy*, and Milton's
Il Penseroso.

HENCE, all you vain delights,
  As short as are the nights
    Wherein you spend your folly!
There's nought in this life sweet.
If man were wise to see't,
    But only melancholy;
    O sweetest melancholy!

Welcome, folded arms and fixèd eyes,
A sigh that piercing mortifies,
A look that's fastened to the ground,
A tongue chained up without a sound!
Fountain heads and pathless groves,
Places which pale passion loves!
Moonlight walks, when all the fowls
Are warmly housed save bats and owls!

A midnight bell, a parting groan,
These are the sounds we feed upon;
Then stretch our bones in a still gloomy valley;
Nothing's so dainty sweet as lovely melancholy.

LOVE'S EMBLEMS.

From *Valentinian*, 1647 (acted 1616?).

NOW the lusty spring is seen;
  Golden yellow, gaudy blue,
  Daintily invite the view,
Everywhere on every green,
Roses blushing as they blow,
  And enticing men to pull,
Lilies whiter than the snow,
    Woodbines of sweet honey full:
    All love's emblems, and all cry,
    "Ladies, if not plucked, we die".

Yet the lusty spring hath stayed;
  Blushing red and purest white
  Daintily to love invite
Every woman, every maid.
Cherries kissing as they grow,
  And inviting men to taste,
Apples even ripe below,
    Winding gently to the waist:
    All love's emblems, and all cry,
    "Ladies, if not plucked, we die".

INVOCATION TO SLEEP.

From *Valentinian*.

CARE-CHARMING Sleep, thou easer of all woes,
  Brother to Death, sweetly thyself dispose
On this afflicted prince; fall like a cloud
In gentle showers; give nothing that is loud
Or painful to his slumbers;—easy, sweet,
And as a purling stream, thou son of Night,

Pass by his troubled senses; sing his pain
Like hollow murmuring wind or silver rain;
Into this prince gently, oh, gently slide,
And kiss him into slumbers like a bride!

SONG TO BACCHUS.

From *Valentinian.*

GOD Lyæus, ever young,
  Ever honoured, ever sung;
Stained with blood of lusty grapes,
In a thousand lusty shapes,
Dance upon the mazer's brim,
In the crimson liquor swim;
From thy plenteous hand divine
Let a river run with wine;
God of youth, let this day here
Enter neither care nor fear!

DRINK TO-DAY.

From the *Bloody Brother*, 1640 (acted 1616?).

DRINK to-day, and drown all sorrow;
  You shall perhaps not do it to-morrow:
Best, while you have it, use your breath;
There is no drinking after death.

Wine works the heart up, wakes the wit,
There is no cure 'gainst age but it:
It helps the headache, cough, and phthisic,
And is for all diseases physic.

Then let us swill, boys, for our health;
Who drinks well, loves the commonwealth.
And he that will to bed go sober
Falls with the leaf still in October.

BEAUTY CLEAR AND FAIR.

From the *Elder Brother*, 1637 (acted 1625?).

BEAUTY clear and fair,
　　Where the air
Rather like a perfume dwells;
　　Where the violet and the rose
　　Their blue veins and blush disclose,
And come to honour nothing else.

Where to live near,
　　And planted there,
Is to live, and still live new;
　　Where to gain a favour is
　　More than light, perpetual bliss,—
Make me live by serving you.

Dear, again back recall
　　To this light,
A stranger to himself and all;
　　Both the wonder and the story
　　Shall be yours, and eke the glory:
I am your servant, and your thrall.

THE CHARM.

From the *Little French Lawyer*, 1647 (acted 1620?).

THIS way, this way come, and hear,
　　You that hold these pleasures dear;
Fill your ears with our sweet sound,
Whilst we melt the frozen ground.
This way come; make haste, O fair!
Let your clear eyes gild the air;
Come, and bless us with your sight;
This way, this way, seek delight!

TO HIS SLEEPING MISTRESS.

From *Women Pleased*, 1647 (acted 1620?).

O, fair sweet face! O, eyes celestial bright,
  Twin stars in heaven, that now adorn the night!
Oh, fruitful lips, where cherries ever grow,
And damask cheeks, where all sweet beauties blow!
O, thou, from head to foot divinely fair!
Cupid's most cunning net's made of that hair;
And, as he weaves himself for curious eyes,
"O me, O me, I'm caught myself!" he cries:
Sweet rest about thee, sweet and golden sleep,
Soft peaceful thoughts, your hourly watches keep,
Whilst I in wonder sing this sacrifice,
To beauty sacred, and those angel eyes!

WEEP NO MORE.

From the *Queen of Corinth*, 1647 (acted 1618?).

WEEP no more, nor sigh, nor groan,
  Sorrow calls no time that's gone;
Violets plucked the sweetest rain
Makes not fresh nor grow again;
Trim thy locks, look cheerfully;
Fate's hid ends eyes cannot see;
Joys as wingèd dreams fly fast,
Why should sadness longer last?

Grief is but a wound to woe;
Gentlest fair, mourn, mourn no mo.

DIRGE.

From the *Maid's Tragedy*, 1619 (acted 1610?).

LAY a garland on my hearse
  Of the dismal yew;

Maidens, willow branches bear;
  Say, I died true.

My love was false, but I was firm
  From my hour of birth.
Upon my buried body lie
  Lightly, gentle earth!

MARRIAGE HYMN.

From *The Two Noble Kinsmen*, 1634 (written 1611?).

ROSES, their sharp spines being gone,
  Not royal in their smells alone,
  But in their hue;
Maiden-pinks, of odour faint,
Daisies smell-less yet most quaint,
  And sweet thyme true;

Primrose, first-born child of Ver
Merry spring-time's harbinger,
  With her bells dim;
Oxlips in their cradles growing,
Marigolds on death-beds blowing,
  Larks'-heels trim.
All, dear Nature's children sweet,
Lie 'fore bride and bridegroom's feet,
  Blessing their sense!
Not an angel of the air,
Bird melodious or bird fair,
  Be absent hence!

The crow, the slanderous cuckoo, nor
The boding raven, nor chough hoar,
  Nor chattering pie,
May on our bride-house perch or sing,
Or with them any discord bring,
  But from it fly!

PHINEAS FLETCHER.
(1582–1648?.)

AN HYMN.

From the *Poems* of Fletcher, 1633.　Reprinted in Chalmers' *Poets*, vol. vi., and in the Fuller Worthies Library (edited by Dr. Grosart).

DROP, drop, slow tears,
　　And bathe those beauteous feet,
Which brought from Heaven
　　The news and Prince of Peace:
Cease not, wet eyes,
　　His mercies to entreat;
To cry for vengeance
　　Sin doth never cease:
In your deep floods
　　Drown all my faults and fears;
Nor let His eye
　　See sin, but through my tears.

JOHN FORD.
(1586?–1639?.)

CALANTHA'S DIRGE.

From the *Broken Heart*, 1633 (acted 1629?).　Dyce has edited Ford's Works.

GLORIES, pleasures, pomps, delights, and ease,
　　Can but please
Outward senses, when the mind
Is untroubled, or by peace refined.
Crowns may flourish and decay,
Beauties shine, but fade away.

Youth may revel, yet it must
Lie down in a bed of dust.
Earthly honours flow and waste,
Time alone doth change and last.
Sorrows mingled with contents prepare
      Rest for care;
Love only reigns in death; though art
Can find no comfort for a Broken Heart.

PENTHEA'S DYING SONG.

OH no more, no more, too late
    Sighs are spent; the burning tapers
Of a life as chaste as fate,
    Pure as are unwritten papers,
Are burnt out; no heat, no light
Now remains; 't is ever night.
    Love is dead; let lovers' eyes
    Locked in endless dreams,
    Th' extremes of all extremes
    Ope no more, for now Love dies.
Now Love dies—implying
Love's martyr must be ever, ever dying.

ROBERT DAVENPORT.
(? –1651?.)

From *King John and Matilda*, 1655 (acted 1636?).

A REQUIEM.

MATILDA, now go take thy bed
    In the dark dwellings of the dead;

And rise in the great waking day,
Sweet as incense, fresh as May.

Rest thou, chaste soul, fixed in thy proper sphere,
Amongst Heaven's fair ones; all are fair ones there.

Chorus.

Rest there, chaste soul, whilst we here troubled say
"Time gives us griefs, Death takes our joys away".

"A. W."

A DIALOGUE BETWEEN THE SOUL AND THE BODY.

"A. W." is a frequent contributor to Davison's *Poetical Rhapsody*, 1602, where the following extract is found. Various conjectures as to his identity are discussed by Mr. Bullen in the Introduction to his edition of the *Rhapsody*.

Soul. AY me, poor soul, whom bound in sinful chains
This wretched body keeps against my will!
Body. Ay me, poor body, whom for all my pains,
This froward soul causeless condemneth still!
Soul. Causeless? Whenas thou striv'st to sin each day!
Body. Causeless? Whenas I strive thee to obey!
Soul. Thou art the means, by which I fall to sin.
Body. Thou art the cause that sett'st this means a-work.
Soul. No part of thee that hath not faulty been.
Body. I show the poison that in thee doth lurk.
Soul. I shall be pure when so I part from thee.
Body. So were I now, but that thou stainest me.

ANONYMOUS LYRICS, 1604–1675.

SUMMER.

From Weelkes' *Madrigals*, 1604.

COLD winter ice is fled and gone,
    And summer brags on every tree;
The red-breast peeps among the throng
Of wood-brown birds that wanton be:
Each one forgets what they have been,
And so doth Phyllis, summer's queen.

IN LAUDEM AMORIS.

From Hume's *First Part of Airs*, 1605.

FAIN would I change that note
    To which fond love hath charmed me
Long, long to sing by rote,
Fancying that that harmed me:
Yet when this thought doth come,
"Love is the perfect sum
    Of all delight",
I have no other choice
Either for pen or voice
    To sing or write.

O Love! they wrong thee much
That say thy sweet is bitter,
When thy rich fruit is such
As nothing can be sweeter.
Fair house of joy and bliss,
Where truest pleasure is,
    I do adore thee:
I know thee what thou art,
I serve thee with my heart,
    And fall before thee.

YE LITTLE BIRDS THAT SIT AND SING.

From the *Fair Maid of the Exchange*, 1607.

YE little birds that sit and sing
    Amidst the shady valleys,
And see how Phyllis sweetly walks
    Within her garden-alleys;
Go, pretty birds, about her bower;
Sing, pretty birds, she may not lower;
Ah, me! methinks I see her frown!
    Ye pretty wantons, warble.

Go, tell her through your chirping bills,
    As you by me are bidden,
To her is only known my love,
    Which from the world is hidden.
Go, pretty birds, and tell her so;
See that your notes strain not too low,
For, still, methinks, I see her frown;
    Ye pretty wantons, warble.

Go, tune your voices' harmony,
    And sing, I am her lover;
Strain loud and sweet, that every note
    With sweet content may move her:
And she that hath the sweetest voice,
Tell her I will not change my choice
Yet still, methinks, I see her frown,
    Ye pretty wantons, warble.

Oh, fly! make haste! see, see, she falls
    Into a pretty slumber.
Sing round about her rosy bed,
    That waking, she may wonder.
Say to her, 't is her lover true
That sendeth love to you, to you;
And when you hear her kind reply
    Return with pleasant warblings.

THERE IS A LADY.

From Thomas Ford's *Music of Sundry Kinds*, 1607.

THERE is a lady sweet and kind,
　　Was never face so pleased my mind;
I did but see her passing by,
And yet I love her till I die.

Her gesture, motion, and her smiles,
Her wit, her voice my heart beguiles,
Beguiles my heart, I know not why,
And yet I love her till I die.

Her free behaviour, winning looks,
Will make a lawyer burn his books;
I touched her not, alas! not I,
And yet I love her till I die.

Had I her fast betwixt mine arms,
Judge you that think such sports were harms;
Were 't any harm? no, no, fie, fie,
For I will love her till I die.

Should I remain confinèd there
So long as Phœbus in his sphere,
I to request, she to deny,
Yet would I love her till I die.

Cupid is wingèd and doth range,
Her country so my love doth change:
But change she earth, or change she sky
Yet will I love her till I die.

REVELS.

From Weelkes' *Airs for Three Voices*, 1608.

COME, let 's begin to revel it out,
　　And tread the hills and dales about;
That hills and dales and woods may sound
An echo to this warbling round.

Lads, merry be with music sweet;
And, fairies, trip it with your feet;
That hills and dales and woods may sound
An echo to this warbling round.

FAIN I WOULD.

From Alfonso Ferrabosco's *Airs,* 1609.

FAIN I would, but O I dare not,
   Speak my thoughts at full to praise her:
"Speak the best," cries Love, "and spare not;
Thy speech can no higher raise her:
Thy speech than thy thoughts are lower,
Yet thy thoughts doth not half know her".

THE BELLMAN'S SONG.

From *Melismata,* 1611.

MAIDS to bed and cover coal;
   Let the mouse out of her hole;
Crickets in the chimney sing
Whilst the little bell doth ring:
If fast asleep, who can tell
When the clapper hits the bell?

TWO IN ONE.

From Dowland's *A Pilgrim's Solace,* 1612.

TO ask for all thy love, and thy whole heart,
         'T were madness!
      I do not sue
      Nor can admit,
   Fairest! from you
      To have all!
Yet who giveth all, hath nothing to impart
         But sadness!

He that receiveth all, can have no more
    Than seeing.
      My love, by length
        Of every hour,
      Gathers new strength!
        New growth, new flower!
You must have daily new rewards in store,
    Still being.

You cannot, every day, give me your heart
    For merit!
      Yet, if you will,
        When yours doth go,
      You shall have still
        One to bestow!
For you shall mine, when yours doth part,
    Inherit!

Yet, if you please, I 'll find a better way,
    Than change them.
      For so, alone,
        Dearest! we shall
      Be one! and one
        Another's all!
Let us join our hearts, that nothing may
    Estrange them!

A-MAYING.

From Francis Pilkington's *First Set of Madrigals*, 1614.

SEE where my love a-maying goes,
    With sweet dame Flora sporting!
She most alone with nightingales
    In wood's delights consorting.
Turn again, my dearest!
    The pleasant'st air 's in meadows:
Else by the rivers let us breathe,
    And kiss amongst the willows.

THE HUNT IS UP.

From Ravenscroft's *A Brief Discourse in Music,* 1614.

Chorus.

THE hunt is up, the hunt is up,
    Sing merrily we, the hunt is up.

Verse

The birds they sing, the deer they fling,
    Hey nony nony no.
The hounds they cry, the hunters fly,
    Hey tro-li-lo-li lo.

The wood resounds to hear the hounds,
The rocks report this merry sport
Then hie apace unto the chase,
Whilst every thing doth sweetly sing.

From Thomas Ravenscroft's *Brief Discourse,* &c., 1614.

THE URCHINS' DANCE.

BY the moon we sport and play,
    With the night begins our day:
As we frisk the dew doth fall;
Trip it, little urchins all!
Lightly as the little bee,
Two by two, and three by three;
And about, about go we.

THE ELVES' DANCE.

ROUND about in a fairy ring-a,
    Thus we dance and thus we sing-a;
Trip and go, to and fro,
    Over this green-a;
All about, in and out,
    Over this green-a.

THE FAIRIES' DANCE.

DARE you haunt our hallowed green?
None but fairies here are seen.
Down and sleep,
Wake and weep;
Pinch him black, and pinch him blue,
That seeks to steal a lover true!
When you come to hear us sing,
Or to tread our fairy ring,
Pinch him black, and pinch him blue!
O thus our nails shall handle you!

THE SATYRS' DANCE.

ROUND-A, round-a, keep your ring:
To the glorious sun we sing,—
Ho, ho!
He that wears the flaming rays,
And th' imperial crown of bays,
Him with shouts and songs we praise,—
Ho, ho!
That in his bounty he'd vouchsafe to grace
The humble sylvans and their shaggy race.

SWEET SUFFOLK OWL.

From Thomas Vautor's *Songs of Divers Airs and Natures*, 1619.

SWEET Suffolk owl, so trimly dight
With feathers like a lady bright,
Thou sing'st alone, sitting by night,
Te whit, te whoo!
Thy note, that forth so freely rolls,
With shrill command the mouse controls,
And sings a dirge for dying souls,
Te whit, te whoo!

THE MERRY BELLS OF OXFORD.

From *The Loyal Garland, or Poesie for Kings*, 1624; reprinted
by the Percy Society, 1850.

OH the merry Christ-Church bells,
    One, two, three, four, five, six;
They troll so wondrous deep,
    So woundy sweet,
And they chime so merrily, merrily.
Hark the first and second bell,
    At every day by four and ten,
Cries, Come, come, come, come, come to prayers,
    And the vergers troop before the deans:
Tinkle, tinkle, tinkle, goes the little bell,
      To call in every soul
      But the devil a man
      Will leave his can,
Till they hear the mighty toll.

LOVE IN THY YOUTH.

From Walter Porter's *Madrigals and Airs*, 1632.

LOVE in thy youth, fair maid, be wise;
    Old Time will make thee colder,
And though each morning new arise
    Yet we each day grow older.
Thou as heaven art fair and young,
    Thine eyes like twin stars shining:
But ere another day be sprung,
    All these will be declining.
Then winter comes with all his fears
    And all thy sweets shall borrow;
Too late then wilt thou shower thy tears,
    And I too late shall sorrow.

PARTING.

From *Egerton MS.*, 2013; printed in vol. iii. of Arber's *Garner*.

WE must not part, as others do,
　　With sighs and tears, as we were two.
Though with these outward forms we part,
We keep each other in our heart.
What search hath found a being where
I am not, if that thou be there?

True love hath wings, and can as soon
Survey the world, as sun and moon;
And everywhere our triumphs keep
Over absence, which makes others weep:
By which alone a power is given
To live on earth, as they in heaven.

HEY NONNY NO!

From *Christ Church MS.*, i. 5. 49.

HEY nonny no!
Men are fools that wish to die!
Is 't not fine to dance and sing
When the bells of death do ring?
Is 't not fine to swim in wine,
　　And turn upon the toe
　　And sing Hey nonny no,
When the winds blow and the seas flow?
　　Hey nonny no!

THE GREAT ADVENTURER.

Quoted in Brome's *Sparagus Garden*, acted 1635.

OVER the mountains
    And over the waves,
Under the fountains
And under the graves;
Under floods that are deepest,
Which Neptune obey;
Over rocks that are steepest,
Love will find out the way.

Where there is no place
For the glow-worm to lie;
Where there is no space
For receipt of a fly;
Where the midge dares not venture
Lest herself fast she lay;
If love come, he will enter,
And soon find out his way.

You may esteem him
A child for his might;
Or you may deem him
A coward from his flight;
But if she whom love doth honour
Be concealed from the day,
Set a thousand guards upon her,
Love will find out the way.

Some think to lose him
By having him confined;
And some do suppose him,
Poor thing, to be blind;

But if ne'er so close ye wall him,
Do the best that you may,
Blind love, if so ye call him,
Will find out his way.

You may train the eagle
To stoop to your fist;
Or you may inveigle
The phœnix of the east;
The lioness, ye may move her
To give o'er her prey;
But you 'll ne'er stop a lover:
He will find out his way.

THE KING'S PROGRESS.

From *Christ Church MS. K.*, 3. 43-5. (Music by Thomas Ford.)

YET if his majesty our sovereign lord
    Should of his own accord
Friendly himself invite,
And say, " I 'll be your guest to-morrow night ",
How should we stir ourselves, call and command
All hands to work! " Let no man idle stand.
Set me fine Spanish tables in the hall;
See they be fitted all;
Let there be room to eat,
And order taken that there want no meat.
See every sconce and candlestick made bright,
That without tapers they may give a light.
Look to the presence: are the carpets spread,
The dais o'er the head,
The cushions in the chairs,
And all the candles lighted on the stairs?
Perfume the chambers, and in any case
Let each man give attendance in his place!"

Thus if the king were coming would we do,
      And 't were good reason too;
For 't is a duteous thing
To show all honour to an earthly king,
      And after all our travail and our cost,
So he be pleased, to think no labour lost.
But at the coming of the King of Heaven
      All 's set at six and seven:
We wallow in our sin,
Christ cannot find a chamber in the inn.
We entertain Him always like a stranger,
And as at first still lodge Him in the manger.

WALY, WALY.

Printed in Thomson's *Orpheus Caledonius*, 1725. The original version
of the song probably dates from circa 1675, where it is brought into
the ballad of Jamie Douglas.   It is possible, however, that it dates from
the sixteenth century.   See Prof. Child's *English and Scottish Popular
Ballads*, part vii. (Boston, 1890).

O WALY, waly, up the bank,
      O waly, waly, doun the brae,
And waly, waly, yon burn-side,
      Where I and my love wont to gae!
I lean'd my back unto an aik,
      I thocht it was a trustie tree;
But first it bow'd and syne it brak',—
      Sae my true love did lichtlie me.

O waly, waly, but love be bonnie
      A little time while it is new!
But when 't is auld it waxeth cauld,
      And fades awa' like morning dew
O wherefore should I busk my heid,
      Or wherefore should I kame my hair?

For my true love has me forsook,
    And says he 'll never lo'e me mair.

Noo Arthur Seat[1] sall be my bed,
    The sheets sall ne'er be press'd by me;
Saint Anton's well sall be my drink;
    Since my true love 's forsaken me.
Martinmas wind, when wilt thou blaw,
    And shake the green leaves off the tree?
O gentle death, when wilt thou come?
    For of my life I am wearie.

'T is not the frost that freezes fell,
    Nor blawing snaw's inclemencie,
'T is not sic cauld that makes me cry;
    But my love's heart grown cauld to me.
When we cam' in by Glasgow toun,
    We were a comely sicht to see;
My love was clad in the black velvet,
    An' I mysel' in cramasie.

But had I wist before I kiss'd
    That love had been sae ill to win,
I 'd lock'd my heart in a case o' goud,
    And pinn'd it wi' a siller pin.
Oh, oh! if my young babe were born,
    And set upon the nurse's knee;
And I mysel' were dead and gane,
    And the green grass growing over me!

[1] The hill near Edinburgh.

JOHN MILTON.

(1608–1674.)

HYMN ON THE NATIVITY.

This *Hymn* is dated in 1629; *L'Allegro* and *Il Penseroso*, 1632–1638; *Arcades*, 1630–1634; *Comus*, 1634; the *Song on May Morning*, 1630 (?); the first sonnet probably soon after 1630; that on the Massacre in Piedmont in 1655; and that on his Blindness at about the same time. Compare with the last the first fifty-five lines of Book III. of *Paradise Lost*.

IT was the winter wild,
  While the heaven-born child
  All meanly wrapt in the rude manger lies;
Nature, in awe of him,
Had doffed her gaudy trim,
  With her great Master so to sympathise:
It was no season then for her
To wanton with the sun, her lusty paramour.

Only with speeches fair
She woos the gentle air,
  To hide her guilty front with innocent snow;
And on her naked shame,
Pollute with sinful blame,
  The saintly veil of maiden-white to throw;
Confounded, that her Maker's eyes
Should look so near upon her foul deformities.

But he, her fears to cease,
Sent down the meek-eyed Peace;
  She, crowned with olive green, came softly sliding
Down through the turning sphere,
His ready harbinger,
  With turtle wing the amorous clouds dividing;
And, waving wide her myrtle wand,
She strikes a universal peace through sea and land.

No war or battle's sound
Was heard the world around.
  The idle spear and shield were high uphung;
The hookèd chariot stood
Unstain'd with hostile blood;
  The trumpet spake not to the armèd throng;
And kings sat still with awful eye,
As if they surely knew their sovran Lord was by.

But peaceful was the night,
Wherein the Prince of Light
  His reign of peace upon the earth began:
The winds, with wonder whist,
Smoothly the waters kissed,
  Whispering new joys to the mild ocean,
Who now hath quite forgot to rave,
While birds of calm sit brooding on the charmèd wave.

The stars, with deep amaze,
Stand fixed in steadfast gaze,
  Bending one way their precious influence;
And will not take their flight,
For all the morning light,
  Or Lucifer that often warned them thence;
But in their glimmering orbs did glow,
Until their Lord himself bespake, and bid them go.

And, though the shady gloom
Had given day her room,
  The sun himself withheld his wonted speed,
And hid his head for shame,
As his inferior flame
  The new-enlightened world no more should need;
He saw a greater Sun appear
Than his bright throne or burning axle-tree could
    bear.

The shepherds on the lawn,
Or ere the point of dawn,
 Sat simply chatting in a rustic row;
Full little thought they than
That the mighty Pan
 Was kindly come to live with them below;
Perhaps their loves, or else their sheep,
Was all that did their silly thoughts so busy keep;

When such music sweet
Their hearts and ears did greet,
 As never was by mortal fingers strook,
Divinely-warbled voice
Answering the stringed noise,
 As all their souls in blissful rapture took:
The air, such pleasure loth to lose,
With thousand echoes still prolongs each heavenly
 close.

Nature, that heard such sound
Beneath the hollow round
 Of Cynthia's seat, the airy region thrilling,
Now was almost won
To think her part was done,
 And that her reign had here its last fulfilling;
She knew such harmony alone
Could hold all heaven and earth in happier union

At last surrounds their sight
A globe of circular light,
 That with long beams the shame-faced night arrayed;
The helmèd cherubim,
And sworded seraphim,
 Are seen in glittering ranks with wings displayed,
Harping in loud and solemn quire,
With unexpressive notes, to Heaven's new-born heir.

Such music, as 't is said,
Before was never made,
   But when of old the sons of morning sung,
While the Creator great
His constellations set,
   And the well-balanced world on hinges hung,
And cast the dark foundations deep,
And bid the weltering waves their oozy channel keep.

Ring out, ye crystal spheres!
Once bless our human ears,
   If ye have power to touch our senses so;
And let your silver chime
Move in melodious time;
   And let the bass of Heaven's deep organ blow;
And, with your ninefold harmony,
Make up full consort to the angelic symphony.

For, if such holy song
Enwrap our fancy long,
   Time will run back and fetch the age of gold;
And speckled Vanity
Will sicken soon and die,
   And leprous Sin will melt from earthly mould;
And Hell itself will pass away,
And leave her dolorous mansions to the peering day.

Yea, Truth and Justice then
Will down return to men,
   Orbed in a rainbow; and, like glories wearing,
Mercy will sit between,
Throned in celestial sheen,
   With radiant feet the tissued clouds down steering;
And Heaven, as at some festival,
Will open wide the gates of her high palace hall.

But wisest Fate says no,
This must not yet be so,
  The babe yet lies in smiling infancy,
That on the bitter cross
Must redeem our loss,
  So both himself and us to glorify:
Yet first, to those ychained in sleep,
The wakeful trump of doom must thunder through
    the deep,

With such a horrid clang
As on Mount Sinai rang,
  While the red fire and smouldering clouds out brake;
The aged earth aghast,
With terror of that blast,
  Shall from the surface to the centre shake;
When, at the world's last session,
The dreadful Judge in middle air shall spread his
    throne.

And then at last our bliss,
Full and perfect is,
  But now begins; for, from this happy day,
The old dragon, underground,
In straiter limits bound,
  Not half so far casts his usurpèd sway;
And, wroth to see his kingdom fail,
Swinges the scaly horror of his folded tail.

The oracles are dumb;
No voice or hideous hum
  Runs through the archèd roof in words deceiving.
Apollo from his shrine
Can no more divine,
  With hollow shriek the steep of Delphos leaving.
No nightly trance, or breathèd spell,
Inspires the pale-eyed priest from the prophetic cell.

The lonely mountains o'er,
And the resounding shore,
  A voice of weeping heard and loud lament;
From haunted spring and dale,
Edged with poplar pale,
  The parting Genius is with sighing sent;
With flower-inwoven tresses torn,
The Nymphs in twilight shade of tangled thickets
    mourn.

In consecrated earth,
And on the holy hearth,
  The Lars and Lemurs mourn with midnight plaint.
In urns and altars round,
A drear and dying sound
  Affrights the flamens at their service quaint;
And the chill marble seems to sweat,
While each peculiar power foregoes his wonted seat.

Peor and Baälim
Forsake their temples dim
  With that twice-battered god of Palestine;
And moonèd Ashtaroth,
Heaven's queen and mother both,
  Now sits not girt with tapers' holy shine;
The Libyac Hammon shrinks his horn;
In vain the Tyrian maids their wounded Thammuz
    mourn.

And sullen Moloch, fled,
Hath left in shadows dread
  His burning idol all of blackest hue:
In vain with cymbals' ring
They call the grisly king,
  In dismal dance about the furnace blue:
The brutish gods of Nile as fast,
Isis, and Orus, and the dog Anubis, haste.

Nor is Osiris seen
In Memphian grove or green,
   Trampling the unshowered grass with lowings loud;
Nor can he be at rest
Within his sacred chest,
   Nought but profoundest Hell can be his shroud;
In vain with timbrelled anthems dark
The sable-stolèd sorcerers bear his worshipped ark.

He feels from Judah's land
The dreaded infant's hand,
   The rays of Bethlehem blind his dusky eyne;
Nor all the gods beside
Longer dare abide,
   Not Typhon huge ending in snaky twine:
Our babe, to show his Godhead true,
Can in his swaddling bands control the damnèd crew.

So, when the sun in bed,
Curtained with cloudy red,
   Pillows his chin upon an orient wave,
The flocking shadows pale,
Troop to the infernal jail,
   Each fettered ghost slips to his several grave;
And the yellow-skirted fays
Fly after the night-steeds, leaving their moon-loved
    maze.

But see! the Virgin blest
Hath laid her babe to rest;
   Time is, our tedious song should here have ending:
Heaven's youngest-teemèd star
Hath fixed her polished car,
   Her sleeping Lord with handmaid lamp attending;
And all about the courtly stable
Bright-harnessed angels sit in order serviceable.

L'ALLEGRO.

HENCE, loathèd Melancholy,
    Of Cerberus and blackest Midnight born,
In Stygian cave forlorn,
    'Mongst horrid shapes, and shrieks, and sights
        unholy!
Find out some uncouth cell,
    Where brooding Darkness spread his jealous wings,
And the night-raven sings;
    There under ebon shades, and low-browed rocks,
As ragged as thy locks,
    In dark Cimmerian desert ever dwell.
But come, thou goddess fair and free,
In heaven yclept Euphrosyne,
And by men heart-easing Mirth;
Whom lovely Venus, at a birth,
With two sister Graces more,
To ivy-crownèd Bacchus bore:
Or whether (as some sager sing)
The frolic wind that breathes the spring,
Zephyr, with Aurora playing,
As he met her once a-Maying;
There on beds of violets blue,
And fresh-blown roses washed in dew,
Filled her with thee, a daughter fair,
So buxom, blithe, and debonair.
    Haste thee, nymph, and bring with thee
Jest, and youthful jollity,
Quips, and cranks, and wanton wiles,
Nods, and becks, and wreathèd smiles,
Such as hang on Hebe's cheek,
And love to live in dimple sleek;
Sport that wrinkled Care derides,

And Laughter holding both his sides.
Come, and trip it as you go,
On the light fantastic toe;
And in thy right hand lead with thee
The mountain-nymph, sweet Liberty;
And, if I give thee honour due,
Mirth, admit me of thy crew,
To live with her, and live with thee,
In unreprovèd pleasures free;
To hear the lark begin his flight,
And singing startle the dull night,
From his watch-tower in the skies,
Till the dappled dawn doth rise;
Then to come, in spite of sorrow,
And at my window bid good-morrow,
Through the sweet-briar, or the vine,
Or the twisted eglantine:
While the cock, with lively din,
Scatters the rear of darkness thin,
And to the stack, or the barn-door,
Stoutly struts his dames before:
Oft listening how the hounds and horn
Cheerly rouse the slumbering morn,
From the side of some hoar hill,
Through the high wood echoing shrill.
    Sometime walking, not unseen,
By hedgerow elms, on hillocks green,
Right against the eastern gate,
Where the great sun begins his state,
Robed in flames and amber light,
The clouds in thousand liveries dight;
While the ploughman, near at hand,
Whistles o'er the furrowed land,
And the milkmaid singeth blithe,
And the mower whets his scythe,

And every shepherd tells his tale,
Under the hawthorn in the dale.

   Straight mine eye hath caught new pleasures,
While the landskip round it measures;
Russet lawns, and fallows grey,
Where the nibbling flocks do stray;
Mountains, on whose barren breast
The labouring clouds do often rest;
Meadows trim, with daisies pied,
Shallow brooks, and rivers wide;
Towers and battlements it sees
Bosomed high in tufted trees,
Where perhaps some beauty lies,
The cynosure of neighbouring eyes.

   Hard by, a cottage chimney smokes
From betwixt two aged oaks,
Where Corydon and Thyrsis met,
Are at their savoury dinner set
Of herbs, and other country messes,
Which the neat-handed Phillis dresses;
And then in haste her bower she leaves,
With Thestylis to bind the sheaves;
Or, if the earlier season lead,
To the tanned haycock in the mead.

   Sometimes with secure delight
The upland hamlets will invite,
When the merry bells ring round,
And the jocund rebecks sound
To many a youth and many a maid,
Dancing in the chequered shade,
And young and old come forth to play
On a sunshine holiday,
Till the livelong daylight fail:
Then to the spicy nut-brown ale,
With stories told of many a feat:

How faery Mab the junkets eat;
She was pinched, and pulled, she said;
And he, by friar's lantern led,
Tells how the drudging goblin sweat
To earn his cream-bowl duly set,
When in one night, ere glimpse of morn,
His shadowy flail hath threshed the corn,
That ten day-labourers could not end;
Then lies him down, the lubber fiend,
And, stretched out all the chimney's length,
Basks at the fire his hairy strength;
And crop-full out of doors he flings,
Ere the first cock his matin rings.
Thus done the tales, to bed they creep,
By whispering winds soon lulled asleep.

   Towered cities please us then,
And the busy hum of men,
Where throngs of knights and barons bold,
In weeds of peace, high triumphs hold,
With store of ladies, whose bright eyes
Rain influence, and judge the prize
Of wit or arms, while both contend
To win her grace whom all commend.
There let Hymen oft appear
In saffron robe, with taper clear,
And pomp, and feast, and revelry,
With mask and antique pageantry;
Such sights as youthful poets dream
On summer eves by haunted stream.
Then to the well-trod stage anon,
If Jonson's learned sock be on,
Or sweetest Shakespeare, Fancy's child,
Warble his native wood-notes wild.

   And ever, against eating cares,
Lap me in soft Lydian airs,

Married to immortal verse,
Such as the meeting soul may pierce,
In notes with many a winding bout
Of linkèd sweetness long drawn out,
With wanton heed and giddy cunning;
The melting voice through mazes running,
Untwisting all the chains that tie
The hidden soul of harmony;
That Orpheus' self may heave his head
From golden slumber on a bed
Of heaped Elysian flowers, and hear
Such strains as would have won the ear
Of Pluto, to have quite set free
His half-regained Eurydice.
　　These delights if thou canst give,
Mirth, with thee I mean to live.

IL PENSEROSO.

HENCE, vain deluding joys,
　　The brood of Folly without father bred!
How little you bested,
　　Or fill the fixèd mind with all your toys!
Dwell in some idle brain,
　　And fancies fond with gaudy shapes possess,
As thick and numberless
　　As the gay motes that people the sunbeams;
Or likest hovering dreams,
　　The fickle pensioners of Morpheus' train.
But hail, thou goddess sage and holy,
Hail, divinest Melancholy!
Whose saintly visage is too bright
To hit the sense of human sight,
And therefore to our weaker view
O'erlaid with black, staid wisdom's hue;

Black, but such as in esteem
Prince Memnon's sister might beseem,
Or that starred Ethiop queen that strove
To set her beauty's praise above
The sea-nymphs, and their powers offended:
Yet thou art higher far descended;
Thee bright-haired Vesta, long of yore,
To solitary Saturn bore;
His daughter she; in Saturn's reign
Such mixture was not held a stain:
Oft in glimmering bowers and glades
He met her, and in secret shades
Of woody Ida's inmost grove,
Whilst yet there was no fear of Jove.
  Come, pensive nun, devout and pure,
Sober, steadfast, and demure,
All in a robe of darkest grain,
Flowing with majestic train,
And sable stole of cypress lawn,
Over thy decent shoulders drawn.
Come, but keep thy wonted state,
With even step, and musing gait,
And looks commercing with the skies,
Thy rapt soul sitting in thine eyes:
There, held in holy passion still,
Forget thyself to marble, till
With a sad leaden downward cast
Thou fix them on the earth as fast;
And join with thee calm Peace, and Quiet,
Spare Fast, that oft with gods doth diet,
And hears the Muses in a ring
Aye round about Jove's altar sing:
And add to these retired Leisure,
That in trim gardens takes his pleasure.
But first, and chiefest, with thee bring,

Him that yon soars on golden wing,
Guiding the fiery-wheelèd throne,
The cherub Contemplation;
And the mute Silence hist along,
'Less Philomel will deign a song,
In her sweetest saddest plight,
Smoothing the rugged brow of night,
While Cynthia checks her dragon yoke,
Gently o'er the accustomed oak:
Sweet bird, that shun'st the noise of folly,
Most musical, most melancholy!
Thee, chantress, oft the woods among
I woo, to hear thy even-song;
And, missing thee, I walk unseen
On the dry smooth-shaven green,
To behold the wandering moon,
Riding near her highest noon,
Like one that had been led astray
Through the heaven's wide pathless way
And oft, as if her head she bowed,
Stooping through a fleecy cloud.
    Oft, on a plat of rising ground,
I hear the far-off curfew sound,
Over some wide-watered shore,
Swinging slow with sullen roar:
Or, if the air will not permit,
Some still removèd place will fit,
Where glowing embers through the room
Teach light to counterfeit a gloom·
Far from all resort of mirth,
Save the cricket on the hearth,
Or the bellman's drowsy charm,
To bless the doors from nightly harm.
    Or let my lamp, at midnight hour,
Be seen in some high lonely tower,

Where I may oft outwatch the Bear,
With thrice-great Hermes, or unsphere
The spirit of Plato, to unfold
What worlds or what vast regions hold
The immortal mind that hath forsook
Her mansion in this fleshly nook:
And of those demons that are found
In fire, air, flood, or underground,
Whose power hath a true consent
With planet or with element.
Sometime let gorgeous tragedy
In sceptred pall come sweeping by,
Presenting Thebes', or Pelops' line,
Or the tale of Troy divine,
Or what (though rare) of later age
Ennobled hath the buskined stage.

    But, O sad virgin, that thy power
Might raise Musæus from his bower!
Or bid the soul of Orpheus sing
Such notes as, warbled to the string,
Drew iron tears down Pluto's cheek,
And made Hell grant what love did seek:
Or call up him that left half-told
The story of Cambuscan bold,
Of Camball, and of Algarsife,
And who had Canace to wife,
That owned the virtuous ring and glass;
And of the wondrous horse of brass,
On which the Tartar king did ride:
And if aught else great bards beside
In sage and solemn tunes have sung,
Of turneys, and of trophies hung,
Of forests, and enchantments drear,
Where more is meant than meets the ear.

    Thus, Night, oft see me in thy pale career,

Till civil-suited Morn appear,
Not tricked and frounced as she was wont
With the Attic boy to hunt,
But kerchieft in a comely cloud,
While rocking winds are piping loud,
Or ushered with a shower still,
When the gust hath blown his fill,
Ending on the rustling leaves,
With minute-drops from off the eaves.
And, when the sun begins to fling
His flaring beams, me, goddess, bring
To archèd walks of twilight groves,
And shadows brown that Sylvan loves,
Of pine, or monumental oak,
Where the rude axe, with heavèd stroke,
Was never heard the nymphs to daunt,
Or fright them from their hallowed haunt.
There in close covert by some brook,
Where no profaner eye may look,
Hide me from day's garish eye,
While the bee with honeyed thigh,
That at her flowery work doth sing,
And the waters murmuring,
With such consort as they keep,
Entice the dewy-feathered Sleep;
And let some strange mysterious dream
Wave at his wings in airy stream
Of lively portraiture displayed,
Softly on my eyelids laid;
And, as I wake, sweet music breathe
Above, about, or underneath,
Sent by some spirit to mortals good,
Or the unseen genius of the wood.
    But let my due feet never fail
To walk the studious cloister's pale,

And love the high-embowèd roof,
With antic pillars massy proof,
And storied windows richly dight,
Casting a dim religious light:
There let the pealing organ blow,
To the full-voiced quire below,
In service high and anthems clear,
As may with sweetness, through mine ear,
Dissolve me into ecstasies,
And bring all heaven before mine eyes.
    And may at last my weary age
Find out the peaceful hermitage,
The hairy gown and mossy cell,
Where I may sit and rightly spell
Of every star that heaven doth shew,
And every herb that sips the dew;
Till old experience do attain
To something like prophetic strain.
    These pleasures, Melancholy, give,
And I with thee will choose to live.

SONG.

O'ER the smooth enamelled green,
    Where no print of step hath been,
Follow me, as I sing
And touch the warbled string:
Under the shady roof
Of branching elm star-proof
    Follow me.
I will bring you where she sits,
Clad in splendour as befits
    Her deity,
Such a rural Queen
All Arcadia hath not seen.

SONG.

NYMPHS and Shepherds, dance no more
    By sandy Ladon's lilied banks;
On old Lycæus, or Cyllene hoar,
    Trip no more in twilight ranks;
Though Erymanth your loss deplore,
    A better soil shall give ye thanks.
From the stony Mænalus
Bring your flocks, and live with us;
Here ye shall have greater grace,
To serve the Lady of this place
Though Syrinx your Pan's mistress were,
Yet Syrinx well might wait on her.
    Such a rural Queen
    All Arcadia hath not seen.

SONG.

SWEET Echo, sweetest Nymph, that livest unseen
    Within thy airy shell,
    By slow Meander's margent green,
And in the violet-embroidered vale
    Where the love-lorn nightingale
Nightly to thee her sad song mourneth well:
Canst thou not tell me of a gentle pair
      That likest thy Narcissus are?
      O, if thou have
    Hid them in some flowery cave,
      Tell me but where,
Sweet queen of parley, daughter of the sphere!
So may'st thou be translated to the skies,
And give resounding grace to all Heaven's harmonies!

INCANTATION.

SABRINA fair,
    Listen where thou art sitting
Under the glassy, cool, translucent wave,
    In twisted braids of lilies knitting
The loose train of thy amber-dropping hair;
    Listen for dear honour's sake,
    Goddess of the silver lake,
        Listen and save!

Listen, and appear to us,
In name of great Oceanus,
By the earth-shaking Neptune's mace,
And Tethys' grave majestic pace;
By hoary Nereus' wrinkled look,
And the Carpathian wizard's hook;
By scaly Triton's winding shell,
And old soothsaying Glaucus' spell;
By Leucothea's lovely hands,
And her son that rules the strands;
By Thetis' tinsel-slippered feet,
And the songs of Sirens sweet;
By dead Parthenope's dear tomb,
And fair Ligea's golden comb,
Wherewith she sits on diamond rocks
Sleeking her soft alluring locks;
By all the nymphs that nightly dance
Upon thy streams with wily glance;
Rise, rise, and heave thy rosy head
From thy coral-paven bed,
And bridle in thy headlong wave,
Till thou our summons answered have.
        Listen and save!

THE LAND OF ETERNAL SUMMER.

TO the ocean now I fly,
    And those happy climes that lie
Where day never shuts his eye,
Up in the broad fields of the sky.
There I suck the liquid air,
All amidst the gardens fair
Of Hesperus, and his daughters three
That sing about the golden tree.
Along the crispèd shades and bowers
Revels the spruce and jocund Spring;
The Graces and the rosy-bosomed Hours
Thither all their bounties bring.
There eternal Summer dwells,
And west winds with musky wing
About the cedarn alleys fling
Nard and cassia's balmy smells.
Iris there with humid bow
Waters the odorous banks, that blow
Flowers of more mingled hue
Than her purpled scarf can shew,
And drenches with Elysian dew
(List, mortals, if your ears be true)
Beds of hyacinth and roses,
Where young Adonis oft reposes,
Waxing well of his deep wound,
In slumber soft, and on the ground
Sadly sits the Assyrian queen.
But far above, in spangled sheen,
Celestial Cupid, her famed son, advanced
Holds his dear Psyche, sweet entranced,
After her wandering labours long,
Till free consent the gods among
Make her his eternal bride,

And from her fair unspotted side
Two blissful twins are to be born,
Youth and Joy; so Jove hath sworn

But now my task is smoothly done:
I can fly, or I can run
Quickly to the green earth's end,
Where the bowed welkin slow doth bend,
And from thence can soar as soon
To the corners of the moon.
Mortals, that would follow me,
Love Virtue: she alone is free.
She can teach ye how to climb
Higher than the sphery chime;
Or if Virtue feeble were
Heaven itself would stoop to her.

SONG ON MAY MORNING.

NOW the bright morning star, day's harbinger,
    Comes dancing from the east, and leads with her
The flowery May, who from her green lap throws
The yellow cowslip and the pale primrose.
    Hail! bounteous May, that dost inspire
    Mirth, and youth, and warm desire!
    Woods and groves are of thy dressing;
    Hill and dale doth boast thy blessing.
Thus we salute thee with our early song,
And welcome thee, and wish thee long.

TO THE NIGHTINGALE.

O NIGHTINGALE, that on yon bloomy spray
    Warblest at eve, when all the woods are still;
Thou with fresh hopes the lover's heart dost fill,
While the jolly hours lead on propitious May.

The liquid notes that close the eye of day
First heard before the shallow cuckoo's bill,
Portend success in love; O, if Jove's will
Have linked that amorous power to thy soft lay,
Now timely sing, ere the rude bird of hate
Foretell my hopeless doom, in some grove nigh:
As thou from year to year hast sung too late
For my relief, yet had'st no reason why:
 Whether the Muse or Love call thee his mate,
 Both them I serve, and of their train am I

ON HIS BLINDNESS.

WHEN I consider how my light is spent,
 Ere half my days, in this dark world and wide,
And that one talent, which is death to hide,
Lodged with me useless, though my soul more bent
To serve therewith my Maker, and present
My true account, lest He, returning, chide;
"Doth God exact day-labour, light denied?"
I fondly ask: but Patience, to prevent
That murmur, soon replied, "God doth not need
Either man's work, or His own gifts; who best
Bear His mild yoke, they serve Him best: His state
Is kingly; thousands at His bidding speed,
 And post o'er land and ocean without rest;
 They also serve who only stand and wait".

ON THE LATE MASSACRE IN PIEDMONT.

AVENGE, O Lord, Thy slaughtered saints, whose bones
 Lie scattered on the Alpine mountains cold;
Ev'n them who kept Thy truth so pure of old,
When all our fathers worshipped stocks and stones,
Forget not: in Thy book record their groans
Who were Thy sheep, and in their ancient fold

Slain by the bloody Piedmontese that rolled
Mother with infant down the rocks.   Their moans
The vales redoubled to the hills, and they
To heaven.   Their martyred blood and ashes sow
O'er all the Italian fields, where still doth sway
The triple tyrant; that from these may grow
A hundred fold, who, having learnt Thy way,
Early may fly the Babylonian woe.

GEORGE WITHER.

(1588–1667.)

Most of Wither's voluminous poetry has been reprinted by the Spenser
Society. Selections from his poems, including "Fair Virtue", the "Shep-
herd's Hunting", and several lyrics, were edited in 1891 by Prof. Henry
Morley in the Companion Poets Series.   Wither's *Hymns and Songs of
the Church*, edited by Edward Farr, are in the Library of Old Authors.
"Fair Virtue" and "Fidelia" are reprinted in Arber's *Garner*.   Both
extracts occur in *Fair Virtue, the Mistress of Philarete*, 1622 (written
about 1610); the first also in "Fidelia", 1617.

THE AUTHOR'S RESOLUTION IN A SONNET.

SHALL I, wasting in despair,
　Die, because a woman's fair?
Or make pale my cheeks with care
'Cause another's rosy are?
　　Be she fairer than the day
　　Or the flowery meads in May,
　　If she think not well of me.
　　What care I how fair she be?

Shall my seely heart be pin'd
'Cause I see a woman kind?
Or a well-disposèd nature
Joinèd with a lovely feature?

Be she meeker, kinder than
Turtle-dove or pelican:
If she be not so to me,
What care I how kind she be?

Shall a woman's virtues move
Me to perish for her love?
Or her well-deservings known
Make me quite forget mine own?
  Be she with that goodness blest
  Which may merit name of best:
  If she be not such to me,
  What care I how good she be?

'Cause her fortune seems too high
Shall I play the fool and die?
She that bears a noble mind,
If not outward helps she find,
  Thinks what with them he would do,
  That without them dares her woo.
  And unless that mind I see
  What care I how great she be?

Great, or good, or kind, or fair,
I will ne'er the more despair:
If she love me (this believe)
I will die ere she shall grieve.
  If she slight me when I woo,
  I can scorn and let her go,
  For if she be not for me
  What care I for whom she be?

THE FLOWER OF VIRTUE.

LET who list (for me) advance
  The admirèd flowers of France;
Let who will praise and behold
The reservèd marigold;

Let the sweet-breathed violet now,
Unto whom she pleaseth, bow;
And the fairest lily spread,
Where she will her golden head:
I have such a flower to wear
That for those I do not care.

Never shall my fancy range,
Nor once think again of change;
Never will I, never more,
Grieve or sigh, as heretofore;
Nor within the lodgings lie
Of despair or jealousy.

WILLIAM HABINGTON.

(1605–1654?.)

TO CASTARA:

THE REWARD OF INNOCENT LOVE.

From *Castara*, 1634; augmented editions 1635 and 1640. The first
selection is from the first edition, the second from that of 1635, and the
last two from that of 1640.   Reprinted in vol. vi. of Chalmers' *Poets*,
and in Arber's English Reprints, 1870.

WE saw and wooed each other's eyes,
    My soul contracted then with thine,
And both burnt in one sacrifice,
By which our marriage grew divine.

Let wilder youth, whose soul is sense,
Profane the temple of delight,
And purchase endless penitence,
With the stolen pleasure of one night.

Time's ever ours while we despise
The sensual idol of our clay,
For though the sun do set and rise,
We joy one everlasting day;

Whose light no jealous clouds obscure,
While each of us shine innocent,
The troubled stream is still impure;
With virtue flies away content.

And though opinion often err,
We'll court the modest smile of fame,
For sin's black danger circles her,
Who hath infection in her name.

Thus when to one dark silent room,
Death shall our loving coffins thrust;
Fame will build columns on our tomb,
And add a perfume to our dust.

TO THE MOMENT LAST PAST.

O WHITHER dost thou fly? cannot my vow
Intreat thee tarry? Thou wert here but now,
And thou art gone, like ships which plough the sea,
And leave no print for man to track their way.
O unseen wealth! who thee did husband, can
Outvie the jewels of the ocean,
The mines of th' earth! One sigh well spent in thee
Had been a purchase for eternity!
We will not lose thee then. Castara, where
Shall we find out his hidden sepulchre?
And we'll revive him. Not the cruel stealth
Of fate shall rob us of so great a wealth
   Undone in thrift! while we besought his stay,
   Ten of his fellow-moments fled away.

NOX NOCTI INDICAT SCIENTIAM.

WHEN I survey the bright
    Celestial sphere,
So rich with jewels hung, that night
Doth like an Ethiop bride appear:

My soul her wings doth spread
    And heavenward flies,
The Almighty's mysteries to read
In the large volumes of the skies.

For the bright firmament
    Shoots forth no flame
So silent, but is eloquent
In speaking the Creator's name.

No unregarded star
    Contracts its light,
Into so small a character,
Removed far from our human sight:

But if we steadfast look
    We shall discern
In it as in some holy book,
How man may heavenly knowledge learn.

It tells the conqueror,
    That far-stretched power,
Which his proud dangers traffic for,
Is but the triumph of an hour.

That from the farthest north
    Some nation may
Yet undiscovered issue forth,
And o'er his new-got conquest sway.

Some nation yet shut in
    With hills of ice,
May be let out to scourge his sin,
Till they shall equal him in vice.

And then they likewise shall
    Their ruin have;
For as yourselves your empires fal
And every kingdom hath a grave.

Thus those celestial fires,
    Though seeming mute,
The fallacy of our desires
And all the pride of life confute.

For they have watched since first
    The world had birth:
And found sin in itself accursed,
And nothing permanent on earth.

COGITABO PRO PECCATO MEO.

IN what dark silent grove
  Profaned by no unholy love,
Where witty melancholy ne'er
Did carve the trees or wound the air,
Shall I religious leisure win,
To weep away my sin?

How fondly have I spent
My youth's unvalued treasure, lent
To traffic for celestial joys;
My unripe years, pursuing toys,
Judging things best that were most gay,
Fled unobserved away.

Grown elder I admired
Our poets as from Heaven inspired;
What obelisks decreed I fit
For Spenser's art, and Sidney's wit?
But waxing sober soon I found
Fame but an idle sound.

Then I my blood obeyed,
And each bright face an idol made:
Verse in an humble sacrifice,
I offered to my mistress' eyes,
But I no sooner grace did win
But met the devil within

But grown more politic
I took account of each state trick:
Observed each motion, judged him wise,
Who had a conscience fit to rise.
Whom soon I found but form and rule
And the more serious fool.

But now my soul prepare
To ponder what and where we are,
How frail is life, how vain a breath
Opinion, how uncertain death;
How only a poor stone shall bear
Witness that once we were.

How a shrill trumpet shall
Us to the bar as traitors call.
Then shall we see too late that pride
Hath hope with flattery belied,
And that the mighty in command
Pale cowards there must stand.

ROBERT HERRICK.

(1591–1674.)

Practically all of Herrick's poetry appeared first in *Hesperides*, 1648, and was probably written 1620–1648.   There are numerous modern editions of Herrick, who, like Campion and so many others of the early lyrists, has only come into favour during the present century.   The best are Dr. Grosart's (3 vols., London, 1877), Mr. A. W. Pollard's (2 vols. 1891, in the Muses' Library), and Mr. Saintsbury's (2 vols. 1893, in the Aldine Poets).   Selections nearly complete have been edited by Prof. E. E. Hale, junr. (Athenæum Press Series, Boston, 1895), by Prof. Palgrave (Golden Treasury Series, 1877), by Prof. Henry Morley (the Universal Library, 1883), and by Mr. H. P. Horne (Canterbury Poets, 1887).

THE ARGUMENT OF THE HESPERIDES.

I SING of brooks, of blossoms, birds, and bowers,
  Of April, May, of June, and July flowers;
I sing of maypoles, hock-carts, wassails, wakes,
Of bridegrooms, brides, and of their bridal cakes.
I write of Youth, of Love;—and have access
By these to sing of cleanly wantonness;
I sing of dews, of rains, and, piece by piece,
Of balm, of oil, of spice, and ambergris.
I sing of times trans-shifting; and I write
How roses first came red, and lilies white.
I write of groves, of twilights, and I sing
The court of Mab, and of the Fairy King.
I write of Hell; I sing, and ever shall
Of Heaven,—and hope to have it after all.

UPON THE LOSS OF HIS MISTRESSES.

I HAVE lost, and lately, these
    Many dainty mistresses:
Stately Julia, prime of all;
Sappho next, a principal;

Smooth Anthea, for a skin
White and heaven-like crystalline;
Sweet Electra, and the choice
Myrrha, for the lute and voice.
Next, Corinna, for her wit,
And the graceful use of it;
With Perilla: all are gone,
Only Herrick's left alone,
For to number sorrow by
Their departures hence, and die.

TO LIVE MERRILY, AND TO TRUST TO GOOD VERSES.

NOW is the time for mirth
   Nor cheek or tongue be dumb;
For the flowery earth,
   The golden pomp is come.

The golden pomp is come;
   For now each tree does wear,
Made of her pap and gum,
   Rich beads of amber here.

Now reigns the Rose, and now
   The Arabian dew besmears
My uncontrollèd brow,
   And my retorted[1] hairs.

Homer, this health to thee,
   In sack of such a kind,
That it would make thee see,
   Though thou wert ne'er so blind.

Next, Virgil I'll call forth,
   To pledge this second health
In wine whose each cup's worth
   An Indian commonwealth.

[1] thrown back.

A goblet next I'll drink
   To Ovid; and suppose
Made he the pledge, he'd think
   The world had all one nose.

Then this immensive cup
   Of aromatic wine,
Catullus, I quaff up
   To that terse muse of thine.

Wild I am now with heat,
   O Bacchus! cool thy rays;
Or frantic I shall eat
   Thy thyrse, and bite the bays.

Round, round, the roof does run;
   And being ravished thus,
Come, I will drink a tun
   To my Propertius.

Now, to Tibullus next,
   This flood I drink to thee;
But stay, I see a text,
   That this presents to me.

Behold! Tibullus lies
   Here burnt, whose small return
Of ashes scarce suffice
   To fill a little urn.

Trust to good verses then:
   They only will aspire,
When pyramids, as men,
   Are lost i' th' funeral fire,

And when all bodies meet
   In Lethe to be drowned;
Then only numbers sweet,
   With endless life are crowned.

AN ODE FOR BEN JONSON.

A H Ben!
　　　Say how or when
　　　　Shall we, thy guests,
　　　Meet at those lyric feasts,
　　　　　Made at the Sun,
　　　The Dog, the Triple Tun;
　　Where we such clusters had,
As made us nobly wild, not mad?
　　And yet each verse of thine
Out-did the meat, out-did the frolic wine.

　　　　　My Ben!
　　　　Or come again,
　　　　　Or send to us
　　　Thy wit's great overplus;
　　　　But teach us yet
　　　Wisely to husband it,
　　Lest we that talent spend;
And having once brought to an end
　　That precious stock,—the store
Of such a wit the world should have no more.

HIS PRAYER TO BEN JONSON.

W HEN I a verse shall make,
　　　Know I have prayed thee,
For old religion's sake,
　　Saint Ben, to aid me.

Make the way smooth for me,
　　When I, thy Herrick,
Honouring thee, on my knee
　　Offer my Lyric.

Candles I 'll give to thee,
  And a new altar;
And thou, Saint Ben, shalt be
  Writ in my psalter.

TO ANTHEA.

BID me to live, and I will live
  Thy Protestant to be;
Or bid me love, and I will give
  A loving heart to thee.

A heart as soft, a heart as kind,
  A heart as sound and free
As in the whole world thou canst find
  That heart I 'll give to thee.

Bid that heart stay, and it will stay
  To honour thy decree
Or bid it languish quite away,
  And 't shall do so for thee.

Bid me to weep, and I will weep,
  While I have eyes to see;
And having none, yet I will keep
  A heart to weep for thee.

Bid me despair, and I 'll despair,
  Under that cypress tree;
Or bid me die, and I will dare
  E'en death, to die for thee.

Thou art my life, my love, my heart,
  The very eyes of me;
And hast command of every part,
  To live and die for thee.

THE NIGHT-PIECE.

HER eyes the glow-worm lend thee,
  The shooting stars attend thee;
    And the elves also,
    Whose little eyes glow
Like the sparks of fire, befriend thee.

No Will-o'-th'-Wisp mislight thee,
Nor snake or slow-worm bite thee;
    But on, on thy way,
    Not making a stay,
Since ghost there's none to affright thee.

Let not the dark thee cumber;
What though the moon does slumber?
    The stars of the night
    Will lend thee their light,
Like tapers clear, without number.

Then Julia, let me woo thee,
Thus, thus to come unto me;
    And when I shall meet
    Thy silvery feet,
My soul I'll pour into thee.

CHERRY-RIPE.

CHERRY-RIPE, ripe, ripe, I cry,
  Full and fair ones; come and buy:
If so be you ask me where
They do grow?   I answer, There
Where my Julia's lips do smile;—
There's the land, or cherry-isle;
Whose plantations fully show
All the year where cherries grow.

TO ELECTRA.

I DARE not ask a kiss,
  I dare not beg a smile;
Lest having that or this,
  I might grow proud the while.

No, no, the utmost share
  Of my desire shall be
Only to kiss that air
  That lately kissèd thee.

DELIGHT IN DISORDER.

A SWEET disorder in the dress
  Kindles in clothes a wantonness;
A lawn about the shoulders thrown
Into a fine distraction;
An erring lace, which here and there
Enthrals the crimson stomacher;
A cuff neglectful, and thereby
Ribbons to flow confusedly;
A winning wave, deserving note,
In the tempestuous petticoat;
A careless shoe-string, in whose tie
I see a wild civility;—
Do more bewitch me, than when art
Is too precise in every part.

UPON JULIA'S CLOTHES.

WHENAS in silks my Julia goes,
  Till then, methinks, how sweetly flows
That liquefaction of her clothes!
Next when I cast mine eyes, and see
That brave vibration each way free;
O how that glittering taketh me!

TO THE ROSE.

GO, happy rose, and interwove
   With other flowers, bind my love.
Tell her, too, she must not be
Longer flowing, longer free,
That so oft has fettered me.

Say, if she's fretful, I have bands
Of pearl and gold, to bind her hands;
Tell her, if she struggle still,
I have myrtle rods at will,
For to tame, though not to kill.

Take thou my blessing thus, and go
And tell her this,—but do not so!
Lest a handsome anger fly
Like a lightning from her eye,
And burn thee up, as well as I.

TO DIANEME.

SWEET, be not proud of those two eyes,
   Which star-like sparkle in their skies;
Nor be you proud that you can see
All hearts your captives, yours yet free;
Be you not proud of that rich hair,
Which wantons with the love-sick air;
Whenas that ruby which you wear,
Sunk from the tip of your soft ear,
Will last to be a precious stone,
When all your world of beauty's gone.

THIS AGE BEST.

PRAISE they that will times past, I joy to see
   Myself now live; this age best pleaseth me.

DIVINATION BY A DAFFODIL.

WHEN a daffodil I see
    Hanging down his head towards me,
Guess I may what I must be:
First, I shall decline my head;
Secondly, I shall be dead;
Lastly, safely burièd.

TO THE VIRGINS.

GATHER ye rosebuds while ye may:
    Old Time is still a-flying;
And this same flower that smiles to-day,
    To-morrow will be dying.

The glorious lamp of heaven, the Sun,
    The higher he's a-getting,
The sooner will his race be run,
    And nearer he's to setting.

That age is best, which is the first,
    When youth and blood are warmer;
But being spent, the worse, and worst
    Times, still succeed the former.

Then be not coy, but use your time,
    And while ye may, go marry;
For having lost but once your prime,
    You may for ever tarry.

TO BLOSSOMS.

FAIR pledges of a fruitful tree,
    Why do ye fall so fast?
    Your date is not so past,
But you may stay yet here awhile,
    To blush and gently smile;
        And go at last.

What, were ye born to be
    An hour or half's delight;
    And so to bid good-night?
'T was pity Nature brought ye forth,
    Merely to show your worth,
        And lose you quite.

But you are lovely leaves, where we
    May read how soon things have
    Their end, though ne'er so brave:
And after they have shown their pride,
    Like you, awhile,—they glide
        Into the grave.

TO DAFFODILS.

FAIR Daffodils, we weep to see
    You haste away so soon;
As yet the early-rising sun
    Has not attained his noon.
        Stay, stay,
    Until the hasting day
        Has run
    But to the even-song;
And, having prayed together, we
    Will go with you along.

We have short time to stay, as you;
    We have as short a spring;
As quick a growth to meet decay,
    As you, or any thing.
        We die
    As your hours do, and dry
        Away,
    Like to the summer's rain;
Or as to the pearls of morning's dew,
    Ne'er to be found again.

TO VIOLETS.

WELCOME, maids of honour,
          You do bring
          In the spring;
And wait upon her.

She has virgins many,
          Fresh and fair;
          Yet you are
More sweet than any

Y' are the maiden posies,
          And so graced,
          To be placed,
'Fore damask roses.

Yet though thus respected,
          By and by
          Ye do lie,
Poor girls, neglected.

TO MEADOWS.

YE have been fresh and green,
    Ye have been filled with flowers;
And ye the walks have been
    Where maids have spent their hours.

You have beheld how they
    With wicker arks did come,
To kiss and bear away
    The richer cowslips home.

You 've heard them sweetly sing,
    And seen them in a round;
Each virgin, like a spring,
    With honeysuckles crowned.

But now, we see none here,
   Whose silvery feet did tread,
And with dishevelled hair
   Adorned this smoother mead.

Like unthrifts, having spent
   Your stock, and needy grown,
You're left here to lament
   Your poor estates alone.

ANACREONTIC.

BORN was I to be old,
   And for to die here;
After that, in the mould
   Long for to lie here.
But before that day comes,
   Still I be bousing;
For I know in the tombs
   There's no carousing.

UPON A CHILD THAT DIED.

HERE she lies, a pretty bud,
   Lately made of flesh and blood;
Who, as soon fell fast asleep,
As her little eyes did peep.
Give her strewings; but not stir
The earth, that lightly covers her.

UPON A CHILD.

HERE a pretty baby lies
   Sung asleep with lullabies;
Pray be silent, and not stir
The easy earth that covers her.

GRACE FOR A CHILD.

HERE, a little child, I stand,
    Heaving up my either hand:
Cold as paddocks though they be,
Here I lift them up to Thee,
For a benison to fall
On our meat, and on our all.   Amen.

THE LITANY.

IN the hour of my distress,
    When temptations me oppress,
And when I my sins confess,
            Sweet Spirit, comfort me!

When I lie within my bed,
Sick in heart, and sick in head,
And with doubts discomforted,
            Sweet Spirit, comfort me!

When the house doth sigh and weep
And the world is drowned in sleep,
Yet mine eyes the watch do keep,
            Sweet Spirit, comfort me!

When the artless doctor sees
No one hope, but of his fees,
And his skill runs on the lees,
            Sweet Spirit, comfort me!

When his potion and his pill
Has or none or little skill,
Meet for nothing but to kill,
            Sweet Spirit, comfort me!

When the passing-bell doth toll,
And the furies in a shoal
Come to fright a parting soul,
    Sweet Spirit, comfort me!

When the tapers now burn blue,
And the comforters are few,
And that number more than true,
    Sweet Spirit, comfort me!

When the priest his last hath prayed,
And I nod to what is said,
'Cause my speech is now decayed,
    Sweet Spirit, comfort me!

When, God knows, I'm tost about,
Either with despair or doubt;
Yet, before the glass be out,
    Sweet Spirit, comfort me!

When the tempter me pursu'th
With the sins of all my youth,
And half damns me with untruth,
    Sweet Spirit, comfort me!

When the flames and hellish cries
Fright mine ears, and fright mine eyes,
And all terrors me surprise,
    Sweet Spirit, comfort me!

When the Judgment is revealed,
And that opened which was sealed;
When to Thee I have appealed,
    Sweet Spirit, comfort me!

THOMAS CAREW.

(1598?–1639?.)

From Carew's *Poems*, 1640. There are modern editions by Mr. W. C. Hazlitt (in the Roxburghe Library), and by the Rev. J. W. Ebsworth (in the Library of Old Authors). They are also reprinted in vol. v. of Chalmers' *Poets*.

SONG.

ASK me no more where Jove bestows,
When June is past, the fading rose;
For in your beauty's orient deep
These flowers, as in their causes, sleep.

Ask me no more whither do stray
The golden atoms of the day,
For, in pure love, heaven did prepare
Those powders to enrich your hair.

Ask me no more whither doth haste
The nightingale when May is past,
For in your sweet dividing throat
She winters and keeps warm her note.

Ask me no more where those stars light
That downwards fall in dead of night,
For in your eyes they sit, and there
Fixed become as in their sphere.

Ask me no more if east or west
The Phœnix builds her spicy nest,
For unto you at last she flies,
And in your fragrant bosom dies.

DISDAIN RETURNED.

HE that loves a rosy cheek,
　　Or a coral lip admires,
Or from star-like eyes doth seek
　　Fuel to maintain his fires,
As old Time makes these decay,
So his flames must waste away.

But a smooth and steadfast mind,
　　Gentle thoughts and calm desires,
Hearts, with equal love combined
　　Kindle never-dying fires;
Where these are not, I despise
Lovely cheeks or lips or eyes.

No tears, Celia, now shall win,
　　My resolved heart to return;
I have searched thy soul within
　　And find nought but pride and scorn;
I have learned thy arts, and now
Can disdain as much as thou!

THE PRIMROSE.

ASK me why I send you here
　　This firstling of the infant year;
Ask me why I send to you
This primrose all bepearled with dew;
I straight will whisper in your ears,
The sweets of love are washed with tears:
Ask me why this flower doth show
So yellow, green, and sickly too;
Ask me why the stalk is weak,
And bending, yet it doth not break;
I must tell you, these discover
What doubts and fears are in a lover.

EPITAPH ON THE LADY MARY VILLERS.

THE Lady Mary Villers lies
  Under this stone; with weeping eyes
The parents that first gave her birth,
And their sad friends, laid her in earth.
If any of them, reader, were
Known unto thee, shed a tear;
Or if thyself possess a gem
As dear to thee as this to them,
Though a stranger to this place,
Bewail in theirs thine own hard case,
For thou, perhaps, at thy return
May'st find thy darling in an urn.

SIR JOHN SUCKLING.

(1609-1641.)

Suckling's Collected Poems were first published in 1646 under the
title of *Fragmenta Aurea.* As in the cases of Carew and Lovelace also,
many of his songs were set to music and circulated long before the for
mal edition of his poems.   They are reprinted in Chalmers' *Poets,* vol.
vi., and have been edited, together with the plays, by Mr. W. C. Haz
(2 vols., London, 1874).

ORSAMES' SONG.

WHY so pale and wan, fond lover?
  Prithee, why so pale?
Will, when looking well can't move her,
  Looking ill prevail?
  Prithee, why so pale?

Why so dull and mute, young sinner?
  Prithee, why so mute?

Will, when speaking well can't win her,
     Saying nothing do 't?
     Prithee, why so mute?

Quit, quit, for shame, this will not move:
     This cannot take her.
If of herself she will not love,
     Nothing can make her:
     The devil take her!

CONSTANCY.

OUT upon it, I have loved,
     Three whole days together;
And am like to love three more,
     If it prove fair weather.

Time shall moult away his wings,
     Ere he shall discover
In the whole wide world again
     Such a constant lover.

But the spite on 't is, no praise
     Is due at all to me:
Love with me had made no stays,
     Had it any been but she.

Had it any been but she,
     And that very face,
There had been at least ere this
     A dozen in her place.

RICHARD LOVELACE.
(1618–1658.)

From the volume entitled *Lucasta*, 1649. His poems have been edited by Mr. W. C. Hazlitt in the Library of Old Authors, 1864.

GOING TO THE WARS.

TELL me not, sweet, I am unkind,
    That from the nunnery
Of thy chaste breast and quiet mind
    To war and arms I fly.

True, a new mistress now I chase,
    The first foe in the field,
And with a stronger faith embrace
    A sword, a horse, a shield.

Yet this inconstancy is such
    As you too shall adore,—
I could not love thee, dear, so much,
    Loved I not honour more.

TO ALTHEA FROM PRISON

WHEN love with unconfinèd wings
    Hovers within my gates,
And my divine Althea brings
    To whisper at the grates;
When I lie tangled in her hair,
    And fettered to her eye,
The birds that wanton in the air
    Know no such liberty.

When flowing cups run swiftly round
    With no allaying Thames,
Our careless heads with roses bound,
    Our hearts with loyal flames;

When thirsty grief in wine we steep,
  When healths and draughts go free,
Fishes that tipple in the deep
  Know no such liberty.

When, like committed linnets, I
  With shriller throat shall sing
The sweetness, mercy, majesty,
  And glories of my King;
When I shall voice aloud, how good
  He is, how great should be,
Enlargèd winds that curl the flood
  Know no such liberty.

Stone walls do not a prison make,
  Nor iron bars a cage;
Minds innocent and quiet take
  That for an hermitage;
If I have freedom in my love,
  And in my soul am free,
Angels alone, that soar above,
  Enjoy such liberty.

THE ROSE.

SWEET, serene, sky-like flower,
  Hasten to adorn her bower,
    From thy long cloudy bed
    Shoot forth thy damask head.

New-startled blush of Flora,
The grief of pale Aurora
  (Who will contest no more),
    Haste, haste to strew her floor!

Vermilion ball that's given
From lip to lip in heaven,

Love's couch's coverled,
Haste, haste to make her bed.

Dear offspring of pleased Venus
And jolly plump Silenus,
    Haste, haste to deck the hair
    Of the only sweetly fair!

See! rosy is her bower,
Her floor is all this flower,
    Her bed a rosy nest
    By a bed of roses pressed!

JAMES SHIRLEY.

(1596–1666.)

The resonant verses on Death's Final Conquest occur in the *Contention of Ajax and Ulysses*, 1659. The second song is from *The Imposture, a Tragi-Comedy*, 1652 (licensed 1640). It was first printed in the 1646 edition of Shirley's *Poems*. Shirley's *Dramatic Works and Poems* have been edited by Gifford and Dyce (6 vols., London, 1833).

A DIRGE.

THE glories of our blood and state
    Are shadows, not substantial things;
There is no armour against fate;
    Death lays his icy hand on kings:
        Sceptre and crown
        Must tumble down,
    And in the dust be equal made
    With the poor crooked scythe and spade.

Some men with swords may reap the field,
    And plant fresh laurels where they kill;
But their strong nerves at last must yield;
    They tame but one another still:

Early or late
They stoop to fate,
And must give up their murmuring breath,
When they, pale captives, creep to death.

The garlands wither on your brow;
Then boast no more your mighty deeds;
Upon Death's purple altar now,
See, where the victor-victim bleeds:
Your head must come
To the cold tomb:
Only the actions of the just
Smell sweet and blossom in their dust.

PEACE RESTORED.

YOU virgins, that did late despair
To keep your wealth from cruel men,
Tie up in silk your careless hair,
Soft peace is come again.

Now lovers' eyes may gently shoot
A flame that will not kill;
The drum was angry, but the lute
Shall whisper what you will.

Sing Iö, Iö! for his sake
That hath restored your drooping heads:
With choice of sweetest flowers make
A garden where he treads;

Whilst we whole groves of laurel bring,
A petty triumph to his brow,
Who is the master of our spring,
And all the bloom we owe.

RICHARD BROME.

(? –1652?.)

THE MERRY BEGGARS.

From *A Jovial Crew, or the Merry Beggars,* 1652 (acted 1641?).

COME, come away! the spring,
　　By every bird that can but sing
Or chirp a note, doth now invite
Us forth to taste of his delight,
In field, in grove, on hill, in dale;
But above all the nightingale,
Who in her sweetness strives to outdo
The loudness of the hoarse cuckoo.
　　"Cuckoo," cries he; "Jug, jug, jug," sings she;
　　From bush to bush, from tree to tree;
　　Why in one place then tarry we?

Come away! why do we stay?
We have no debt or rent to pay;
No bargains or accompts to make,
Nor land or lease to let or take:
Or if we had, should that remore[1] us
When all the world's our own before us,
And where we pass and make resort,
It is our kingdom and our court?
　　"Cuckoo," cries he, &c.

[1] hinder.

CHARLES COTTON.

(1630–1687.)

ODE: LAURA SLEEPING.

From his *Poems on Several Occasions*, 1689, reprinted in
Chalmers' *Poets*, vol. vi.

WINDS, whisper gently whilst she sleeps,
    And fan her with your cooling wings;
Whilst she her drops of beauty weeps,
    From pure, and yet-unrivalled springs.

Glide over beauty's field, her face,
    To kiss her lip and cheek be bold,
But with a calm and stealing pace,
    Neither too rude, nor yet too cold.

Play in her beams, and crisp her hair,
    With such a gale as wings soft love,
And with so sweet, so rich an air,
    As breathes from the Arabian grove.

A breath as hushed as lover's sigh,
    Or that unfolds the morning's door;
Sweet as the winds that gently fly,
    To sweep the Spring's enamelled floor.

Murmur soft music to her dreams,
    That pure and unpolluted run,
Like to the new-born crystal streams,
    Under the bright enamoured sun

But when she waking shall display
    Her light, retire within your bar:
Her breath is life, her eyes are day,
    And all mankind her creatures are.

WILLIAM STRODE.

(1600?–1644.)

SONG: IN COMMENDATION OF MUSIC.

From a seventeenth-century miscellany entitled *Wit Restored*, 1658.

WHEN whispering strains do softly steal
    With creeping passion through the heart,
And when at every touch we feel
    Our pulses beat, and bear a part;
      When threads can make
      A heart-string quake;—
      Philosophy
      Can scarce deny
    The soul consists of harmony.

    .   .   .   .

Oh, lull me, lull me, charming air,
    My senses rocked with wonder sweet!
Like snow on wool thy fallings are,
    Soft like a spirit are thy feet.
      Grief who need fear
      That hath an ear?
      Down let him lie,
      And slumbering die,
    And change his soul for harmony.

SAMUEL SHEPPARD. (?)

(Fl. 1650.)

EPITHALAMIUM.

From *The Loves of Amandus and Sophronia*, 1650.

HEAVENLY fair Urania's son,
   Thou that dwell'st on Helicon,
Hymen, O thy brows impale,
To the bride the bridegroom hale
Take thy saffron robe and come
With sweet-flowered marjoram;
Yellow socks of woollen wear,
With a smiling look appear;
Shrill Epithalamiums sing,
Let this day with pleasure spring;
Nimbly dance; the flaming tree
Take in that fair hand of thine.
Let good auguries combine
For the pair that now are wed;
Let their joys be nourishèd
Like a myrtle, ever green,
Ownèd by the Cyprian queen,
Who fosters it with rosy dew,
Where her nymphs their sport pursue.
Leave th' Aonian cave behind
(Come, O come with willing mind!)
And the Thespian rocks, whence drill
Aganippe waters still.
Chastest virgins, you that are
Either for to make or mar,
Make the air with Hymen ring,
Hymen, Hymenæus sing!

GEORGE DIGBY, EARL OF BRISTOL. (?)
(1612–1676.)

SONG.

From the comedy of *Elvira*, 1667; in Hazlitt's Dodsley, vol. xv.

SEE, O see!
   How every tree,
Every bower,
Every flower,
A new life gives to others' joys,
   Whilst that I
   Grief-stricken lie,
   Nor can meet
   With any sweet
But what faster mine destroys.
What are all the senses' pleasures,
When the mind has lost all measures?

   Hear, O hear!
   How sweet and clear
   The nightingale
   And waters' fall
In concert join for others' ears,
   Whilst to me,
   For harmony,
   Every air
   Echoes despair,
And every drop provokes a tear.
What are all the senses' pleasures,
When the mind has lost all measures?

EDMUND WALLER.
(1605–1687.)

Three editions of Waller's *Poems*, in which the first three selections given below were published, appeared in 1645. The contents do not vary. The last extract was written by Waller when he was over eighty years of age. Waller's *Poems* are reprinted in Chalmers' *Poets*, vol. viii., also in the Muses' Library, 1892, edited by Mr. G. Thorn Drury.

ON A GIRDLE.

THAT which her slender waist confined,
   Shall now my joyful temples bind;
No monarch but would give his crown
His arms might do what this has done.

It was my heaven's extremest sphere,
The pale which held that lovely deer;
My joy, my grief, my hope, my love,
Did all within this circle move.

A narrow compass, and yet there
Dwelt all that's good and all that's fair;
Give me but what this ribband bound,
Take all the rest the sun goes round.

SONG.

GO, lovely Rose,
Tell her that wastes her time and me,
   That now she knows
When I resemble her to thee
How sweet and fair she seems to be.

   Tell her that's young,
And shuns to have her graces spied,
   That had'st thou sprung
In deserts where no men abide,
Thou must have uncommended died.

Small is the worth
Of beauty from the light retired;
Bid her come forth,
Suffer herself to be desired,
And not blush so to be admired.

Then die, that she
The common fate of all things rare
May read in thee,
How small a part of time they share
Who are so wondrous sweet and fair.

TO A LADY IN RETIREMENT.

SEES not my love, how Time resumes
The glory which he lent these flowers?
Though none should taste of their perfumes
Yet must they live but some few hours:
Time, what we forbear, devours!

Had Helen, or the Egyptian queen,
Been ne'er so thrifty of their graces,
Those beauties must at length have been
The spoil of age, which finds out faces
In the most retired places.

Should some malignant planet bring
A barren drought, or ceaseless shower,
Upon the autumn, or the spring,
And spare us neither fruit nor flower;
Winter would not stay an hour.

Could the resolve of Love's neglect
Preserve you from the violation
Of coming years, then more respect
Were due to so divine a fashion;
Nor would I indulge my passion.

THE LAST PROSPECT.

THE seas are quiet when the winds give o'er;
　　So, calm are we when passions are no more!
For then we know how vain it was to boast
Of fleeting things, so certain to be lost.
Clouds of affection from our younger eyes
Conceal that emptiness which age descries.

　　The soul's dark cottage, battered and decayed,
Lets in new light, through chinks that time has made;
Stronger by weakness, wiser, men become,
As they draw near to their eternal home:
Leaving the old, both worlds at once they view,
That stand upon the threshold of the new.

ABRAHAM COWLEY.

(1618–1667.)

ON SOLITUDE.

Accompanying the prose Essay on Solitude, in the *Essays in Verse
and Prose*, 1668.　Cowley's Works, edited by Dr. Grosart, occupy two
volumes of the Chertsey Worthies Library.　His poems are included in
vol. vii. of Chalmers' *Poets*.

HAIL, old patrician trees, so great and good!
　　Hail, ye plebeian underwood!
　　Where the poetic birds rejoice,
And for their quiet nests and plenteous food,
　　Pay with their grateful voice.

Hail, the poor muse's richest manor seat!
　　Ye country houses and retreat
　　Which all the happy gods so love,
That for you oft they quit their bright and great
　　Metropolis above.

Here nature does a house for me erect,
 Nature the wisest architect,
  Who those fond artists does despise
That can the fair and living trees neglect,
  Yet the dead timber prize.

Here let me careless and unthoughtful lying,
 Hear the soft winds above me flying
  With all their wanton boughs dispute,
And the more tuneful birds to both replying,
  Nor be myself too mute.

A silver stream shall roll his waters near,
 Gilt with the sunbeams here and there,
  On whose enamelled bank I 'll walk,
And see how prettily they smile, and hear
  How prettily they talk.

Ah wretched, and too solitary he
 Who loves not his own company!
  He 'll feel the weight of 't many a day
Unless he call in sin or vanity
  To help to bear 't away.

O Solitude, first state of human-kind!
 Which blest remained till man did find
  Even his own helper's company.
As soon as two (alas!) together joined,
  The serpent made up three.

The god himself, through countless ages thee
 His sole companion chose to be,
  Thee, sacred Solitude alone,
Before the branchy head of number's tree
  Sprang from the trunk of one.

Thou (though men think thine an unactive part)
 Dost break and tame the unruly heart,
  Which else would know no settled pace,

Making it more well managed by thy art,
    With swiftness and with grace.

Thou the faint beams of reason's scattered light,
    Dost like a burning-glass unite,
    Dost multiply the feeble heat,
And fortify the strength, till thou dost bright
    And noble fires beget.

Whilst this hard truth I teach, methinks, I see
    The monster London laugh at me;
    I should at thee too, foolish city,
If it were fit to laugh at misery,
    But thy estate I pity.

Let but thy wicked men from out thee go,
    And all the fools that crowd thee so,
    Even thou who dost thy millions boast,
A village less than Islington wilt grow,
    A solitude almost.

JAMES GRAHAM, MARQUIS OF MONTROSE.

(1612–1650.)

MY DEAR AND ONLY LOVE.

See Scott's *Legend of Montrose*, and Napier's *Memoirs of Montrose*.
Other specimens of Montrose are given in Hannah's *Courtly Poets*.

MY dear and only love, I pray,
    This little world of thee
Be governed by no other sway
    But purest monarchy.
For if confusion have a part,
    Which virtuous souls abhor,

And hold a synod in thy heart,
 I 'll never love thee more.

Like Alexander I will reign,
 And I will reign alone,
My thoughts shall evermore disdain
 A rival on my throne.
He either fears his fate too much,
 Or his deserts are small,
That dares not put it to the touch,
 To win or lose it all.

But I must rule and govern still,
 And always give the law,
And have each subject at my will,
 And all to stand in awe.
But 'gainst my battery if I find
 Thou shunn'st the prize so sore
As that thou sett'st me up a blind,
 I 'll never love thee more.

If in the empire of thy heart,
 Where I should solely be,
Another do pretend a part,
 And dares to vie with me;
Or if committees thou erect,
 And go on such a score,
I 'll sing and laugh at thy neglect,
 And never love thee more.

But if thou wilt be constant then,
 And faithful of thy word,
I 'll make thee glorious by my pen,
 And famous by my sword.
I 'll serve thee in such noble ways
 Was never heard before;
I 'll crown and deck thee all with bays,
 And love thee evermore.

EDWARD, LORD HERBERT OF CHERBURY.

(1581–1648.)

LOVE'S ETERNITY.

Portions of *An Ode, upon a Question moved whether Love should
Continue for Ever*, published among his *Occasional Verses*, 1665.   His
Poems have been edited by Mr. Churton Collins (London, 1881).

O NO, Beloved: I am most sure
    These virtuous habits we acquire,
    As being with the soul entire,
Must with it evermore endure.

Else should our souls in vain elect,
    And vainer yet were Heaven's laws,
    When to an everlasting cause
They gave a perishing effect.

These eyes again thine eyes shall see,
    And hands again these hands enfold,
    And all chaste pleasures can be told
Shall with us everlasting be.

For if no use of sense remain,
    When bodies once this life forsake
    Or they could no delight partake,
Why should they ever rise again?

An if every imperfect mind
    Make love the end of knowledge here,
    How perfect will our love be, where
All imperfection is refined!

So when from hence we shall be gone,
    And be no more, nor you, nor I,
    As one another's mystery,
Each shall be both, yet both but one.

GEORGE HERBERT.

(1593–1633.)

VIRTUE.

From *The Temple, Sacred Poems and Private Ejaculations*, 1633.
Dr. Grosart's edition of the *Complete Works* of Herbert in the Fuller
Worthies Library, 3 vols., 1874, is the standard modern edition.

SWEET day, so cool, so calm, so bright!
    The bridal of the earth and sky,—
The dew shall weep thy fall to-night:
    For thou must die.

Sweet rose, whose hue, angry and brave,
    Bids the rash gazer wipe his eye,
Thy root is ever in its grave,
    And thou must die.

Sweet spring, full of sweet days and roses,
    A box where sweets compacted lie,
My music shows ye have your closes
    And all must die.

Only a sweet and virtuous soul,
    Like seasoned timber, never gives;
But though the whole world turn to coal,
    Then chiefly lives.

THE COLLAR.

I STRUCK the board, and cried, "No more;
    I will abroad!
What, shall I ever sigh and pine?
My lines and life are free; free as the road,
  Loose as the wind, as large as store.
      Shall I be still in suit?

Have I no harvest but a thorn
To let me blood, and not restore
What I have lost with cordial fruit?
        Sure there was wine
Before my sighs did dry it; there was corn
    Before my tears did drown it;
Is the year only lost to me?
        Have I no bays to crown it,
No flowers, no garlands gay? all blasted,
            All wasted?
    Not so, my heart; but there is fruit,
            And thou hast hands.
    Recover all thy sigh-blown age
On double pleasures; leave thy cold dispute
Of what is fit and not; forsake thy cage,
            Thy rope of sands
Which petty thoughts have made; and made to thee
    Good cable, to enforce and draw,
            And be thy law,
    While thou didst wink and wouldst not see.
            Away! take heed;
            I will abroad.
Call in thy death's-head there, tie up thy fears:
            He that forbears
        To suit and serve his need
            Deserves his load."
But as I raved, and grew more fierce and wild
            At every word,
    Methought I heard one calling, "Child";
        And I replied, "My Lord".

LOVE.

LOVE bade me welcome; yet my soul drew back,
　　Guilty of dust and sin.
But quick-eyed Love, observing me grow slack
　　From my first entrance in,
Drew nearer to me, sweetly questioning,
　　If I lacked anything.

"A guest," I answered, "worthy to be here":
　　Love said, "You shall be he".
"I, the unkind, ungrateful? Ah, my dear,
　　I cannot look on Thee!"
Love took my hand and smiling did reply,
　　"Who made the eyes but I?"

"Truth, Lord; but I have marred them: let my shame
　　Go where it doth deserve."
"And know you not," says Love, "Who bore the blame?"
　　"My dear, then I will serve."
"You must sit down," says Love, "and taste my meat."
　　So I did sit and eat.

FRANCIS QUARLES.

(1592–1644.)

"PHOSPHOR, BRING THE DAY."

From the *Emblems, Divine and Moral,* 1635. Quarles's *Works,*
edited by Dr. Grosart, are in the Chertsey Worthies Library
(3 vols., 1880).

WILL'T ne'er be morning? Will that promised light
　Ne'er break, and clear those clouds of night?
　　Sweet Phosphor, bring the day,
　　Whose conquering ray
May chase these fogs: sweet Phosphor, bring the day.

How long, how long shall these benighted eyes
    Languish in shades, like feeble flies
Expecting spring?   How long shall darkness soil
    The face of earth, and thus beguile
Our souls of sprightful action?   When, when will day
    Begin to dawn, whose new-born ray
May gild the weathercocks of our devotion,
    And give our unsouled souls new motion?
        Sweet Phosphor, bring the day:
        The light will fray
These horrid mists: sweet Phosphor, bring the day.

Let those whose eyes, like owls, abhor the light—
    Let those have night that love the night:
        Sweet Phosphor, bring the day.
        How sad delay
Afflicts dull hopes!   Sweet Phosphor, bring the day.

Alas! my light-in-vain-expecting eyes
    Can find no objects but what rise
From this poor mortal blaze, a dying spark
    Of Vulcan's forge, whose flames are dark,—
A dangerous, dull, blue-burning light,
    As melancholy as the night:
Here's all the suns that glister in the sphere
    Of earth: Ah me! what comfort's here!
        Sweet Phosphor, bring the day.
        Haste, haste away
Heaven's loitering lamp: sweet Phosphor, bring the day.

Blow, Ignorance.   O thou, whose idle knee
    Rocks earth into a lethargy,
And with thy sooty fingers hast benight
    The world's fair cheeks, blow, blow thy spite;
Since thou hast puffed our greater taper, do
    Puff on, and out the lesser too.

If e'er that breath-exiléd flame return,
　　Thou hast not blown, as it will burn.
　　　　Sweet Phosphor, bring the day:
　　　　Light will repay
The wrongs of night: sweet Phosphor, bring the day.

HENRY MORE.
(1614–1687.)
THE PHILOSOPHER'S DEVOTION.

From *Philosophical Poems*, 1647; it also appears in the *Divine Dialogues*, 1668. More's Poems, edited by Dr. Grosart, 1878, are n the Chertsey Worthies Library.

SING aloud! His praise rehearse
　Who hath made the universe.
He the boundless heavens has spread,
All the vital orbs has kned;
He that on Olympus high
Tends his flocks with watchful eye,
And this eye has multiplied
Midst each flock for to reside[1].
Thus, as round about they stray,
Toucheth each with outstretched ray;
Nimble they hold on their way,
Shaping out their night and day.
Summer, winter, autumn, spring,
Their inclinèd axes bring.
Never slack they; none respires,
Dancing round their central fires.
In due order as they move,
Echoes sweet be gently drove
Thorough heaven's vast hollowness
Which unto all corners press:

　　　　[1] the suns in their systems.

Music that the heart of Jove
Moves to joy and sportful love;
Fills the listening sailers' ears
Riding on the wandering spheres:
Neither speech nor language is
Where their voice is not transmiss.

God is good, is wise, is strong,
Witness all the creature throng,
Is confessed by every tongue;
All things back from whence they sprung,
As the thankful rivers pay
What they borrowed of the sea.

Now myself I do resign;
Take me whole: I all am thine.
Save me, God, from self-desire,
Death's pit, dark hell's raging fire,
Envy, hatred, vengeance, ire;
Let not lust my soul bemire.

Quit from these, thy praise I 'll sing,
Loudly sweep the trembling string.
Bear a part, O Wisdom's sons,
Freed from vain religions!
Lo! from far I you salute,
Sweetly warbling on my lute—
India, Egypt, Araby,
Asia, Greece, and Tartary,
Carmel-tracts, and Lebanon,
With the Mountains of the Moon,
From whence muddy Nile doth run,
Or wherever else you won[1]:
Breathing in one vital air,
One we are though distant far.
Rise at once; let 's sacrifice:

[1] dwell.

Odours sweet perfume the skies;
See how heavenly lightning fires
Hearts inflamed with high aspires!
All the substance of our souls
Up in clouds of incense rolls.
Leave we nothing to ourselves
Save a voice—what need we else!
Or an hand to wear and tire
On the thankful lute or lyre!

Sing aloud! His praise rehearse
Who hath made the universe.

RICHARD CRASHAW.
(1613?-1649.)

The Wishes first appeared in Crashaw's *The Delights of the Muses,*
1646. *The Flaming Heart: upon the Book and Picture of the Sera-*
phical Saint Teresa first appeared in the second edition of *Steps to the*
Temple, Sacred Poems, in 1648. The next piece is Crashaw's own trans-
lation, in 1646, of his Latin epigram No. 1, *Pharisæus et Publicanus,*
in his *Epigrammatum Sacrorum Liber,* 1634. Crashaw's *Works,* edited
by Dr. Grosart, 1872, are in the Fuller Worthies Library; his Poems are
included in vol. vi. of Chalmers' *Poets.*

WISHES: TO HIS SUPPOSED MISTRESS.

WHOE'ER she be,
    That not impossible she
That shall command my heart and me;

Where'er she lie,
Locked up from mortal eye,
In shady leaves of Destiny;

Till that ripe birth
Of studied Fate stand forth,
And teach her fair steps tread our Earth;

Till that divine
Idea take a shrine
Of crystal flesh, through which to shine;

Meet you her, my wishes,
Bespeak her to my blisses,
And be ye called, my absent kisses.

I wish her, beauty
That owes not all its duty
To gaudy tire or glistering shoe tie.

    .   .   .   .   .   .

A face that 's best
By its own beauty drest,
And can alone commend the rest.

    .   .   .   .   .   .

A cheek where Youth,
And blood, with pen of Truth
Write, what their reader sweetly ru'th.

    .   .   .   .   .   .

Lips, where all day
A lover's kiss may play
Yet carry nothing thence away.

    .   .   .   .   .

Eyes, that displace
The neighbour diamond, and out-face
That sunshine, by their own sweet grace.

Tresses, that wear
Jewels, but to declare
How much themselves more precious are.

    .   .   .   .   .   .

Days, that need borrow,
No part of their good morrow
From a forespent night of sorrow.

    .   .   .   .   .

Life, that dares send
A challenge to his end
And when it comes say, Welcome friend!

.   .   , ...

I wish her store
Of worth may leave her poor
Of wishes; and I wish—no more.

Now if Time knows
That her, whose radiant brows
Weave them a garland of my vows;

.   .   .   .

Her that dares be,
What these lines wish to see:
I seek no further: it is she.

THE FLAMING HEART.

L IVE in these conquering leaves; live all the same;
    And walk through all tongues one triumphant flame.
Live here, great heart; and love and die and kill;
And bleed and wound and yield and conquer still.
Let this immortal life where'er it comes
Walk in a crowd of loves and martyrdoms.
Let mystic deaths wait on 't; and wise souls be
The love-slain witnesses of this life of thee.
O sweet incendiary! show here thy art,
Upon this carcass of a hard cold heart;
Let all thy scattered shafts of light, that play
Among the leaves of thy large books of day,
Combined against this breast at once break in,
And take away from me my self and sin;
This gracious robbery shall thy bounty be,
And my best fortunes such fair spoils of me.
O thou undaunted daughter of desires!
   (M 349)

By all thy dower of lights and fires;
By all the eagle in thee, all the dove;
By all thy lives and deaths of love ;
By thy large draughts of intellectual day;
And by thy thirsts of love more large than they;
By all thy brim-filled bowls of fierce desire;
By thy last morning's draught of liquid fire;
By the full kingdom of that final kiss
That seized thy parting soul, and sealed thee His;
By all the heaven thou hast in Him
(Fair sister of the seraphim);
By all of Him we have in thee,
Leave nothing of my self in me.
Let me so read thy life, that I
Unto all life of mine may die.

TWO WENT UP INTO THE TEMPLE TO PRAY.

TWO went to pray?   O rather say
    One went to brag, the other to pray:

One stands up close and treads on high,
Where the other dares not send his eye.

One nearer to God's altar trod,
The other to the altar's God.

———————

HENRY VAUGHAN.

(1621–1695).

The *Works* of Henry Vaughan, "Silurist", fill four volumes of the
Fuller Worthies Library, edited by Dr. A. B. Grosart, 1871; they also
appear in the Muses' Library, edited by Mr. E. K. Chambers, 1896. His
Sacred Poems have been reprinted also in the Aldine Poets, 1847, edited
by the Rev. H. F. Lyte, and his *Secular Poems* have been edited by
Mr. J. R. Tutin, Hull, 1893. The first three selections are found in
Silex Scintillans, 1650; the next in Part II. of the same title, 1655; and
the last from *Thalia Rediviva*, 1678.

THE RETREAT.

HAPPY those early days, when I
   Shined in my angel-infancy!
Before I understood this place
Appointed for my second race,
Or taught my soul to fancy ought
But a white, celestial thought;
When yet I had not walked above
A mile or two from my first love,
And looking back—at that short space—
Could see a glimpse of His bright face;
When on some gilded cloud or flower
My gazing soul would dwell an hour,
And in those weaker glories spy
Some shadows of eternity;
Before I taught my tongue to wound
My conscience with a sinful sound,
Or had the black art to dispense,
A several sin to every sense,
But felt through all this fleshly dress
Bright shoots of everlastingness.
   O how I long to travel back,
And tread again that ancient track!
That I might once more reach that plain,
Where first I left my glorious train;

From whence the enlightened spirit sees
That shady city of palm trees.
But ah! my soul with too much stay
Is drunk, and staggers in the way!
Some men a forward motion love,
But I by backward steps would move;
And when this dust falls to the urn,
In that state I came, return.

THE WORLD.

I SAW Eternity the other night,
  Like a great ring of pure and endless light,
All calm, as it was bright;
And round beneath it Time in hours, days, years,
  Driven by the spheres
Like a vast shadow moved; in which the world
  And all her train were hurled.

PEACE.

MY soul, there is a country
    Far beyond the stars,
Where stands a wingèd sentry
    All skilful in the wars;
There, above noise and danger,
    Sweet Peace sits crowned with smiles,
And One born in a manger
    Commands the beauteous files.
He is thy gracious friend,
    And, O my soul awake!
Did in pure love descend
    To die here for thy sake,
If thou canst get but thither,
    There grows the flower of peace,

The rose that cannot wither,
    Thy fortress and thy ease.
Leave then thy foolish ranges,
    For none can thee secure,
But One, who never changes,
    Thy God, thy life, thy cure.

BEYOND THE VEIL.

THEY are all gone into the world of light!
    And I alone sit lingering here;
Their very memory is fair and bright,
    And my sad thoughts doth clear.

It glows and glitters in my cloudy breast,
    Like stars upon some gloomy grove,
Or those faint beams in which this hill is drest,
    After the sun's remove.

I see them walking in an air of glory,
    Whose light doth trample on my days:
My days, which are at best but dull and hoary,
    Mere glimmering and decays

O holy Hope! and high Humility,
    High as the heavens above!
These are your walks, and you have showed them me,
    To kindle my cold love.

Dear, beauteous Death! the jewel of the just,
    Shining no where, but in the dark;
What mysteries do lie beyond thy dust;
    Could man outlook that mark!

He that hath found some fledged bird's nest, may know
    At first sight if the bird be flown;
But what fair well or grove he sings in now,
    That is to him unknown.

And yet as angels in some brighter dreams
   Call to the soul, when man doth sleep,
So some strange thoughts transcend our wonted themes,
   And into glory peep.

If a star were confined into a tomb,
   The captive flames must needs burn there;
But when the hand that locked her up, gives room,
   She'll shine through all the sphere.

O Father of eternal life, and all
   Created glories under Thee!
Resume Thy spirit from this world of thrall
   Into true liberty.

Either disperse these mists, which blot and fill
   My perspective—still—as they pass:
Or else remove me hence unto that hill,
   Where I shall need no glass.

THE CHOSEN PATH.

WELCOME, pure thoughts and peaceful hours,
   Enriched with sunshine and with showers!
Welcome fair hopes and holy cares,
The not-to-be-repented shares
Of time and business; the sure road
Unto my last and loved abode!
   O supreme bliss!
The circle, centre, and abyss
Of blessings, never let me miss
Nor leave that path, which leads to Thee,
Who art alone all things to me!
I hear, I see, all the long day,
The noise and pomp of the 'broad way';
I note their coarse and proud approaches,

Their silks, perfumes, and glittering coaches.
But in the 'narrow way' to Thee
I observe only poverty,
And despised things; and all along
The ragged, mean, and humble throng
Are still on foot; and as they go
They sigh, and say their Lord went so!

Give me my staff then, as it stood
When green and growing in the wood.
(Those stones, which for the altar served
Might not be smoothed nor finely carved:)
With this poor stick, I'll pass the ford,
As Jacob did.   And Thy dear word,
As Thou hast dressed it, not as wit
And depraved tastes have poisoned it,
Shall in the passage be my meat,
And none else will Thy servant eat.
Thus, thus, and in no other sort,
Will I set forth, though laughed at for't;
And leaving the wise world their way,
Go through, though judged to go astray.

JOHN WILMOT, EARL OF ROCHESTER.
(1647–1680.)

From his *Poems on Several Occasions,* 1680.   His Selected Poems are reprinted in vol. viii. of Chalmers' *Poets.*

SONG.

DEAR, from thine arms then let me fly,
    That my fantastic mind may prove
The torments it deserves to try,
    That tears my fixed heart from my love.

When wearied with a world of woe
   To thy safe bosom I retire,
Where love, and peace, and truth, do flow,
   May I contented there expire!

Lest, once more wandering from that heaven,
   I fall on some base heart unblest,
Faithless to thee, false, unforgiven,
   And lose my everlasting rest.

TO HIS MISTRESS.

MY light thou art, without thy glorious sight
   My eyes are darkened with eternal night;
My love, thou art my way, my life, my light.

Thou art my way, I wander if thou fly;
Thou art my light, if hid, how blind am I!
Thou art my life, if thou withdraw'st I die.

Thou art my life, if thou but turn away,
My life 's a thousand deaths.   Thou art my way;
Without thee, love, I travel not, but stray.

LOVE AND LIFE.

ALL my past life is mine no more,
   The flying hours are gone;
Like transitory dreams given o'er,
Whose images are kept in store
   By memory alone.

The time that is to come is not;
   How can it then be mine?
The present moment 's all my lot;
And that, as fast as it is got,
   Phillis, is only thine.

Then talk not of inconstancy,
  False hearts, and broken vows;
If I, by miracle, can be
This live-long minute true to thee,
  'T is all that Heaven allows.

SIR CHARLES SEDLEY.

(1639–1701.)

TO CELIA.

Sedley's first publication, a comedy, appeared in 1668. His works
were collected in 1702. There is no edition in this century. This song
first appeared in *A Collection of Poems by Several Hands*, 1693.

NOT, Celia, that I juster am
  Or better than the rest;
For I would change each hour, like them,
  Were not my heart at rest.

But I am tied to very thee
  By every thought I have;
Thy face I only care to see,
  Thy heart I only crave.

All that in woman is adored
  In thy dear self I find;
For the whole sex can but afford
  The handsome and the kind

Why then should I seek further store,
  And still make love anew?
When change itself can give no more,
  'T is easy to be true.

JOHN DRYDEN.
(1631–1700.)

The best edition of Dryden's *Poetical Works* is that of Mr. W. D. Christie (London, 1893), in which the "Songs, Odes, and Lyrical Pieces" occupy pages 367–384. *Alexander's Feast* was written in 1697, and the *Song for St. Cecilia's Day* just ten years earlier. The songs are from *The Indian Emperor*, 1665, from *Œdipus* (by Dryden and Lee), 1679, and from *King Arthur*, 1691, respectively.

ALEXANDER'S FEAST; OR, THE POWER OF MUSIC.

A SONG IN HONOUR OF ST. CECILIA'S DAY, 1697.

'TWAS at the royal feast for Persia won
    By Philip's warlike son:
    Aloft in awful state
    The godlike hero sate
    On his impartial throne;
His valiant peers were placed around;
Their brows with roses and with myrtles bound:
(So should desert in arms be crowned).
The lovely Thais, by his side,
Sate like a blooming Eastern bride,
In flower of youth and beauty's pride.
    Happy, happy, happy pair!
      None but the brave,
      None but the brave,
    None but the brave deserves the fair.

Chorus.

    Happy, happy, happy pair!
      None but the brave,
      None but the brave,
    None but the brave deserves the fair.

Timotheus, placed on high
　　Amid the tuneful quire,
With flying fingers touched the lyre:
　　The trembling notes ascend the sky,
　　　And heavenly joys inspire.
The song began from Jove,
Who left his blissful seats above,
(Such is the power of mighty love).
A dragon's fiery form belied the god:
Sublime on radiant spires he rode,
When he to fair Olympia pressed;
And while he sought her snowy breast,
Then round her slender waist he curled,
And stamped an image of himself, a sovereign of the world.
The listening crowd admire the lofty sound,
A present deity, they shout around;
A present deity, the vaulted roofs rebound:
　　　With ravished ears
　　　The monarch hears,
　　　Assumes the god,
　　　Affects to nod,
　　And seems to shake the spheres.

Chorus.
　　　With ravished ears
　　　The monarch hears,
　　　Assumes the god,
　　　Affects to nod,
　　And seems to shake the spheres.

The praise of Bacchus then the sweet musician sung,
　Of Bacchus ever fair, and ever young,
　　The jolly god in triumph comes;
　Sound the trumpets, beat the drums;
　　Flushed with a purple grace
　　He shows his honest face:

Now give the hautboys breath; he comes, he comes.
 Bacchus, ever fair and young,
  Drinking joys did first ordain;
   Bacchus' blessings are a treasure,
   Drinking is the soldier's pleasure;
    Rich the treasure,
    Sweet the pleasure,
   Sweet is pleasure after pain.

Chorus.

   Bacchus' blessings are a treasure,
   Drinking is the soldier's pleasure;
    Rich the treasure,
    Sweet the pleasure,
   Sweet is pleasure after pain.

 Soothed with the sound the king grew vain;
  Fought all his battles o'er again;
And thrice he routed all his foes, and thrice he slew the
 slain.
  The master saw the madness rise,
  His glowing cheeks, his ardent eyes;
  And while he heaven and earth defied,
   Changed his hand, and checked his pride.
   He chose a mournful Muse,
   Soft pity to infuse;
  He sung Darius great and good,
   By too severe a fate,
  Fallen, fallen, fallen, fallen,
   Fallen from his high estate,
  And weltering in his blood;
  Deserted at his utmost need
  By those his former bounty fed,
   On the bare earth exposed he lies,
   With not a friend to close his eyes.

With downcast looks the joyless victor sate,
   Revolving in his altered soul
      The various turns of chance below;
   And, now and then, a sigh he stole,
     And tears began to flow.

Chorus.

   Revolving in his altered soul
      The various turns of chance below;
   And, now and then, a sigh he stole,
     And tears began to flow.

  The mighty master smiled to see
  That love was in the next degree
  'T was but a kindred-sound to move,
  For pity melts the mind to love.
    Softly sweet, in Lydian measures,
    Soon he soothed his soul to pleasures.
  War, he sung, is toil and trouble;
  Honour but an empty bubble;
    Never ending, still beginning,
  Fighting still, and still destroying:
    If the world be worth thy winning,
  Think, O think, it worth enjoying:
    Lovely Thais sits beside thee,
    Take the goods the gods provide thee
The many rend the skies with loud applause,
So Love was crowned, but Music won the cause.
  The prince, unable to conceal his pain,
       Gazed on the fair
       Who caused his care,
  And sighed and looked, sighed and looked,
  Sighed and looked, and sighed again;
At length, with love and wine at once oppressed,
The vanquished victor sunk upon her breast.

Chorus.

The prince, unable to conceal his pain,
   Gazed on the fair
   Who caused his care,
 And sighed and looked, sighed and looked,
 Sighed and looked, and sighed again;
At length, with love and wine at once oppressed,
The vanquished victor sunk upon her breast.

Now strike the golden lyre again;
A louder yet, and yet a louder strain.
Break his bands of sleep asunder,
And rouse him, like a rattling peal of thunder.
  Hark, hark, the horrid sound
   Has raised up his head;
   As awaked from the dead,
  And, amazed, he stares around.
 "Revenge, revenge!" Timotheus cries;
  "See the Furies arise;
  See the snakes that they rear
  And how they hiss in their hair,
 And the sparkles that flash from their eyes!
  Behold a ghastly band,
  Each a torch in his hand!
Those are Grecian ghosts, that in battle were slain,
   And unburied remain
   Inglorious on the plain:
   Give the vengeance due
   To the valiant crew.
Behold how they toss their torches on high,
 How they point to the Persian abodes,
And glittering temples of their hostile gods."
The princes applaud with a furious joy;
And the king seized a flambeau with zeal to destroy;

Thais led the way,
To light him to his prey,
And, like another Helen, fired another Troy.

Chorus.

And the king seized a flambeau with zeal to destroy;
Thais led the way,
To light him to his prey,
And, like another Helen, fired another Troy.

Thus long ago,
Ere heaving bellows learned to blow,
While organs yet were mute,
Timotheus, to his breathing flute
And sounding lyre,
Could swell the soul to rage, or kindle soft desire.
At last divine Cecilia came,
Inventress of the vocal frame;
The sweet enthusiast, from her sacred store,
Enlarged the former narrow bounds,
And added length to solemn sounds,
With Nature's mother-wit, and arts unknown before.
Let old Timotheus yield the prize,
Or both divide the crown:
He raised a mortal to the skies:
She drew an angel down.

Grand Chorus

At last divine Cecilia came,
Inventress of the vocal frame;
The sweet enthusiast, from her sacred store,
Enlarged the former narrow bounds,
And added length to solemn sounds,
With Nature's mother-wit, and arts unknown before
Let old Timotheus yield the prize,
Or both divide the crown:

He raised a mortal to the skies:
She drew an angel down.

A SONG FOR ST. CECILIA'S DAY,

NOVEMBER 22, 1687.

FROM harmony, from heavenly harmony
This universal frame began:
When Nature underneath a heap
Of jarring atoms lay,
And could not heave her head,
The tuneful voice was heard from high:
Arise, ye more than dead.

Then cold and hot and moist and dry
In order to their stations leap,
And Music's power obey.
From harmony, from heavenly harmony,
This universal frame began:
From harmony to harmony
Through all the compass of the notes it ran,
The diapason closing full in Man.

What passion cannot Music raise and quell?
When Jubal struck the chorded shell,
His listening brethren stood around,
And, wondering, on their faces fell
To worship that celestial sound:
Less than a god they thought there could not dwell
Within the hollow of that shell,
That spoke so sweetly, and so well.
What passion cannot Music raise and quell?

The trumpet's loud clangour
Excites us to arms
With shrill notes of anger
And mortal alarms.

The double double double beat
          Of the thundering drum
          Cries, Hark! the foes come;
Charge, charge, 't is too late to retreat
          The soft complaining flute
          In dying notes discovers
          The woes of hopeless lovers,
Whose dirge is whispered by the warbling lute.

          Sharp violins proclaim
Their jealous pangs and desperation,
Fury, frantic indignation,
Depth of pains and height of passion,
          For the fair, disdainful dame.
          But Oh! what art can teach,
          What human voice can reach
               The sacred organ's praise?
          Notes inspiring holy love,
Notes that wing their heavenly ways
          To mend the choirs above.

Orpheus could lead the savage race,
And trees unrooted left their place,
          Sequacious of the lyre;
But bright Cecilia raised the wonder higher:
When to her organ vocal breath was given,
An angel heard, and straight appeared,
          Mistaking earth for heaven.

                Grand Chorus.
     As from the power of sacred lays
          The spheres began to move,
     And sung the great Creator's praise
          To all the blessed above;
     So when the last and dreadful hour
     This crumbling pageant shall devour,
     The trumpet shall be heard on high,

The dead shall live, the living die,
And Music shall untune the sky.

AH, FADING JOY!

AH, fading joy! how quickly art thou past!
    Yet we thy ruin haste.
As if the cares of human life were few,
    We seek out new:
And follow fate which would too fast pursue.

See how on every bough the birds express
In their sweet notes their happiness.
They all enjoy and nothing spare,
But on their mother nature lay their care:
Why then should man, the lord of all below,
Such troubles choose to know,
As none of all his subjects undergo?
    Hark, hark, the waters fall, fall, fall;
And with a murmuring sound
Dash, dash, upon the ground,
        To gentle slumbers call.

INCANTATION.

The Invocation of the Ghost of Laius by Tiresias.   From the
Tragedy of *Œdipus*.

Tiresias. CHOOSE the darkest part o' the grove;
        Such as ghosts at noonday love.
    Dig a trench, and dig it nigh
    Where the bones of Laius lie:
    Altars raised of turf or stone
    Will the infernal powers have none.—
    Answer me, if this be done.
            Chorus. 'T is done.

Tir.   Is the sacrifice made fit?
      Draw her backward to the pit;

Draw the barren heifer back:
Barren let her be, and black.
Cut the curlèd hair that grows
Full betwixt her horns and brows.
And turn your faces from the sun.—
Answer me, if this be done.
   Chor. 'T is done.

Tir. Pour in blood, and blood-like wine,
To mother Earth and Proserpine;
Mingle milk into the stream;
Feast the ghosts that love the steam:
Snatch a brand from funeral pile;
Toss it in to make them boil:
And turn your faces from the sun.—
Answer me, if all be done.

   Chor. All is done.

  . . . . .

    Song.

1. Hear, ye sullen powers below!
 Hear, ye taskers of the dead!
2. You that boiling cauldrons blow!
 You that scum the molten lead!
3. You that pinch with red-hot tongs!
1. You that drive the trembling hosts
Of poor poor ghosts
With your sharpened prongs!
2. You that thrust them off the brim!
3. You that plunge them when they swim
1. Till they drown;
 Till they go
 On a row
Down, down, down,
Ten thousand, thousand, thousand fathoms low—
Chor. Till they drown, &c.

1. Music for a while
   Shall your cares beguile:
     Wondering how your pains were eased!
2.   And disdaining to be pleased!
3. Till Alecto free the dead
     From their eternal bands;
   Till the snakes drop from her head,
     And whip from out her hands.

1. Come away,
   Do not stay,
   But obey,
   While we play,
   For hell's broke up, and ghosts have holiday.
Chor. Come away, &c.
    1. Laius!   2. Laius!   3. Laius!
    1. Hear!   2. Hear!   3. Hear!
Tir.   Hear and appear!
      By the Fates that spun thy thread!
Chor.   Which are three—
Tir.   By the Furies fierce and dread!
Chor.   Which are three—
Tir.   By the judges of the dead!
Chor.   Which are three—
      Three times three—
Tir.   By hell's blue flame!
      By the Stygian lake!
      And by Demogorgon's name
      At which ghosts quake!
      Hear and appear!

HARVEST HOME.

Comus. YOUR hay it is mowed, and your corn is
          reaped:
       Your barns will be full, and your hovels heaped:
         Come, my boys, come;
         Come, my boys, come;

And merrily roar out harvest home!
            Harvest home,
            Harvest home;
And merrily roar out harvest home!
        Chor. Come, my boys, come, &c.

1. We ha' cheated the parson, we'll cheat him again,
    For why should a blockhead ha' one in ten?
            One in ten,
            One in ten;
    For why should a blockhead ha' one in ten,

2. For prating so long like a book-learned sot,
    Till pudding and dumpling burn to pot,
            Burn to pot,
            Burn to pot,
    Till pudding and dumpling burn to pot?
        Chor. Burn to pot, &c.

3. We'll toss off our ale till we cannot stand,
    And hoigh for the honour of Old England;
            Old England,
            Old England;
    And hoigh for the honour of Old England.
        Chor. Old England, &c.

INDEX OF FIRST LINES.

	Page
Absence, hear thou my protestation,	115
Adieu, farewell earth's bliss,	59
Ah, Ben! Say how or when,	208
Ah, fading joy! how quickly art thou past!	263
Ah! I remember well (and how can I,	96
Ah! my Lord, leave me not,	11
Ah, sweet Content! where is thy mild abode?	106
Ah, were she pitiful as she is fair,	54
All my past life is mine no more,	254
All the flowers of the spring,	147
All ye that lovely lovers be,	57
And wilt thou leave me thus?	6
Are they shadows that we see?	95
A rose, as fair as ever saw the North,	139
Art thou poor, yet hast thou golden slumbers?	111
As I in hoary winter's night stood shivering in the snow,	103
Ask me no more where Jove bestows,	219
Ask me why I send you here,	220
As virtuous men pass mildly away,	113
A sweet disorder in the dress,	211
As you came from the holy land,	43
Avenge, O Lord, Thy slaughtered saints, whose bones,	197
A very phœnix in her radiant eyes,	63
Ay me, poor soul, whom bound in sinful chains,	162
Be a merchant, I will freight thee,	112
Beauty clear and fair,	157
Beauty, sweet love, is like the morning dew,	94
Behold, out walking in these valleys,	105
Bid me to live, and I will live,	209
Blow, blow, thou winter wind,	83
Born was I to be old,	216

Page

Bright star of beauty, on whose eyelids sit, - - - 97
Brown is my love, but graceful, - - - - 75
Buzz! quoth the Blue-fly, - - - - - 123
By a fountain where I lay, - - - - - 78
By the moon we sport and play, - - - - 168

Call for the robin redbreast and the wren, - - - 146
Calm was the day, and through the trembling air, - - 18
Care-charmer Sleep, son of the sable Night, - - 95
Care-charming Sleep, thou easer of all woes, - - 155
Cherry-ripe, ripe, ripe, I cry, - - - - 210
Choose the darkest part o' the grove, - - - 264
Clear Ankor, on whose silver-sanded shore, - - 98
Cold's the wind, and wet's the rain, - - - 109
Cold winter ice is fled and gone, - - - - 163
Come away, come away, death, - - - - 85
Come away, come, sweet love! - - - - 75
Come, cheerful day, part of my life to me, - - 130
Come, come away! the spring, - - - - 227
Come, let's begin to revel it out, - - - - 165
Come, list and hark, - - - - - - 108
Come, little babe, come, silly soul, - - - - 65
Cupid and my Campaspe played, - - - - 50

Dare you haunt our hallowed green? - - - 169
Dear chorister, who from those shadows sends, - 139
Dear, from thine arms then let me fly, - - - 253
Death, be not proud, though some have callèd thee, - 119
Drink to-day, and drown all sorrow, - - - 156
Drink to me only with thine eyes, - - - 122
Drop, drop, slow tears, - - - - - 160

Even such is time, that takes in trust, - - - 45
Eye of the garden, queen of flowers, - - - 104

Fain I would, but oh I dare not, - - - - 166
Fain would I change that note, - - - - 163
Fair and fair, and twice so fair, - - - - 56
Fair daffodils, we weep to see, - - - - 214
Fair pledges of a fruitful tree, - - - - 213
Fair stood the wind for France, - - - - 99

Page

Fair summer droops, droop men and beasts therefore, - 60
Fear no more the heat o' the sun, - - - - 86
Follow thy fair sun, unhappy shadow! - - - 128
Follow your saint, follow with accents sweet! - - 134
Forget not yet the tried intent, - - - - 5
For her gait if she be walking, - - - - 137
Fresh Spring, the herald of love's mighty king, - - 17
From harmony, from heavenly harmony, - - - 262
From Tuskane came my lady's worthy race, - - - 4
Full fathom five thy father lies, - - - - 87
Full many a glorious morning have I seen, - - - 89

Gather ye rosebuds while ye may, - - - - 213
Gentle nymphs, be not refusing, - - - - 135
Give Beauty all her right, - - - - - 128
Glories, pleasures, pomps, delights, and ease, - - 160
God Lyæus, ever young, - - - - - 156
Go, happy rose, and interwove, - - - - 212
Go, heart, unto the lamp of light, - - - - 10
Golden slumbers kiss your eyes, - - - - 111
Go, lovely rose, - - - - - - - 232

Hail, old patrician trees, so great and good, - - 234
Happy those early days, when I, - - - - 249
Happy were he could finish forth his fate, - - 112
Hark, hark! the lark at heaven's gate sings, - - 86
Hark, now everything is still, - - - - 146
Hear me, O God! - - - - - - 125
Heavenly fair Urania's son, - - - - - 230
Hence all you vain delights, - - - - - 154
Hence, loathèd Melancholy, - - - - - 183
Hence, vain deluding joys, - - - - - 187
Here, a little child, I stand, - - - - - 217
Here a pretty baby lies, - - - - - 216
Here she lies, a pretty bud, - - - - - 216
Her eyes the glow-worm lend thee, - - - 210
He that loves a rosy cheek, - - - - - 220
Hey nonny no! - - - - - - - 171
His golden locks time hath to silver turned, - - 57
How happy is he born and taught, - - - 149

                                                    Page
How happy was I when I saw her lead, -   -   -   - 14
How near to good is what is fair! -   -   -   - 123
How should I your true love know,   -   -   - 85

I dare not ask a kiss,   -   -   -   -   -   - 211
I have done one braver thing,   -   -   -   - 117
I have lost, and lately, these, -   -   -   - 205
I never drank of Aganippe well,   -   -   - 47
In hope to 'scape the law, do nought amiss,   -   - 104
In the hour of my distress,   -   -   -   - 217
In vain he seeks for beauty that excelleth,   -   - 70
In what dark silent grove,   -   -   -   - 203
I saw Eternity the other night,   -   -   - 250
I saw my lady weep,   -   -   -   -   - 76
I saw my lady weeping, and Love did languish,   - 70
I sing of brooks, of blossoms, birds, and bowers,   - 205
I struck the board, and cried, "No more",   -   - 239
It is not growing like a tree,   -   -   -   - 125
It is too clear a brightness for man's eye,   -   - 68
It was the winter wild, -   -   -   -   - 176
I would thou wert not fair, or I were wise,   -   - 66

Jolly shepherd, shepherd on a hill,   -   -   - 151

Lady, when I behold the roses sprouting,   -   - 76
Lay a garland on my hearse, -   -   -   - 158
Leave me, O Love, which reachest but to dust,   - 48
Let me not to the marriage of true minds,   -   - 93
Let who list (for me) advance,   -   -   - 199
Like as a ship, that through the ocean wide, -   - 16
Like as the damask rose you see, -   -   - 145
Like as the waves make towards the pebbled shore,   - 89
Like to the clear in highest sphere,   -   - 61
Like to the falling of a star, -   -   -   - 152
Little think'st thou, poor flower, -   -   - 118
Live in these conquering leaves; live all the same,   - 247
Look how the flower which lingeringly doth fade, - 140
Love bade me welcome; yet my soul drew back,   - 241
Love in thy youth, fair maid, be wise,   -   - 170
Lovely kind, and kindly loving,   -   -   - 67
Love, that liveth and reigneth in my thought,   -   - 4

Page

Maids to bed and cover coal, - - - - - - 166
Martial, the things that do attain, - - - - - 5
Matilda, now go take thy bed, - - - - - 161
May! be thou never graced with birds that sing, - - 137
Men call you fair, and you do credit it, - - - - 18
More than most fair, full of the living fire, - - - 16
Mortality, behold and fear! - - - - - - 153
Most glorious Lord of life! that, on this day, - - - 17
My dear and only love, I pray, - - - - - 236
My Girl, thou gazest much, - - - - - - 9
My light thou art, without thy glorious sight, - - - 254
My love in her attire doth shew her wit, - - - 78
My maiden Isabel, - - - - - - - 2
My mind to me a kingdom is, - - - - - 48
My soul, there is a country, - - - - - - 250
My sweetest Lesbia, let us live and love, - - - 126
My true-love hath my heart, and I have his, - - - 46

No longer mourn for me when I am dead, - - - 90
No more, my dear, no more these counsels try, - - 47
Not, Celia, that I juster am, - - - - - 255
Not mine own fears, nor the prophetic soul, - - - 92
Now is the gentle season, freshly flowering, - - - 77
Now is the month of maying, - - - - - 74
Now is the time for mirth, - - - - - - 206
Now the bright morning star, day's harbinger, - - 196
Now the lusty Spring is seen, - - - - - 155
Now winter nights enlarge, - - - - - - 132
Nymphs and Shepherds, dance no more, - - - 193

O'er the smooth enamelled green, - - - - - 192
O, fair sweet face! O, eyes celestial bright, - - - 158
Of Neptune's empire let us sing, - - - - - 131
Of Pan we sing, the best of singers, Pan, - - - 121
O mistress mine, where are you roaming? - - - 84
O, never say that I was false of heart, - - - - 92
O, nightingale, that on yon bloomy spray, - - - 196
O no, Beloved; I am most sure, - - - - - 238
O no more, no more, too late, - - - - - 161
O the merry Christ-Church bells, - - - - - 170

Page

O the month of May, the merry month of May, - 110
Out upon it, I have loved, - - - - - 222
Over hill, over dale, - - - - - - 80
Over the mountains, - - - - - - 172
O waly, waly, up the bank, - - - - 174
O whither dost thou fly? cannot my vow, - - 201

Pack clouds away, and welcome day, - - - 108
Phœbus, arise, - - - - - - 143
Pinch him, pinch him, black and blue, - - - 52
Pipe, merry Annot, - - - - - - 12
Pluck the fruit and taste the pleasure, - - - 63
Poor soul, the centre of my sinful earth, - - 93
Praised be Diana's fair and harmless light, - - 71
Praise they that will times past, I joy to see, - - 212

Queen and huntress, chaste and fair, - - - 121

Rose-cheeked Laura, - - - - - 134
Roses, their sharp spines being gone, - - - 159
Round about in a fairy ring-a, - - - 168
Round-a, round-a, keep your ring, - - - 169

Sabrina fair, - - - - - - - 194
See, O see! - - - - - - - 231
Sees not my love how Time resumes, - - - 233
See the chariot at hand here of Love! - - - 124
See where my love a-maying goes, - - - 167
See where she issues in her beauty's pomp, - - 104
Set me where Phœbus' heat the flowers slayeth, - - 70
Shall I, wasting in despair, - - - - 198
Sigh no more, ladies, sigh no more, - - - 84
Since, there's no help, come, let us kiss and part, - - 98
Sing aloud! His praise rehearse, - - - 243
Sing Lullaby, as women do, - - - - 8
Sing to Apollo, god of day, - - - - 51
Sing we and chant it, - - - - - 73
Sitting by a river's side, - - - - - 55
Slow, slow, fresh fount, keep time with my salt tears, - 120
Spring, the sweet Spring, is the year's pleasant king, - 58
Steer hither, steer your wingèd pines, - - - 136
Sweet, be not proud of those two eyes, - - - 212

Page

Sweet bird, that sing'st away the early hours,   -   - 141
Sweet day, so cool, so calm, so bright!   -   -   - 239
Sweet Echo, sweetest Nymph, that livest unseen,   -   - 193
Sweetest love, I do not go,   -   -   -   -   - 116
Sweet rose, whence is this hue,   -   -   -   - 144
Sweet, serene, sky-like flower,   -   -   -   - 224
Sweet Spring, thou com'st with all thy goodly train,   - 140
Sweet Suffolk owl, so trimly dight,   -   -   - 169
Sweet thrall, first step to Love's felicity,-   -   - 64
Sweet violets, Love's paradise, that spread,   -   - 72

Take, O take those lips away,   -   -   -   - 86
Tell me not, sweet, I am unkind,   -   -   -   - 223
Tell me where is fancy bred, -   -   -   -   - 82
That time of year thou mayst in me behold,   -   - 90
That which her slender waist confined,   -   -   - 232
The expense of spirit in a waste of shame,   -   - 93
The fairy beam upon you,   -   -   -   -   - 123
The glories of our blood and state,   -   -   - 225
The hunt is up, the hunt is up,   -   -   -   - 168
The Lady Mary Villers lies, -   -   -   -   - 221
The last and greatest herald of heaven's King,   - 142
The man of life upright,   -   -   -   -   - 130
The means, therefore, which unto us is lent, -   - 42
The nightingale, as soon as April bringeth,   -   - 45
There is a lady sweet and kind,   -   -   -   - 165
There is none, O none but you,   -   -   -   - 133
The seas are quiet when the winds give o'er, -   - 234
The sootë season, that bud and bloom forth brings,   - 3
The world's a bubble, and the life of man,   -   - 148
They are all gone into the world of light!   -   - 251
They flee from me that sometime did me seek,   -   - 7
This Life, which seems so fair,   -   -   -   - 143
This way, this way come, and hear,   -   -   - 158
Though I have twice been at the doors of death,   - 142
Thrice happy he who by some shady grove,   -   - 141
Thrice toss these oaken ashes in the air,   -   - 132
Tired with all these, for restful death I cry,   -   - 89
To ask for all thy love, and thy whole heart, 't were mad-
    ness!   -   -   -   -   -   -   -   - 166

Page

To me, fair friend, you never can be old,   -   -   - 91
To the ocean now I fly, -   -   -   -   -   - 195
'T was at the royal feast for Persia won,-   -   -   - 256
Two went to pray?   O rather say, -   -   -   - 248

Underneath this sable hearse,   -   -   -   - 137
Under the greenwood tree,   -   -   -   -   - 82

Weep no more, nor sigh, nor groan,   -   -   - 158
Weep not, my wanton, smile upon my knee, -   -   - 53
Weep you no more, sad fountains, -   -   -   - 79
Welcome, maids of honour,   -   -   -   - 215
Welcome pure thoughts and peaceful hours, -   -   - 252
Welcome, welcome, do I sing,   -   -   -   - 138
We must not part, as others do,   -   -   -   - 171
We saw and wooed each other's eyes,   -   -   - 200
What bird so sings, yet so does wail?   -   -   - 51
What pleasure have great princes, -   -   -   - 69
What! shall I ne'er more see those halcyon days! -   - 73
What sing the sweet birds in each grove?   -   - 135
What then is love but mourning?   -   -   - 127
What thing is Beauty?   "Nature's dearest Minion!"   - 107
What time this world's great Workmaster did cast,   - 37
When a daffodil I see,   -   -   -   -   - 213
Whenas in silks my Julia goes,   -   -   -   - 211
When I a verse shall make,   -   -   -   - 208
When icicles hang by the wall,   -   -   -   - 80
When I consider how my light is spent,   -   - 197
When in disgrace with fortune and men's eyes,   - 88
When in the chronicle of wasted time, -   -   - 91
When I survey the bright,   -   -   -   - 202
When love on time and measure makes his ground,   - 77
When Love with unconfinèd wings,   -   -   - 223
When thou must home to shades of underground, -   - 129
When to the sessions of sweet silent thought,   - 88
When whispering strains do softly steal,   -   - 229
Where the bee sucks, there suck I,   -   -   - 87
Whoe'er she be,   -   -   -   -   -   - 245
Whoever comes to shroud me, do not harm,   - 114
Who is Silvia? what is she,   -   -   -   - 81

Page

Who travels by the weary wandering way, - - - 13
Why so pale and wan, fond lover, - - - - - 221
Will't ne'er be morning? Will that promised light, - 241
Wilt Thou forgive that sin, where I begun, - - - 119
Winds, whisper gently whilst she sleeps, - - - 228
With how sad steps, O Moon, thou climbst the skies, - 46
With marjoram gentle, - - - - - - - 1

Ye have been fresh and green, - - - - - 215
Ye learnèd sisters, which have oftentimes, - - - 24
Ye little birds that sit and sing, - - - - 164
Yet if his majesty our sovereign lord, - - - 173
You meaner beauties of the night, - - - - 150
Your hay it is mowed, and your corn it is reaped, - - 266
You spotted snakes with double tongue, - - - 81
You virgins, that did late despair, - - - - 226